ALAS IT SEEMS CRUEL

THE MOUNT MULLIGAN COAL MINE DISASTER OF 1921

PETER BELL

First published 2013

National Library of Australia Cataloguing-in-Publication entry:

Author:	Bell, Peter, 1948-
Title:	Alas it seems cruel : the Mount Mulligan Coal Mine Disaster of 1921 / Peter Bell.
ISBN:	9781922109514 (pbk.)
Subjects:	Coal mine accidents--Queensland--Mount Mulligan. Mine explosions--Queensland--Mount Mulligan. Mulligan, Mount (Qld.)--History.
Dewey Number:	622.809943

Typeset in Cambria 11pt.

Cover Design by Boolarong Press

Published by Boolarong Press, Salisbury, Brisbane, Australia.

Printed and bound by Watson Ferguson & Company, Salisbury, Brisbane, Australia.

CONTENTS

Line Illustrations		iv
Photographs		v
Abbreviations		vi
Preface		vii
Introduction		1
Chapter I	Discovery and Development	9
Chapter II	The Disaster	37
Chapter III	The Royal Commission	67
Chapter IV	The Aftermath	101
Chapter V	Prosperity and Decline	135
Chapter VI	Postscript	167
Appendix A	Walter Filer Letter	175
Appendix B	Herbert Smithson Letter	178
Appendix C	Australian Coal Mine Disasters	180
Appendix D	Population of Mount Mulligan in 1921	182
Appendix E	Annual Coal Production at Mount Mulligan	184
Appendix F	The Dead	185
Sources		189

LINE ILLUSTRATIONS

Map of Lower Cape York Peninsula 11

Plan of Mining Leases at Mount Mulligan 18

Plan of Coal Mining Methods 30

Plan of Mount Mulligan Township 35

Facsimile of Cavil Sheet for 19 September 1921 39

Plan of Mount Mulligan Mine Workings 50

Plan of Explosion's Suspected Origin 73

Contemporary Newspaper Cartoons:

- "In Memoriam" 130
- "Death Declares a Dividend" 131
- "The Profit and the Loss" 132

PHOTOGRAPHS

Mount Mulligan, 2004 2

Mount Mulligan, 1956 8

James Watson 21

Sullivan Coal-Cutting Machine 32

Harris Street, Mount Mulligan, 1921 33

Mount Mulligan School 36

Older School Pupils, 1921 36

Mine Entrance, about 1919 40

Mine Entrance After Explosion 43

Mine Entrance After Explosion 48

Blacksmith's Hut After Explosion 49

Cable drums After Explosion 54

Ventilating Fan Motor After Explosion 55

Recovery Workers Emerging from Mine 59

Recovery Workers Wheeling Coffin Down Ropeway 62

Cemetery Shortly After Disaster 63

Members of the Royal Commission 69

Women and Recovery Workers Near Mine Entrance 107

Mine Surface Workings, about 1930 141

Miners in Underground Workings, about 1930 152

King Cole Mine 157

Mine Entrance, 1977 162

Chillagoe smelter ruins from the air 163

2004 Drier family grave, 2004 164

Ruins of the ventilating adit, 2004 165

ABBREVIATIONS

A.R.	*Annual Report of the Under-Secretary for Mines*
G.S.Q.	Geological Survey of Queensland
I.W.W.	Industrial Workers of the World
M.L.A.	Member of the Legislative Assembly
M.L.C.	Member of the Legislative Council
N.Q.R.	*North Queensland Register*
Oxley	John Oxley Memorial Library
Q.C.E.U.	Queensland Colliery Employees' Union
Q.G.G.	*Queensland Government Gazette*
Q.G.M.J.	*Queensland Government Mining Journal*
Q.I.G.	*Queensland Industrial Gazette*
Q.N.	Queensland Newspapers Library
Q.P.D.	*Queensland Parliamentary Debates*
Q.P.P.	*Queensland Parliamentary Papers*
Q.S.A.	Queensland State Archives
R.C.	*Report of the Royal Commission on the Mount Mulligan Colliery Disaster*
V. & P.	*Votes and Proceedings*

PREFACE

TO THE THIRD EDITION, 2011

This book was written as a History honours thesis at James Cook University in 1977 under the supervision of the late Professor Brian Dalton, first published as a monograph in 1978, and reprinted in a new edition in 1996 to commemorate the seventy-fifth anniversary of the Mount Mulligan disaster.

The book has evolved over those years, but it has not changed fundamentally. I have learned a little more, corrected some errors, changed some emphases, and I may have become a little more forthright in attributing praise or blame, but the story is essentially the same.

When I started writing about Mount Mulligan as a neophyte historian thirty-five years ago, I felt like a lone figure standing on an empty plain stretching to the horizon. There was almost no literature in the field of disasters, and very little on coal mining; there was no historiography to consult. Much has been written in the meantime. Mount Mulligan itself has become famous in Australian prehistory, as Bruno David's archaeological research in the rock shelters on top of the mountain has pushed the known story of Ngurrabullgan back to the limit of carbon dating, 37,000 years ago. Noreen Kirkman's thesis on the Palmer goldfield, and several of the papers in Kett Kennedy's two volumes of readings on North Queensland mining history have put early mining in the region into a much clearer context. Ray Whitmore's three-volume history of coal mining in Queensland has provided the wider state context, Don Dingsdag's book on the Bulli disaster of 1887, and Stuart Piggin's book on the Mount Kembla disaster of 1902 have filled in the picture of the two other major Australian coal mine explosions. Pete Thomas' books on the Coalminers' Union has provided the industrial picture which was missing earlier.

And unfortunately since 1978 there have been three more major disasters in Australian coal mines, with three more enquiries, and thirty-seven more dead miners.

My own research since that time has made me better-informed about some aspects of Mount Mulligan's history and the disaster. I have learned much more about the supply of fuel to the early smelting industry, and how the Chillagoe Company's hopeless enterprise figured in that economy; I have also pursued the theme of myths and legends about mining and disasters, gained some further insights into the politics of the period, and made an extensive study of coal mine safety legislation in Queensland, both before and after Mount Mulligan. This additional knowledge and insight is reflected in the new text. In particular, I have become far more critical of the Mount Mulligan Royal Commission, whose members I believe were hand-picked to give the results that the government wanted, and I express my loss of faith in the reactive process of improving coal mine safety which continues to the present.

The other thing I have lost is the assistance of the people I interviewed then. Thirty-five years ago I was able to speak to nine people who were present in Mount Mulligan on the day of the disaster over fifty years before. There are many more questions which I would have loved to put to them during the preparation of this new edition of their story, but all of their voices are long silent. On the other hand, I can now be a little more frank in telling parts of the story which people alive then might have found embarrassing or painful to see in print.

Peter Bell

Adelaide

INTRODUCTION

"a mountain once seen never to be forgotten."

(James Mulligan, 3 November 1874)

Mount Mulligan is 100km west of Cairns, an impressive natural landmark whose sandstone cliffs look as though a part of the Blue Mountains of New South Wales has somehow been transported 2,000km north. Underlying the mountain are coal deposits that supported a small mining town from 1914 until 1958. There is not much left of the township now. The best place to learn about Mount Mulligan's history is the cemetery, where nearly a quarter of the little town's population was buried in less than one week. On 19 September 1921 a massive coal dust explosion in the Mount Mulligan mine killed all 75, or perhaps 76, men and boys who were working underground.

This is the story of a horrible event in a remote and beautiful location ninety years ago. Of all peacetime jobs, underground mining is one of the most destructive of human life. Most people are vaguely aware that mining is a hazardous occupation, but probably few understand the scale of that hazard. If one were to ask what was the greatest disaster ever to occur in Australia, measured in terms of loss of human life, a well-informed answer might mention the Bathurst Bay cyclone of 1899 which took the lives of at least 239 crew members of wrecked pearling

001 Mount Mulligan from the air, 2004 (Peter Bell)

luggers[1], or perhaps the wreck of the immigrant ship *Cataraqui* on King Island in Bass Strait in 1845 when 400 were drowned.[2] But very few people know that 623 miners were killed in the day-to-day operations of the Broken Hill mines between 1888 and 1964.[3] They died mostly in ones and twos, unreported outside their immediate community, and no-one ever refers to their collective loss as the Broken Hill disaster.

In addition to the dangers in all underground mines, coal mining has its own distinctive hazards because many coal seams generate flammable, toxic and asphyxiating gases. The most feared mine gas is methane, which leaks invisibly from coal seams and can form an explosive mixture with oxygen. Also present in every mine is coal dust, which in the right circumstances is highly explosive.

The ferocity of a coal dust explosion is difficult to imagine. It is nothing like the leisurely dull "whoomp" familiar from Hollywood special effects. The explosion's shock wave can flash through a mine at a kilometre per second: that is the speed of a rifle bullet, or ten

1 Register of Deaths, Cook District, entries for 5 March 1899

2 A. Lemon and M. Morgan, *Poor Souls, They Perished*, Melbourne 1986.

3 O. H. Woodward, *Review of the Broken Hill Lead-Silver-Zinc Industry*, Sydney 1965, p. 391.

times the wind velocity of the most destructive tornado. Its victims hear nothing, for it travels much faster than sound. In its wake the underground workings are filled with orange flame at the temperature of a blast furnace; lead and aluminium instantly turn to liquid. When the flame dies a few moments later, it has consumed all the oxygen in the mine atmosphere. The aftermath is complete darkness, with all lighting destroyed and the mine filled with toxic black smoke. In the last 90 years there have been five coal dust explosions in Queensland mines, which killed 128 coal miners. No-one who has been caught in one has ever lived to describe the experience.

The gases and coal are not hazardous in their natural environment. Methane by itself in a coal seam is quite benign, and there is no dust present before mining begins. It is the miners who create the dust and bring in the oxygen. Unfortunately but inevitably, the process of extracting coal has the potential to turn underground mines into large methane and coal dust bombs. For the last hundred years, a major part of daily coal mine management has been focussed on ensuring those bombs do not go off.

The Mount Mulligan disaster was the greatest industrial accident that Queensland has ever seen. It seemed incomprehensible at the time, and still does, that such an event could happen in a sleepy country town. Because of the isolation and small size of the community in which it occurred - perhaps also because of the romantic splendour of its setting - the story of the disaster has become a part of North Queensland folklore.

Despite the strength of this oral tradition, no substantial account of the Mount Mulligan disaster had been written before 1977. Occasional commemorative newspaper articles had described the disaster, usually drawing on the more sensational features of the 1921 press reports. Regional histories gave Mount Mulligan and the disaster only passing mention. Writers could not make sense of such an event, and treated it as a chance event unconnected with the more coherent passage of human activities, outside any visible causal pattern.[4]

4 See for example, G.C. Bolton, *A Thousand Miles Away*, Brisbane 1963, p.318; D. Jones, *Trinity Phoenix*, Cairns 1976, p.453; G. Pike, *Pioneers' Country*, Mareeba 1976, p.176.

This study takes the approach of treating the disaster as an integral part of North Queensland mining history. The explosion was not an incomprehensible random intrusion into the explicable domain of human affairs, but the logical result of geographic, economic, social, political and technological forces. This account thus necessarily describes at some length not only the rise of Mount Mulligan, and its progress and decline in the decades following the disaster, but also some events further afield in the Australian coal industry. Chance is given very little role in this description of events. A random element undoubtedly influenced the immediate initiation of the explosion at that particular time and place, but the circumstances favouring a coal dust explosion were established long before, and chance to that extent plays a part in most human activities.

When the first version of this study was written in 1977, one recent paper made up the entire historical literature on Australian mine disasters.[5] Since then, monographs have been written on both the other major Australian coal mine disasters, Mount Kembla in 1902[6] and Bulli in 1887[7].

A wealth of published contemporary material describes the Mount Mulligan disaster. The Report of the Royal Commission is a valuable source, and a chapter of this study is devoted to a critical examination of the Royal Commission's proceedings and findings. Contemporary newspapers gave the disaster wide, although not always accurate, coverage; and archival material exists, concerned largely with administrative problems in the disaster's aftermath. Interviews with witnesses of the disaster provided much more detail and also wider information of a social nature.

The history of Mount Mulligan before and after the disaster relies on three principal types of sources: historical literature on North Queensland generally, while rarely treating Mount Mulligan at any length, allows the development of the coal mine and the community to be put in context. By the nature of its single industry, Mount Mulligan was always highly susceptible to economic forces affecting the region as a whole. The development of the mine can be traced through publications of the Queensland Mines Department, supplemented by reference to contemporary mining textbooks. The Mount Mulligan

5 G. Mitchell and S. Piggin, "The Mount Kembla Mine Explosion of 1902", *Journal of Australian Studies*, No.1, 1977, pp.52-69.

6 S. Piggin & H. Lee, *The Mt Kembla Disaster*, Oxford University Press, Sydney 1992.

7 D. Dingsdag, *The Bulli Mining Disaster 1887*, Sydney 1993.

community receives little attention in any written source, and information depends chiefly on interviews with former residents.

Mount Mulligan's place in North Queensland folklore is assured by its very topography. The township was situated at the foot of the mountain, a flat-topped, red-brown precipice which rarely failed to attract comment from visitors, either as a natural spectacle: "elongated; sombre; forbidding; yet withal fascinating by reason of its curious formation - inaccessible except to the most adventurous..."[8], or after 1921 simply as "the coffin-shaped mountain of coal".[9]

Until recent decades what was known of the Aboriginal heritage of Mount Mulligan came from the slim writings of late nineteenth and early twentieth century ethnographers, but new research has established a long and vigorous period of occupation. Archaeological excavation in Ngarrabullgan Cave on top of the mountain has discovered occupational deposits dated to before 37,000 years ago, at the limit of the carbon dating technique.[10] This result, which surprised even the archaeologist in charge of the project, makes Ngarrabullgan the oldest dated site in Queensland and puts it among a number of widely-separated early sites which together convincingly establish a very long Aboriginal presence extending across all of Australia.

Ngarrabullgan (historical sources sometimes give variants such as Narabullgin or Narawoolgin) is the Kuku Djungan name for Mount Mulligan, which in some traditions had been built by the rainbow serpent Goorialla on his travels northward during the creation of the present world.[11] Aboriginal legend also tells of the jealous and evil spirit Eekoo (or Iku) who lived on Mount Mulligan. Eekoo is said to have threatened to destroy the white men if they interfered with the mountain, but this threat of supernatural retribution was

8 H. Borland, "Mt Mulligan", *Cairns Post*, 17 September 1929.

9 *Disaster!*, Melbourne 1977, p.46. This lurid and geologically absurd description exemplifies the worst of the press articles on the disaster.

10 B. David, "Narabullgin Cave", *Archeology in Oceania 28*, 1993, pp. 50-54.

11 P.J. Trezise, *Quinkan Country*, Sydney 1969, p.67. Trezise attributes the story to a Koko jelandji source. A variation on the story from a Koko mini source was given by Jack Watson (interviewed Slade Point, 6 March 1977).

not documented until five years after the disaster, and may reflect a European interpretation of the Eekoo legends.[12]

The dark and dangerous nature of mining renders its practitioners susceptible to supernatural dread, and similar beliefs in spirits who contest the miner's presence have been common for centuries. Nearly every mining district in Europe has its own traditions about beings in the mine, some evil, others simply mischievous: gnomes, basilisks, German kobolds, Cornish knockers, Welsh coblynau. Agricola writing in the sixteenth century in his entirely practical mining treatise *De Re Metallica*, listed difficulties which might arise in underground workings, most of them familiar to miners today: flooding; deterioration of ore quality; poor ventilation; difficulty in timbering. One problem on Agricola's list strikes the modern reader as incongruous, but was clearly seen as a real threat four centuries ago:

> In some of our mines...there are other pernicious pests. These are demons of ferocious aspect, about which I have spoken in my book *De Animantibus Subterraneis*. Demons of this kind are expelled and put to flight by prayer and fasting.[13]

Underground coal miners and their families are subject to unusual social and emotional forces because of the danger inherent in the work. The Australian coal mining tradition originates from that of Britain, which for two centuries has had an appalling record of major disasters, and a greater but less conspicuous attrition in smaller coal mine accidents. It is necessary in coal mining communities to face this constant threat of violent death through a fatalistic ethos: "We live in fear every time they go down, but it is in the blood of an underground miner. My husband says that if you take something from Mother Earth, she will retaliate."[14]

Mount Mulligan was a distinctive town because it was concerned entirely with coal mining, which was conducted nowhere else in the North. Situated at the terminus of a railway branch line, Mount Mulligan was "the absolute dead end",[15] attracting no incidental travellers or diversity of commerce; and was always a state or company town, thus presenting an institutional atmosphere somewhat at odds with the rough-hewn North Queensland mining ethos. Coal miners have never enjoyed the picturesque individualism traditionally associated with gold

---

12 F. Richards, "Customs and Language of the Western Hodgkinson Aboriginals", *Memoirs of the Queensland Museum*, vol.8, 1926, p.256.

13 G. Agricola, *De Re Metallica*, 1558, (trans. H.C. & L.H. Hoover, New York 1950), p.217.

14 Miner's wife after Kianga disaster, quoted in *Courier Mail*, 24 September 1975.

15 Interview with Mary Wardle, Ravenshoe, 13 August 1976.

or tin fields. Collieries are prosaic and corporate; the domain of the wage miner and the public company.

Mount Mulligan was always a rather depressed town, at first supplying the fuel requirements of the luckless Chillagoe Company, with its "over-smart speculation and queer business deals",[16] and after this dream faded, settling into the austere bureaucratic existence of a state mine. Never profitable, the mine spent much of its life in the shadow of financial ruin, awaiting the day when more efficient mines elsewhere would supply coal to the local market at a lower price than Mount Mulligan could match.

Apart from a few former residents of the town at Collinsville and elsewhere, Mount Mulligan is chiefly remembered for the day 75 miners died. The horror of that day, and the deep impression it made on those who went to Mount Mulligan to help or to stare, have left their mark on North Queensland legend. Stories are still told: that the explosion was heard faintly in Townsville; that a huge smokeless fire still rages in the mine; that millions of tonnes of high-grade coal lie untouched because no-one dares enter the mine. Raconteurs in Cairns hotels will tell you of the man never found - blown to atoms in the explosion - or of the one miner who felt a strange premonition on his way to work on the morning of the disaster and returned home. These tales are not fiction, but legends; each has some recognizable origin in fact.[17] Significantly though, they were not repeated by the people who were present in 1921.

One legend was told by those who were there: that after the disaster the date "1921" appeared on the mountain face in numerals a hundred metres high. This part of Mount Mulligan's folklore is readily verifiable - the date can still be read on the mountain, although much depends on the angle of the light and the willingness of the viewer to believe. The inscription is the work of differential weathering which no-one thought to scrutinise before the disaster, but which took on sudden new significance in the year it named - no supernatural hand need be invoked to explain its appearance.

Fortuitously, the research for this account was begun in the mid-1970s during the relatively short interval when due to the passage of time government correspondence had become freely available and the painful memory of the disaster had reduced sufficiently to allow

16 Bolton, *op. cit.*, p.279.

17 Mitchell and Piggin, *op. cit.*, comment on the formulation of legends about the Mount Kembla disaster.

002 Mount Mulligan township, 1956 (Dixon report/CRA 1957)

witnesses to describe it and make personal documents available; and while these events of 1921 were still clearly recalled, and those documents still existed. Ten years earlier much of the information used in this study was not accessible; and now much more has been lost. More attention ought to be paid to such critical intervals of historical accessibility in the selection of topics for research.

1.
DISCOVERY AND DEVELOPMENT

Enough coal for "something like 3,000 years."

(*Cairns Post*, 19 September 1912)

Mount Mulligan is situated at about 16° 50'S, 144° 50'E, in the south-east corner of Cape York Peninsula, a hundred kilometres west of Cairns. Topographically, the Cairns region is a complex one.[1] In the east, a narrow strip of fertile coastal plain rises abruptly to densely-forested ranges 600 to 1500 metres in height. Rainfall near the coast is high, around two hundred centimetres annually near Cairns and much greater in the coastal ranges.

West of the mountains lies a chain of plateaux, notably the rich basalt Atherton Tableland, and to the north of it the drier Mareeba-Dimbulah plain. These tablelands extend roughly to the continental divide, which in this region is a relatively insignificant range of hills, dwindling to

1 This description of the topography and climate of the Cairns hinterland is chiefly derived from *Resources and Industry of Far North Queensland*, Canberra 1971.

imperceptibility where it divides Barron water from Walsh water on the Mareeba plain.

These areas east of the divide are fertile and well-watered, and in this century have provided the economic bases of the Cairns hinterland - sugar cane, beef, tobacco, maize and milk. West of the divide, the landscape declines through rugged hills into the immense flat flood plain of the Gulf of Carpentaria. From Dimbulah to the Gulf, annual rainfall is below one hundred centimetres, most of it falling in the brief, dramatic wet season; agriculture is thus prohibited, and a sparse beef cattle industry provides the only means of livelihood along the rivers flowing westward. The largest of these, the Mitchell, extends its tributaries in a great fan to the divide for four hundred kilometres north and south of Cairns. These tributaries, the Palmer, Mitchell, Hodgkinson, Walsh, Tate and Lynd, rise in the western foothills of the dividing range, and it is in their head-waters that the original economic base of the Cairns hinterland lay.

From Palmerville in the north to Forsayth in the south runs a great crescent of metalliferous country. The gold, tin, silver, copper, lead and tungsten of this region first attracted European settlement to Cape York Peninsula, and from the 1870s to around 1914 provided the livelihood of most of the people living to the west of Cairns. These mining industries, some conducted in inaccessible and unpleasant locations, established the port of Cairns and the network of railways that nurtured it. As these mining industries declined their place was taken by the agricultural and pastoral industries that dominate the Cairns hinterland today.

Mount Mulligan stands in the broken, hilly country west of the divide, fifty kilometres north of Dimbulah. Forming the western watershed of the Hodgkinson River for sixteen kilometres, it dominates the Hodgkinson valley with its dramatic red escarpment. The country visible from Mount Mulligan consists of flat river valleys and low, sharp ranges of granitic and metamorphic rocks, all covered in sparse Eucalypt forest. The average annual rainfall is below one hundred centimetres and the normal temperature range is from 11°C to 33°C. In a region quite monotonous in appearance, the mountain is an overwhelming landmark. Although only four hundred metres higher than the valley fronting it, the mountain's vertical eastern face runs apparently endlessly into the distance, giving an impression of vast, dominating bulk. The mountain is composed of Mesozoic sandstone and conglomerate layers, bedded

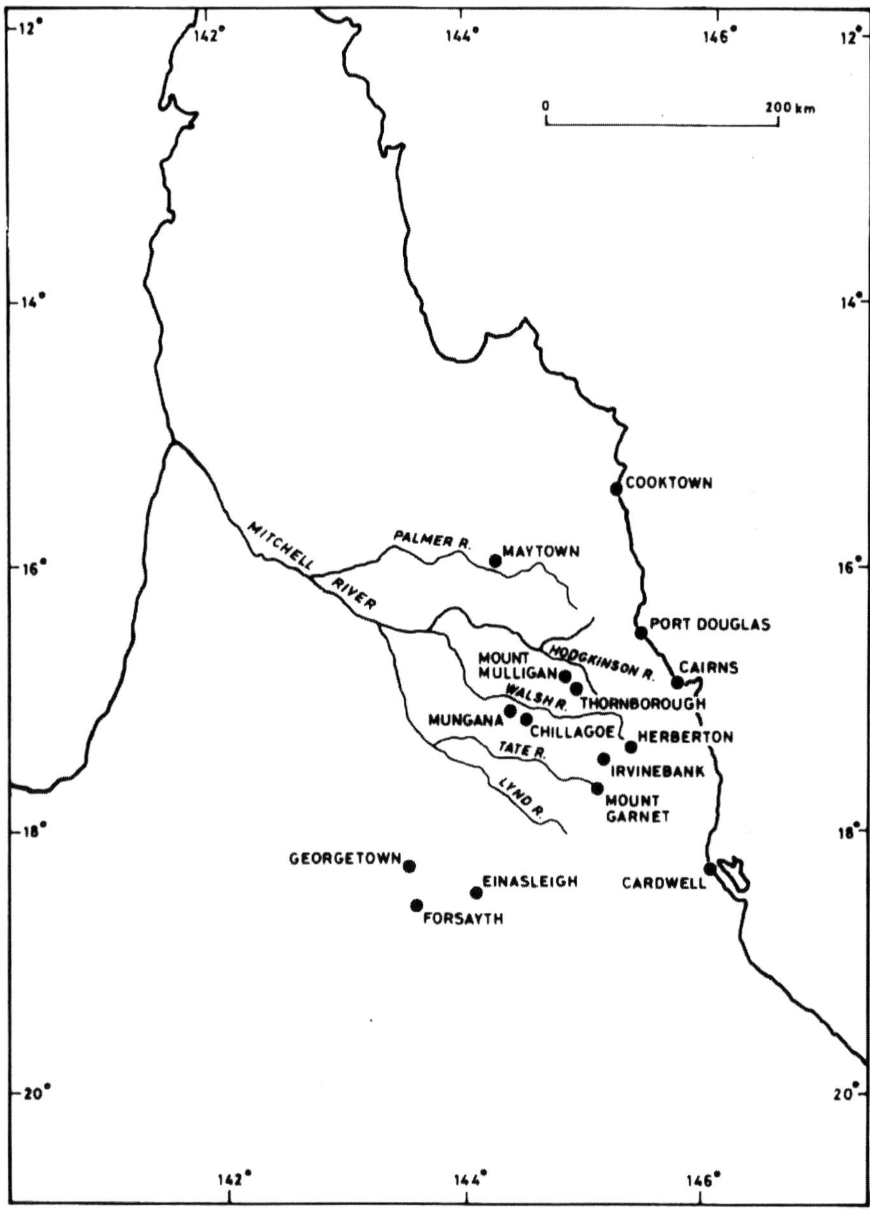

003 Lower Cape York Peninsula, showing the Mitchell River system and major ports and mining towns

with a slight dip to the west, and is thus quite distinct geologically and visually from its surroundings. It is probably a vestigial fragment of the floor of a down-faulted rift valley which roughly extended between the sites of modern Laura and Dimbulah in Mesozoic times.[2] In other words, it is a remnant from a time when the entire landscape looked like it.

Beneath Mount Mulligan lie three coal seams which outcrop on its eastern face below the escarpment, a short distance above the valley floor. These coal deposits, a small remnant preserved from a much more extensive ancient field by down-faulting of the mountain, are of Late Permian origin, roughly contemporary in formation with the Bowen Basin and eastern New South Wales coalfields about two hundred million years ago and older than most other eastern Australian coals.[3] The Mount Mulligan coal varies in quality and is thus potentially useful in a wide range of commercial applications, but the seams are mixed making it difficult to extract the individual grades of coal in sufficiently pure form to realise this potential. The coal seams vary in thickness, approaching two metres in places, but elsewhere much thinner, and inter-layered with shale bands. The total reserves under Mount Mulligan can never be known, but an early estimate was eighty-four million tonnes.[4]

European penetration of the Mount Mulligan region began in 1873 when James Venture Mulligan's report of payable gold on the Palmer River brought alluvial miners into Cape York Peninsula. Initially, these goldseekers travelled either by sea to Cooktown on the Endeavour River or overland from the Etheridge along Mulligan's route well to the west of Mount Mulligan. Mulligan was one of the near-legendary figures of North Queensland history. Irish by birth, he distinguished himself as an explorer, although his life was largely spent as a marginally successful miner and entrepreneur on Queensland gold-fields. He seems to have been driven to discover gold rather than to exploit it: in a series of expeditions between 1873 and 1880, he discovered two major gold-fields and a number of lesser tin and silver deposits.[5]

The first indisputable European sighting of Mount Mulligan was on 2 September 1874 when Mulligan's third expedition camped on the Hodgkinson at the foot of the mountain, and members of the

---

2 L.C. Ball, *Mount Mulligan Coalfield*, G.S.Q. 237, 1912, p.13.

3 A.T. Wells, "Late Permian Coal Measures", in Harrington, Permian Coals, Canberra 1989, pp.175-177; D. Hill and W.G.H. Maxwell, *Elements of the Stratigraphy of Queensland*, Brisbane 1967, p.49.

4 Ball, *op. cit.*, p.16. This was later shown to be a gross over-estimate - see chapter five.

5 Bolton, *op. cit.*, p.52, and R.L. Jack, *Northmost Australia*, vol. II, Melbourne 1922, pp.413-65. On 3 November 1874, Mulligan wrote in his journal: 'The fascination as well as the charm is broken once I return to ground travelled before, though I expect more gold.' (*Guide to the Palmer River...*, Brisbane 1875, p.24).

party conferred the present name on it in the face of their leader's protestations of professional modesty:[6]

> The bluff or notable landmark stands more than 1500 feet high, and as we have just now rounded it, can see that it is a mount on the top of a range... The river Hodgkinson comes down the south-east side; bending round, flows on north-west down that range to the junction of the Mitchell. Our party still persists in calling this Mount Mulligan.[7]

When Mulligan's fifth expedition of 1876 discovered gold on the Hodgkinson itself, a further rush brought mining settlement to the foot of the mountain. The towns of Thornborough and Kingsborough flourished briefly on the upper Hodgkinson and small townships spread north-west along the river to within two or three kilometres of the mountain. Woodville and Stewart's Town (sometimes Stuartstown), the northernmost outposts of the Hodgkinson field, stood near the junction of the Hodgkinson River and Richards Creek, which drains a gorge in the face of Mount Mulligan.

The Hodgkinson boom was short-lived. Mining operations contracted to the deep reefs around Kingsborough and Thornborough within a few years, and the town of Woodville had shrunk to a population of one determined digger by 1891.[8] But the difficulty of overland transport from the ports of Cardwell and Cooktown to the Hodgkinson had led to the establishment of two closer ports in 1876 - Cairns and Port Douglas. The further incentive of tin discoveries in the Herberton district after 1880 brought a railway across the range from Cairns to Mareeba in 1893 and eventually to Herberton in 1910. The expansion of base metal discoveries west and north of Herberton in the 1880s and the 1890s caused the development of a flourishing hinterland of small-scale mining enterprises, dependent on the Cairns-Mareeba railway for market, plant and fuel.

---

6 The first European sighting of Mount Mulligan is problematical. Jack places Kennedy's journey of 26 August 1848 along the Hodgkinson under the face of Mount Mulligan (Jack, *op. cit.*, vol. I, p.215), but this interpretation of Kennedy's fragmentary journal is not supported by others (e.g. E. Beale, *Kennedy of Cape York*, Adelaide 1970, p.194), and is flatly refuted by the only other surviving account of the Kennedy expedition (W. Carron, *Narrative of an Expedition...*, Sydney 1849, pp.42-44). Mount Mulligan was for a time thought to be the feature named Mount Lilley by the Hann expedition on 30 July 1872, but the vagueness of the Hann's navigation left this in dispute. (Jack, *op. cit.*, vol. II, p.383). Mulligan and Hann later concluded that "it was impossible for Mount Lilley to be Mount Mulligan." (Mulligan's reminiscences, *Queenslander* 31 December 1904, p. 8)

7 Mulligan, *op. cit.*, pp.15-16.

8 Sub-Inspector Lamond to Commissioner of Police, 27 November 1891. (Letter refers to investigation of a complaint about Aborigines on the upper Hodgkinson.) Q.S.A. COL 139, 91/14183.

As gold declined in economic significance, the Hodgkinson valley was left to the deep miners and the pastoralists. At least two cattle properties, the Wason's and Crowley's, were established near Woodville by the 1890s,[9] in the face of sporadic Aboriginal resistance. In March 1883, a stockman, Charles Desailly, had been fatally speared at Mount Mulligan while mustering cattle on foot in the Richards Creek gorge.[10] A state of armed watchfulness seems to have been taken for granted among settlers at the time, for Desailly was dismissed in a police report as being "himself entirely to blame for his untimely end".[11] In the early 1890s the European community of the Woodville district mounted a punitive expedition against an Aboriginal camp, inflicting an unknown number of casualties.[12]

Operations resumed at the gold-town of Woodville in 1892 when Bill Richards commenced mining at the Dagworth mine assisted by his son, Frank, and five stepsons surnamed Harris from his wife's previous marriage. The Richards-Harris family was to play a major role in the subsequent development of Mount Mulligan.

In early 1907, after prospecting for gemstones in the gorge of Richards Creek at Mount Mulligan, Bill Harris of Woodville brought home small samples of a sooty black mineral. The mountain was geologically an improbable site for gems, but Bill Harris' discovery was of considerably greater economic significance - it was coal.[13] The existence of coal under Mount Mulligan had been predicted in 1878 in a public lecture at Thornborough by the Reverend Tenison Woods.[14] None of the thousands of miners who had passed through the Hodgkinson had sought to investigate this prophecy.

Bill Harris' find aroused interest in the two great mining empires which by 1907 had risen to dominate North Queensland. That of John Moffat operated the Great Northern tin mine at Herberton, the Great Southern tin mine and smelters at Irvinebank, and a number of smaller mines linked by a network of light railways. The Chillagoe Company, which had bought Moffat's western interests in 1898, operated a large

---

9 J.W. Crowley to Colonial Secretary, 28 December 1892. Q.S.A. COL 139, 93/00248.

10 Thomas McCarthy to Edwin Desailly, 14 March 1883. Letter in the possession of Norman Desailly, Noble Park, Victoria.

11 Sub-Inspector Carr to Colonial Secretary, 16 July 1883. Q.S.A. COL/A366, 83/3847.

12 Police Magistrate Zillman to Under Colonial Secretary, 30 January 1893, Q.S.A. COL 139, 93/01407; and Richards, *op. cit.*, p.255. Both accounts are vague, and may possibly refer to separate but similar punitive expeditions.

13 H.A. Borland, 'First Years of Mt. Mulligan Colliery', *Cairns Post*, 5 June 1941.

14 *Walsh and Tinaroo Miner*, 21 May 1913.

smelter at Chillagoe and a railway system extending from the state railhead at Mareeba to the copper mines at Einasleigh and Forsayth and the copper, silver and lead mines of the Chillagoe and Mungana district. The Chillagoe smelters drew the bulk of their ore from the Mungana Company, closely allied to the Chillagoe Company, whose principal workings were the Girofla and Lady Jane mines at Mungana.[15]

The Chillagoe Company had spent its life in a precarious financial state, with a history of repeated reconstruction.[16] In 1900 it had launched an ambitious program of development at Chillagoe before doing an adequate geological assessment of its resources. Financed largely by London debenture and share-holders, it had concluded two advantageous agreements with Queensland governments leading to the construction of the Chillagoe railway in 1900 and the Etheridge railway in 1906, and had subsisted on the promise of a number of small base metal deposits for ten years without ever paying a dividend.

In 1907 base metal prices went through the floor; the copper price plunged from £112 in March to £62 in December.[17] Both the Irvinebank and Chillagoe companies sought to make economies in every way possible, and one option was to reduce fuel costs. Coal and coke for smelters and locomotives had to be shipped from the West Moreton and Newcastle fields. Local timber was burned where possible but in 1907, 7,179 tons of coke was unloaded in the port of Cairns, the bulk of it intended for mineral smelting.[18] The Chillagoe Company's demand for cheaper fuel was particularly great since in 1907 it was expanding its smelting capacity to treat the growing silver-lead output of the Mungana mines.[19]

The existence of a new source of fuel close to the Mareeba-Chillagoe railway was obviously of great interest to both companies. Soon after the discovery of coal at Mount Mulligan, an initial prospecting lease of six hundred and forty acres was taken up by John Moffat and exploratory mining began. The outcrop in the gorge pinched out within six metres from the surface, and operations shifted to the eastern face of the

---

15 Bell, "History", Chillagoe Smelter Conservation Plan, 1993, pp. 6-24.

16 Chillagoe Proprietary Limited was registered in Queensland in 1897. Subsequent reconstructions of the company were: 1898 Chillagoe Railways and Mines Limited, 1902 New Chillagoe Railways and Mines Limited, 1905 Chillagoe Company Limited, 1913 Chillagoe Limited; wound up in 1923. (Compiled from documents in JUS 54 and JUS 55, and Company Registers 23/1913 and 227 book 11, all in Q.S.A.)

17 *A.R.* 1907, p.3.

18 *A.R.* 1907, p.117.

19 *A.R.* 1906, p.72.

mountain. By September 1907 the new tunnel, which was to be known as Number One Adit, had been driven twenty metres into the coal seam near the southern side of the gorge entrance. Six tonnes of coal were tested in a local furnace[20] and a larger consignment was taken by dray to Irvinebank for more extensive testing in smelters and locomotives. A government geologist, L.C. Ball, cursorily inspected the coal seams in 1909.[21]

Despite Moffat's early initiative in exploring the coalfield, it was the Chillagoe Company which took over its development. In 1910, after a curiously sluggish period of development financed by Moffat, the Chillagoe Company commenced prospecting in earnest. Moffat had by this time registered four prospecting leases, each of one square mile, covering the most obvious coal-bearing area. The Chillagoe Company employed Jim Harris of Woodville, a mining engineer, to supervise operations on the field, and took up leases extending north and south of Moffat's along the coal out crop. Harris opened two further tunnels, Adits Two and Three, on the eastern face of the mountain a mile north of Number One.[22]

The Chillagoe smelters were now working at greatly increased capacity, but were struggling with metallurgical difficulties. The company was producing blister copper from a new plant completed in 1908, and installed a state-of-the-art but highly inefficient silver-lead smelting process employing Huntington-Heberlein roasting ovens and Edwards blast furnaces.[23] During 1910 the Chillagoe Company imported 10,588 tones of coke and 6,000 tons of coal through Cairns, and consumed in addition some 40,000 tons of firewood.[24]

The significance of the Chillagoe Company's enterprises and the steady decline in output from earlier northern mineral fields was reflected in administrative terms in February 1909, when the Hodgkinson Gold and Mineral Field and the Walsh and Tinaroo Mineral Field were abolished, and their territory amalgamated into the Chillagoe Gold and Mineral Field.[25] However, the Chillagoe Company, never a profitable concern, was coming under increased pressure from several directions; a succession of falls in lead and copper prices

20 Borland, 'First Years...', *op. cit.*
21 Ball, *Notes on Coal at Mount Mulligan*, G.S.Q. 222, 1909.
22 *Ibid.*, G.S.Q. 237, p.34.
23 *A.R.* 1908, p.72.
24 Ball, G.S.Q. 237, p.37.
25 *A.R.* 1909, p.38.

from 1907 to 1911 reduced the smelters' financial returns, and led to a reduction in the quantity of ore bought by the smelters. Many of the small, independently-owned mines of the Mungana district were forced to close. The Company's position was not assisted by the formation of the Amalgamated Workers' Association in May 1908, which gave rise to a period of industrial militancy in the Company's mines and railway works.[26]

The company was described by the Under-Secretary for Mines in 1908 as existing under 'a burden of depression'.[27] Faced with declining profitability at a time when it was massively over-capitalised at the smelters and on the Etheridge railway, the company approached the Queensland Government for assistance early in 1911, at the same time embarking on development at Mount Mulligan in readiness for production. The supply of cheaper fuel must at the time have seemed a panacea for the smelters' financial troubles but in retrospect was simply an exacerbation of the company's chief problem - excessive spending in pursuit of a diminishing return.

A mining engineer, S. Manwaring, apparently from Tasmania, was engaged to report on the Mount Mulligan operation, but had the misfortune to ship north on the SS *Yongala* which sank with no survivors between Mackay and Townsville on the night of 23 March 1911.[28] In his place the company employed colliery manager James Watson of Wollongong, "a man of considerable note in the coal world", who had experience as a coal mine manager in New South Wales and New Zealand, and as a government Inspector of Collieries, sent to investigate the aftermath of two mine disasters. He visited Mount Mulligan in June 1911, and made recommendations for the mine's future.[29] Development on the site was placed in the hands of a Lancashire mine manager, G.B. Stones.

26 K.H. Kennedy, The Public Life of William McCormack, PhD Thesis, James Cook University 1973, pp.10-12.

27 *A.R.* 1908, p.72.

28 *Brisbane Courier*, 31 March 1911.

29 *Cairns Post*, 25 September 1912. James Thomas Watson, born Ballarat 1872, N.S.W. mine manager's certificate no. 169, 1898. Manager, Stockton colliery, Newcastle, 1898-1900; lecturer in coalmining 1900-1902; Government Inspector of Collieries, N.S.W., 1902-1906; prominent in Mount Kembla Disaster aftermath, 1902; Manager Paparoa colliery, N.Z., 1907-1911; Corrimal colliery, Wollongong, 1911-1914; Mount Mulligan colliery 1914-1922. Awarded Clarke Medal for services in Mount Mulligan disaster aftermath, 1922. Died 1938. (P. Bell, "Watson, James Thomas 1872-1938", *Australian Dictionary of Biography Supplementary Volume*, Melbourne University Press, 2005, pp. 398-399; Interview with Jack Watson, Slade Point, 6 March 1977; and *R.C.* pp.4-5.)

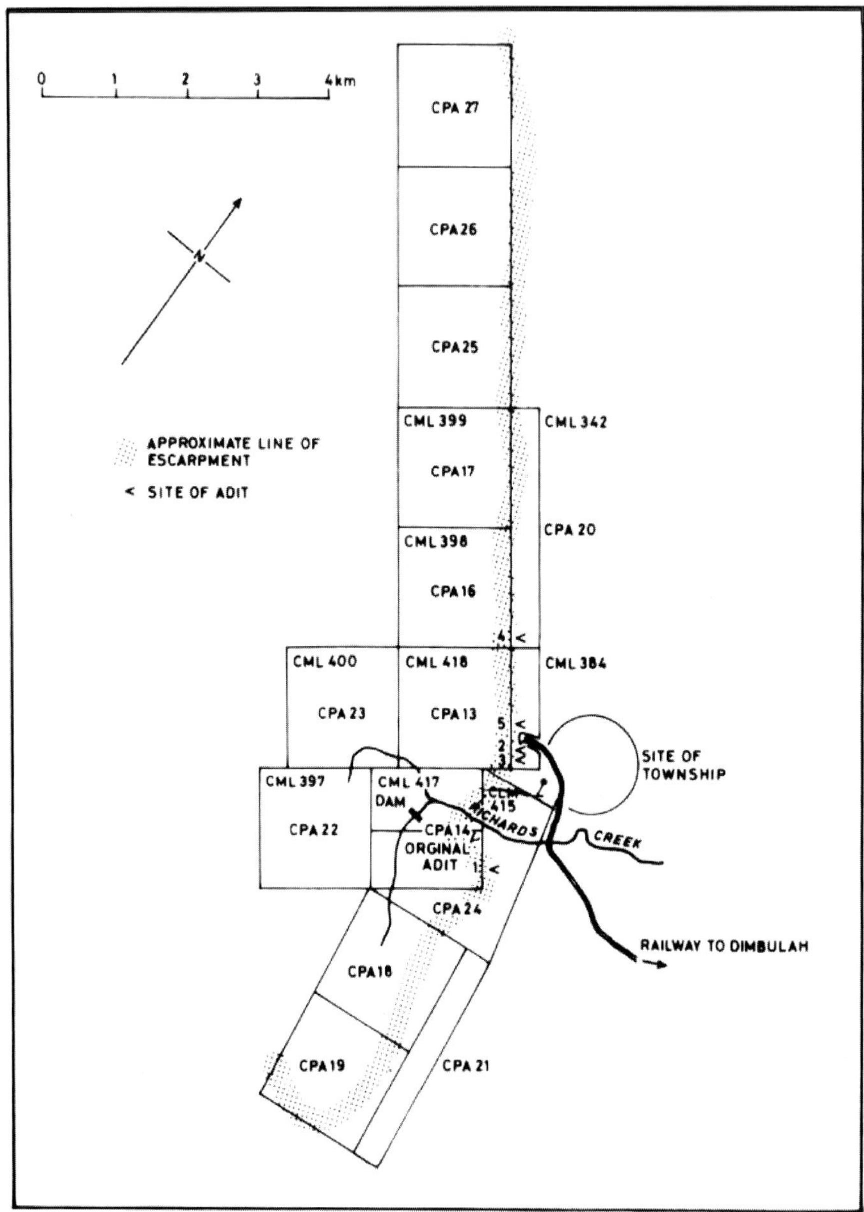

004 Coal Prospecting Areas (CPA) and Coal Mining Leases (CML) registered at Mount Mulligan. CPAs 13, 14, 22, 23 & 24, and CMLs 397, 400, 417 & 418 were registered by John Moffat, the remainder by the Chillagoe Company

Initial work concentrated on Number Two Adit. The decomposed coal close to the surface was poor in quality, the unstable ground required much costly timbering, and constant pumping was needed to clear the tunnel of water seepage.[30] In August 1911, Lionel Ball returned to the field and carried out an extensive geological survey of the coal deposits. His report, published the following year, showed that at least one of the Mount Mulligan seams was suitable for coking, and that, given the accessibility and shallow dip of the seams, no great difficulties were likely to be encountered in extracting coal. He calculated the annual demand for Mount Mulligan coal at 60,000 tons per year, supporting the rate of production of 1,000 tons per week which the Chillagoe Company proposed, and concluded: "The future of the field depends wholly on the construction of a railway."[31]

In 1911 the Chillagoe Company had surveyed a route for a railway from Mount Mulligan to connect with the Chillagoe line at Dimbulah, thirty miles south. The proximity of the route to the fading town of Thornborough aroused local hopes of a revival of the Hodgkinson goldfield, which had officially closed in 1909.[32] The Chillagoe Company's sole concern, however, was with the transportation of coal, and ultimately coke, from Mount Mulligan to Chillagoe. Indications were that the quality of the coal would improve, and the difficulties of extracting it diminish, as Adits Two and Three reached more stable ground under the escarpments of Mount Mulligan. But the coal was valueless until it was connected by rail with the furnaces at Chillagoe.

In April 1911, the Chillagoe Company had approached the Queensland Premier, D.F. Denham, and the Secretary for Railways, W.T. Paget, with a proposition for the construction of a railway from Dimbulah to Mount Mulligan.[33] The Government responded with a grant of two thousand pounds for further exploratory development at Mount Mulligan, and a degree of encouragement for the prospect of a railway. Presumably the visit of Ball to the field in August 1911 stemmed from these negotiations.

Popular agitation for the construction of the Mount Mulligan railway soon followed. The campaign was led by the *Cairns Post* whose owner, A.J. Draper, was chairman of the Cairns Stock Exchange, had mining interests, and had been in the 1880s Secretary of the Cairns Railway League and a vocal Separationist.[34] In 1911, the Cairns Chamber of Commerce urged the government to enact the railway legislation

30 *A.R.* 1910, p.48.
31 Ball, G.S.Q. 237, p.39.
32 Borland, 'First Years...', *op. cit.*
33 *Q.P.D.* vol.113, 1912, p.2539.
34 *Life of A.J. Draper*, Cairns 1931.

during the current session.[35] As railway excitement heightened, the lions of the Cairns business community were entertained on a visit to Mount Mulligan in September 1912, as guests of the Woothakata Shire Council.[36] The Chillagoe Company's manager there, Stones, informed the assembled entrepreneurs that the estimated life of the coalfield was "something like 3,000 years".[37]

The *Cairns Post*'s editorials grew steadily more shrill throughout late 1912 in their demands for a railway to Mount Mulligan. The benefits the editor envisaged as emanating from the coalfield grew steadily to embrace all of Queensland, then the Commonwealth, finally culminating in an extraordinary fantasy in which Mount Mulligan coal, a transcontinental railway and the Panama Canal would combine to make Cairns the economic hub of the continent:

> If...the transcontinental line connects with the western terminus of the Cairns line, and a short line 29 miles in length is constructed between the Mount Mulligan coal field and the Chillagoe line, abundant supplies of cheap and excellent steaming coal will be available at a point where it will be most required .... as soon as the Panama Canal is open for traffic, Cairns will be the most direct port connected by rail with the rest of Australia for all European and American shipping .... it will act as a distinct inducement to much of the shipping to make Cairns its terminal Australian port.[38]

The enthusiasm was not shared by all the North. The Atherton Tableland resented the recent curtailment of construction on the Millaa Millaa and Cedar Creek (Ravenshoe) lines running through agricultural districts, and gave only qualified support to this proposal for a railway to yet another lonely mine.[39]

Nonetheless, in October 1912 a meeting of local authorities and business interests in Cairns found sufficient local enthusiasm for the projected railway to send a deputation to meet Denham in Brisbane. The apparent success of this deputation in eliciting from the premier a promise to introduce the Mount Mulligan railway legislation before the end of the session caused the *Post* to wax fulsome over the magnanimous response of the Liberal government to the entreaties

35 *Cairns Post*, 21 November 1911.

36 The Woothakata Divisional Board was established at Thornborough in 1876, became the Woothakata Shire in 1907, moved its office to Mareeba in 1919, and was renamed Mareeba Shire on 20 December 1947. Woothakata is reputedly another Aboriginal name for Mount Mulligan, but this seems unverifiable.

37 *Cairns Post*, 19 September 1912.

38 *Ibid.*, 26 October 1912.

39 *Ibid.*, 8 and 9 October 1912.

005 James Watson, about 1921 (Doris Smith)

of northern citizens.[40] No mention was made of the equally influential negotiations the Chillagoe Company had been conducting with Denham to the same end for eighteen months past.

Queensland Railways commenced locomotive tests of Mount Mulligan coal in October 1911 and these continued intermittently for over a year. Initial results were highly encouraging, and Railways Commissioner Evans wired to J.S. Reid, chairman of the Chillagoe Company, an enthusiastic if slightly ambiguous report: "My locomotive officer reports Mount Mulligan coal equal to Newcastle. I congratulate you hope you are better".[41] Further tests were less exhilarating, but demonstrated that

40 *Ibid.*, 31 October 1912.
41 Evans to Reid, telegram 24 October 1911. Q.S.A. A/9230, batch 1.

Mount Mulligan coal compared favourably with the Ipswich coal then used in northern locomotives. The prolonged duration of the locomotive tests reflects a lingering suspicion that the samples supplied by the Chillagoe Company were handpicked, and not typical of the mine's output.[42] The Cairns Gas Company also tested Mount Mulligan coal and found it suitable for its own purposes.[43]

The Chillagoe Company's representative in Brisbane, A.J. Thynne, found himself under increased pressure to conclude the Mount Mulligan railway negotiations as 1912 proceeded. The Lady Jane mine at Mungana, one of the Company's most important sources of silver-lead ore, had been closed since 1909 by a succession of misfortunes including an underground fire and a massive fall of rock.[44] The shareholders were becoming restless, and in October Reid cabled to Thynne: "Time flying trust nearing settlement put me in position if possible to recommend on Tuesday some satisfactory public announcement here and London necessary to allay growing anxiety."[45]

Negotiations were concluded in November. The Queensland Government agreed to build the Mount Mulligan railway at an estimated cost of over £114,000, and the Chillagoe Company was to purchase Treasury Bills at 4% to reimburse the state as construction proceeded. The Company was also required to provide coal to satisfy Queensland Railways' requirements on the Cairns-Mareeba line.[46]

Despite the *Cairns Post*'s editorial fears of Labor opposition, debate in the Legislative Assembly on the Mount Mulligan railway proposal centred as much on regional partisanship as on opposition to the advancement of a Chillagoe Company fuel monopoly. The recent curtailment of government spending on railway construction drew criticism of the Mount Mulligan proposal from members in whose electorates railway proposals had recently been shelved - the Dawson Valley line, the Miles-Taroom railway and the Atherton Tableland extensions. Where the nature of the proposal was more clearly understood, there was opposition to the highly favourable terms granted to the Chillagoe Company. It was pointed out that the government

42 State Mining Engineer to Under Secretary for Mines, memorandum 23 August 1912, and annotation 'Seen - but I am not convinced - as the Mulligan coal may have been a *picked* lot. C.R. 28/12/11' on Chief Mechanical Engineer to Commissioner for Railways, 22 December 1911, which gives details of tests showing the superiority of Mount Mulligan coal. Both in Q.S.A. A/9230, batch 1.

43 *Cairns Post*, 16 October 1912.

44 *A.R.* 1912, p.38.

45 Reid to Thynne, telegram 8 October 1912. Q.S.A. A/9230, unnumbered batch.

46 Thynne to Paget, 11 November 1912. Q.S.A. A/9230, unnumbered batch.

intended to pay the Company 4% interest on its own expenses in constructing the line. Ideological opposition to private railways and coal mines was expressed by Labor members but influenced few of their votes.

Supporters of the line argued that the opening up of Mount Mulligan's vast coal reserves would revive mining in the Cairns hinterland; huge bodies of metal ore lay in the ground with lack of fuel the chief obstacle to their exploitation. Northern members hailed the line as a small redress of perennial neglect of North Queensland and, in a stirring advocacy of pouring good money after bad, several members pointed out the necessity of ensuring the continued viability of the Chillagoe Company to safeguard the Government's investments, especially that in the Etheridge Railway of 1906. The proposal passed easily after two lengthy days of debate in November 1912.[47] The Legislative Council referred the proposal to a Select Committee which sat for one day and produced a glowing report in favour of the railway. The proposal passed the Council without opposition.[48]

With legislative sanction effected, Railway Commissioner Evans concluded final negotiations with the Chillagoe Company in Melbourne and preparations began for construction of the railway. Parochial jealousy on a more local level now arose. An organization styling itself the Wolfram Railway League lobbied H.A.C. Douglas, MLA for Cook, and E.G. Theodore, MLA for Chillagoe, to have the railway survey shifted westward to pass through the moribund town of Wolfram Camp, without success.[49] On an even more minute scale, the Woothakata Shire complained that the survey passed through land gazetted as a cemetery reserve at Thornborough, and requested that the line be moved to a new route they proposed in order to preserve the sanctity of the burial ground. In a letter to Douglas, however, the shire clerk made the true motivation of this complaint more explicit by confiding: "If the deviation was allowed it would make communication with the town more complete."[50]

The commencement of the railway on which so many hopes depended was done with proper ceremony. On the 19th May 1913 Sir William MacGregor, Governor of Queensland, was drawn majestically

47 *Q.P.D.* vol.113, 1912, pp.2531-63 and 2583-2611.

48 *Ibid.*, p.2865.

49 Secretary, Wolfram Railway League to Douglas, 13 January 1913, and to Theodore, 18 January 1913. Q.S.A. A/9230, batch 2A.

50 J. Rank to Douglas, 14 October 1913. Q.S.A. A/9231, batch 2C.

into Dimbulah by a lavishly decorated locomotive.[51] In an afternoon of speeches and gourmandising, hosted by the Woothakata Shire Council, the Governor turned the first sod of the Mount Mulligan Railway, and in the course of his speech he described the event as one of "historical importance to the whole of the Commonwealth", and also predicted that Britain would not go to war against Germany.[52] The Chillagoe Company underwent reconstruction to finance the Mount Mulligan railway; in March 1913 the Chillagoe Company was liquidated and its assets passed to Chillagoe Limited, which called up capital from shareholders to finance the purchase of government bonds.[53]

Construction of the Mount Mulligan line was delayed by repeated strikes and difficulty in obtaining labour, and dragged on for sixteen months. The workers on the line, strengthened by labour shortage, refused piecework and successfully struck for a flat wage of ten shillings a day.[54] Not until September 1914 was the line inspected as "practically finished", and then the quality of much of the work done was so deficient as to require immediate remedial attention.[55]

As the railway progressed, development continued at the Mount Mulligan mine, and Chillagoe Limited took up extensive coalmining leases on the land north and south of the Moffat claims in place of its prospecting licences. A township was surveyed, and land sold at auction at the Thornborough court house in April 1914 began to be occupied as tents and modest homes spread slowly along Watson and Harris streets. A brickmaking plant and a dam on Richards Creek on top of Mount Mulligan were built, and operations were commenced on the construction of a powerhouse, utilizing boilers and generator from Chillagoe Limited's copper mine at Forsayth.[56]

But as the railway neared the township of Mount Mulligan, the combined burdens of reduced ore capacity and increased expenditure weighed increasingly on Chillagoe Limited. Finally, over-capitalisation expressed itself in a shortage of operating funds. The smelters closed in

51 General Traffic Manager, Townsville, to General Traffic Superintendent, 8 September 1913. Q.S.A. A/9231, batch 7.

52 *Walsh and Tinaroo Miner*, 21 May 1913.

53 C.L. Hewitt to Registrar of Joint Stock Companies, 7 March 1913. Q.S.A. Company Register 277 book 11, and *Queensland Statutes*, vol.10, p.8629.

54 Evans, minute 21 May 1913, Q.S.A. A/9231, batch 8.

55 Inspecting Engineer to Commissioner of Railways, 5 September 1914. Q.S.A. A/9231, batch 2C. A distinctive feature of the surviving Mount Mulligan railway works is the use of earth embankments across creeks where bridges might normally be expected. Apparently horse labour for earthworks was preferred to more expensive skilled human labour for trestle carpentry.

56 *Q.G.M.J.* 15 May 1914, p.274.

March 1914; the Mount Mulligan mine fell idle in July, and the township which had sprung to life in April was rapidly deserted.[57] In August, the railway arrived in a ghost town.

Faced with the embarrassment of an expensive railway to nowhere, the Denham government pressed on Chillagoe Limited its obligation to supply railway coal, and the mine re-opened in 1915, supplying fuel to Queensland Government and Chillagoe Limited railways and the Irvinebank smelters. The Mount Mulligan railway officially opened on 7 April 1915.[58] Forty-five miners were employed in 1915 as operations resumed on a restricted scale. The Babcock and Wilcox boiler and 300 KW generator from Forsayth were in operation and work had commenced on a coke plant. A ventilating fan was installed at the entrance to Number Three Adit, expelling air which entered the mine at Number Two and passed through the workings. Even with the limited market available, however, mining operations were restricted by the unavailability of labour,[59] a problem which was to plague the Mount Mulligan mine throughout its operation. While experienced miners were plentiful in North Queensland, most were trained in metalliferous mining which employed techniques quite different from those practised in coal mines. Mount Mulligan was too remote from the established coalmining areas of Australia to attract enough miners with the necessary skills:

> As in the previous year, the only serious difficulty met with was in connection with the supply of skilled labour. A number of the best of our miners enlisted, and are now on the front, and we have found the greatest difficulty in filling their places. In view of the fact that the miners earn a higher average wage than in any other district in Australia...it is difficult to understand why men do not settle down here.[60]

Watson had been appointed Superintending Engineer at Mount Mulligan in 1914, in charge of the mine's development. Aware of recent technical innovations in British and American coal mines, he sought to reduce the mine's dependence on manpower by installing mechanical coal-cutters and developing the underground workings for their use.

There were two principal methods of extracting coal from underground workings: the older "Welsh bord", or "bord-and-pillar" system, involved the extraction of coal from parallel straight galleries, or

57 *A.R.* 1914, p.43.

58 Q.S.A. A/9232, batch 33.

59 *A.R.* 1915, p.54.

60 *Chillagoe Limited Annual Report*, 1916, p.7.

bords, on a square grid plan, so that a regular pattern of square pillars of coal was left to support the roof. Only about half the coal in a seam could initially be extracted by this method. The coal remaining in the pillars could subsequently be removed and the roof simply allowed to collapse if the district was to be abandoned. Alternatively, the pillars could be progressively removed and replaced by packed columns of stone and waste coal, called goaf. Bord-and-pillar mining was highly labour-intensive, although electric coal-cutters, called shortwall machines, reduced the labour required in actually hewing the coal.

The technique which Watson introduced to the mine was new and rather radical: in the "longwall system", coal was extracted by a bigger coal-cutter, the longwall machine, which moved along an uninterrupted face of the coal-seam perhaps two or three hundred metres in length, removing coal as it travelled. The mine roof was left unsupported by this complete extraction of coal from large areas of the seam, and was normally simply allowed to collapse under the weight of the overburden. This process was not as horrifying as it sounds since the coal-bearing rock strata in most mines are quite plastic; rather than falling abruptly, the roof descended almost imperceptibly, progressively filling the space some distance behind the working-face. If necessary, this crushing process could be retarded by artificial props or packs of goaf. For access to the face, roadways were kept open by timbering and by regularly cutting away, or 'brushing', rock from the descending roof.[61] The longwall system had the advantage of requiring less labour for cutting coal, timbering roadways and building packwalls, and also simplified the mine layout, thus reducing the effort expended in wheeling coal from the working-face to the pit-head.

Longwall and shortwall coal-cutting machines were essentially similar in function. They operated like huge horizontal chainsaws, travelling along the working-face and undercutting the coal at ground level. Thus, separated from its foundation, the coal usually fell outward from the face in large blocks, under pressure from the roof. Where the coal did not fall, it was drilled near the roof and dislodged by blasting. The detached blocks of coal were broken up by hand tools or by further blasting, loaded into skips and wheeled from the face.

The Sullivan coal-cutting machines installed at Mount Mulligan were of American manufacture and electrically operated. Their use demanded extensive electrical installations in the mine workings. One disadvantage

61 G.L. Kerr, *Practical Coal Mining*, London 1922, pp.209-224.

of the machines was that they greatly increased the amount of coal dust present in a mine already unpleasantly dry and dusty for most of the year, but economy of operation out-weighed this consideration. Two Sullivan machines were in use at Mount Mulligan by 1917, and a third was installed in 1919.[62]

The collapse of Chillagoe Limited's operations in 1914 had brought depression to much of the Cairns hinterland, whose hand-to-mouth mining enterprises were heavily dependent on the Chillagoe smelters and railway for processing and marketing of their products. However, two distant events combined to bring the North Queensland base metal industry back to life. During the Great War there was a steady increase in the prices of copper and lead, improving prospects for viable operation of the smelters. And in 1915, the Denham Liberal government was defeated by the Labor party under T.J. Ryan, giving Queensland a government with an expressed ideological commitment to the establishment of state enterprises. Before the outbreak of war, the Denham government had lost patience with Chillagoe Limited, which after an expenditure of nearly six million pounds on its North Queensland projects still sought government assistance in its financial straits.[63] But the new Labor government, flushed with victory and encouraged by wartime metal prices, sought to advance its own policy and solve the Chillagoe problem in a single bold stroke - the purchase of Chillagoe Limited's enterprise.

Shortly after the election of the Ryan government in May 1915, Chillagoe Limited began negotiations through its strategically-situated Brisbane solicitor, A.J. Thynne, MLC, for the sale of its North Queensland assets to the Queensland government. The Company's initial price was £950,000. In August 1915, Ryan approached Prime Minister Fisher for Federal funds to re-open the Chillagoe smelters as a state enterprise, but without success.[64] During the course of its negotiations with the Queensland Government, Chillagoe Limited consolidated its position on the Mount Mulligan coal-field. The heart of the coal-bearing area was still under John Moffat's four leases. In September 1915, rights to these leases passed to Chillagoe Limited at a price of £50,000, to be paid as a royalty of one shilling per ton of coal extracted from the field.[65]

62 *A.R.* 1917, p.25, and 1919, p.49.

63 *Worker*, 4 January 1917.

64 *Q.P.D.* vol.125, 1916, p.2398.

65 Moffat to Queensland National Bank, letter of escrow, 6 September 1915. Copy attached to letter from Flower and Hart to Crown Solicitor, 12 April 1919. Q.S.A. JUS 55, 19/3482.

Ryan went to London in March 1916 and by May had obtained the backing of the Imperial Government for his plan to remedy "the idleness of certain copper propositions".[66] Britain was facing a serious base metal shortage caused by the unexpectedly high consumption of munitions on the western front, and the price of copper was rising dramatically. He next approached the trustees for Chillagoe Limited's debenture holders, and found them more amenable than Thynne. Uneasy at the Company's declining fortunes, the London trustees had delayed foreclosure only on the Melbourne directors' assurance that the Queensland Government was eager to buy and that a high price was possible. Disabused of this belief by Ryan, the trustees agreed to Queensland's purchase of Chillagoe Limited's assets for £450,000, less than half Thynne's original proposal, though the amount owed debenture holders alone was £670,000.[67]

Buoyed by this coup, Ryan in December 1916 placed before Parliament the Chillagoe and Etheridge Railways Purchase Bill, under which the state was empowered to purchase the railways and "any other property" of Chillagoe Limited for a sum not exceeding £450,000 in Queensland Government debentures.[68] The Bill was rejected by the Legislative Council in February 1917 after a Select Committee had reported unfavourably.

A second attempt, the Chillagoe and Etheridge Railways Bill, was introduced in November 1917. This second bill was far more specific than that of 1916, covering the purchase of all Chillagoe Limited's assets except the Mount Mulligan mine, and providing for a loan of £90,000 to the company to develop a coke plant and other improvements at Mount Mulligan. Because of the central importance of Mount Mulligan in the proposal, debate on the 1917 purchase bill sounded eerily like that on the Mount Mulligan railway five years earlier. The viability of Chillagoe Limited's assets, and specifically of Mount Mulligan coal, dominated the debate. The bill's opponents argued that the Chillagoe operations were inherently unsound: "The copper is not there. That is the problem. If the copper were there, there would be no necessity for the debenture holders to go hawking such a valuable concession as this is supposed to be all around the country ...."[69]

66 Queensland Agent-General, London, to Acting Premier, Brisbane. Telegram 11 May 1916. Q.S.A. PRE A524, 16/5778.

67 *Q.P.D.* vol.125, 1916, p.2506, and M. Birrell, T.J. Ryan and the Queensland Labour Party, B.A. Hons. thesis, University of Queensland 1951, pp.91-92.

68 *Q.P.D.* 1916-1917, vol.3, pp.478-88.

69 Speech by J. Tolmie (Liberal, Toowoomba), *Q.P.D.* vol.128, 1917, p.2816.

Theodore, now State Treasurer, spear-headed the government's case. He stressed the potential of fuel from Mount Mulligan for reversing the fortunes of the smelters, and quoted at length from a third geological report by Ball on the coal-field and its mining operations[70]: "... all this depends on the success or otherwise of Mount Mulligan, and whether we can get cheap coal and coke from there."[71] This bill, too, was passed by the Assembly and rejected by the Council in November 1917. The Council concluded that no further evidence had been produced to alter the findings of the Select Committee in February.[72]

The second bill was reintroduced in unaltered form in June 1918. Having passed the Assembly, it was referred by the Council to another Select Committee, which recommended against the bill in early September. However, after the tabling of this report, the Select Committee belatedly travelled to North Queensland and took evidence there from 24 September to 4 October. In a surprising about-face, the Committee convinced itself on the spot that the Chillagoe enterprises were viable, and in a Further Report recommended passage of the bill subject to minor amendments, over which the Assembly did not quibble.[73] The Chillagoe and Etheridge Railways Act received assent on 15 November 1918.[74] The Queensland Government had acquired the metals industry it had sought on the basis of wartime metal prices, but the Great War had ended four days previously, and metal prices were already falling.

Final negotiations proceeded for the handover of Chillagoe Limited's smelters, mines and railways to the state. Mount Mulligan was the sole remaining property in the Company's hands, and began to be developed with the £90,000 the Act provided for this purpose. £25,000 was advanced in late 1918 to pay £10,000 owing to Einasleigh debenture holders, and to discharge a £15,000 loan from the Bank of Australasia in 1914.[75] The Queensland Government took mortgages on the Company's Mount Mulligan property as security on these loans. By July 1919, the mortgages had grown as further Government advances were made: £5,000 for the construction of workmen's cottages, £4,831 for work on

70 Ball, 'Mount Mulligan Coalfield', *Q.G.M.J.* 15 September 1917, pp.444-53.
71 *Q.P.D.* vol.128, 1917, p.2821.
72 *Ibid.*, p.3566.
73 *Q.P.P.* 1918, vol.2, p.1470.
74 *Q.P.P.* vol.131, 1918, p.3646.
75 Crown Solicitor's Office Memorandum 24 December 1918. Q.S.A. JUS 56, 18/20568.

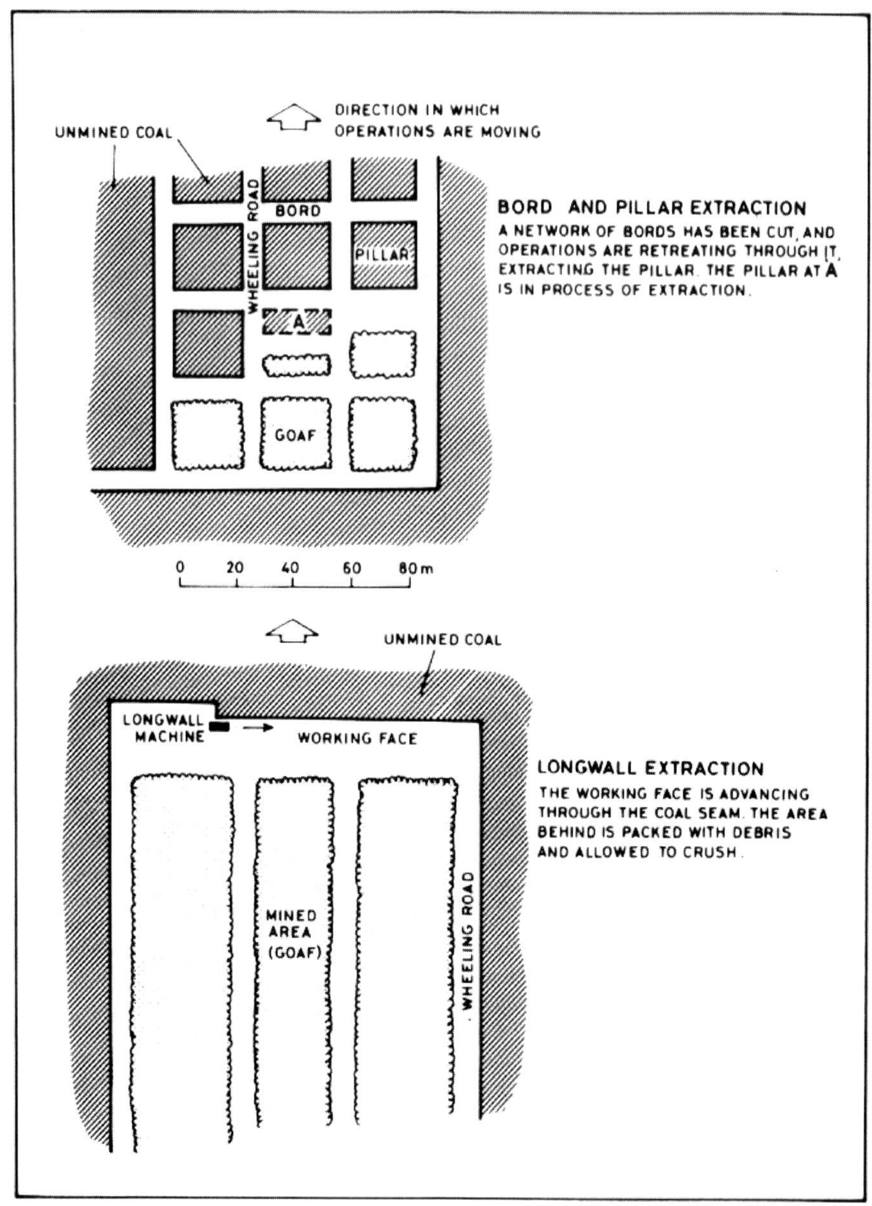

006 Methods of coal extraction

the construction of coke ovens, and £11,524 for installation of a picking belt and shaker plant.[76]

76 Memorandum of mortgage, 15 July 1919, Q.S.A. JUS 54, and Gibson Battle to Chillagoe Limited, 19 June 1919, Q.S.A. JUS 55.

As Chillagoe Limited sank slowly beneath the weight of its mortgages, the purchase of the smelters was effected on 19 June 1919, and P.L. Goddard assumed management of the state's operations.[77] Renovation of the abandoned smelters and pumping out of mines took some months, and it was 1920 before the smelters were blown in and limited production recommenced.[78] When the smelters re-opened, however, they were still firing Newcastle coke, for nothing existed yet of the Mount Mulligan coke works but foundation holes - despite the £60,000 advanced by the state for its construction.

Production of coal at Mount Mulligan, even so, was nearly 24,000 tonnes. Chillagoe Limited had installed an endless ropeway to replace the earlier cumbersome winding-drum haulage of coal from the mine. Coal-skips were drawn from the mine on a two feet gauge tramway to a tippler which emptied them directly into coal trucks on the railway line. The empty skips were re-attached to the moving endless cable and returned to the mine along a second parallel tramway. The dam on top of the mountain was being raised in height to improve water supply capacity, the earlier level having proved inadequate to cope with the dry season demand for water for coal-washing, steam-raising, dust-laying and township consumption. New workers' cottages were under construction.[79] By the standards of 1920, Mount Mulligan, with its electric coal-cutting machines, efficient power generation, longwall extraction methods and endless haulage system was an advanced and progressive mine.

During that same year, Chillagoe Limited commenced work on Number Four Adit, further north along the mountain face. The site was one which Watson had recommended as promising in his report of May 1911, but it was also a few yards north of the Irvinebank Company's leases, on Chillagoe Limited's land. In view of the shilling per ton royalty which Chillagoe was paying to the Irvinebank Company, the motivation for the siting of Number Four Adit is open to speculation. The tunnel was driven some hundred metres, but never developed for production and seems to have been abandoned in 1921.

A stable township of over 300 citizens was established below the cliffs of Mount Mulligan by 1921. 175 voters were registered as living

77 *Q.P.D.* vol.139, 1922, p.698.
78 *A.R.* 1920, p.42.
79 *Ibid.*, p.51.

007 Sullivan shortwall coal-cutting machine with Jeffrey drill in background (*A.R.* 1909, p. 150)

in the town in that year.[80] 90 miners were on the books of the Mount Mulligan branch of the Queensland Colliery Employees' Union.[81] The manager, engineer and a few other dignitaries occupied substantial houses on the slopes of the mountain, and many of the miners were housed in simple iron-roofed timber frame dwellings. The less fortunate, however, lived in corrugated iron huts, uninhabitable during most of the daylight hours. A few recent arrivals had recourse to tents.

The town boasted two hotels, the *Mount Mulligan* and the *Federal*, universally referred to as the "top" hotel and the "bottom" hotel, apparently with reference both to their positions in relation to the mountain and their social standing. O'Brien's *Mount Mulligan* hotel - a two-story corrugated iron edifice - dominated the town; it was made all the more attractive by the recent installation of electric lights powered by the company's generator. [82]

80 This figure is far too low for the adult population of the town. The majority of the names of the miners killed in 1921 do not appear on the electoral roll. Itinerant miners probably did not bother to register. Even so, the 1921 enrolment is a dramatic increase over the 68 voters enrolled in 1920, probably as a result of Labor canvassing before the October 1920 state election.

81 *Worker*, 6 October 1921.

82 Chillagoe Limited ledger, entry 14 September 1921.

008 Harris Street, Mount Mulligan, 1921, looking southwest. The buildings from left are: Post Office, Grainer's grocery, Hutton's drapery, cafe, O'Brien's *Mount Mulligan* (top) hotel and at right the billiards saloon. (QN)

There were five stores and regular out-door film shows. No one in Mount Mulligan owned a motor vehicle, as the only access to the town was by the twice-weekly train to Cairns. An ambulance rail car provided transport to Mareeba hospital in an emergency, although it was kept in regular use for less urgent purposes, and the miners made frequent social visits to Thornborough by pump-car. A predominantly masculine community with a high proportion of short-term residents, Mount Mulligan's social life was naturally somewhat rough around the edges. Spontaneous, unembittered fist-fights between miners were common and the consumption of alcohol was high: "I'm not going to tell you how we lived. We lived on beer mostly," one former miner said.[83] But the town was by no means simply a community of drunken brawlers. The piano was a more important focal point for social activity than the keg, and dance and song evenings were a nightly occurrence in homes and hotels. Because young female dancing partners were in short supply, the girls of Mount Mulligan were in a position to impose a high standard of decorum upon the miners who attended.

A school had opened in August 1915, and by 1921, with two teachers and 74 pupils, was bulging from its tiny classroom. In August 1921 the secretary of the school committee, Frank Grant, complained to Brisbane

83 Interview with Alf Leary, Brisbane, 21 January 1976.

of "the overcrowded condition of the local school" and requested that the building be enlarged.[84] The town also had a church where visiting clergymen from Mareeba and Cairns preached. However, in the early hours of 3 February 1920 a tropical cyclone struck Mount Mulligan. Damage was extensive among the corrugated iron buildings of the town and most were severely damaged; among those destroyed was the church.[85] It tells us much about the community spirit of Mount Mulligan that the unroofed hotels were operating normally within hours, and rebuilt within days. The church was not rebuilt until 1947.

Mount Mulligan in 1921 had outgrown the raw hardships of a pioneer mining town and settled into a relatively stable maturity. Isolation ensured that life was often difficult, but by no means harsh, and a close-knit loyalty, induced by that isolation, was universally recalled by former residents of the town. This sleepy little township, the last remnant of the Chillagoe Company's mining empire, was about to become the setting for the greatest land disaster in Queensland's history.

84 Grant to Minister for Public Instruction, 26 August 1921, Q.S.A. EDU Z1930, 21/41220.
85 Brisbane *Telegraph*, 9 February 1920.

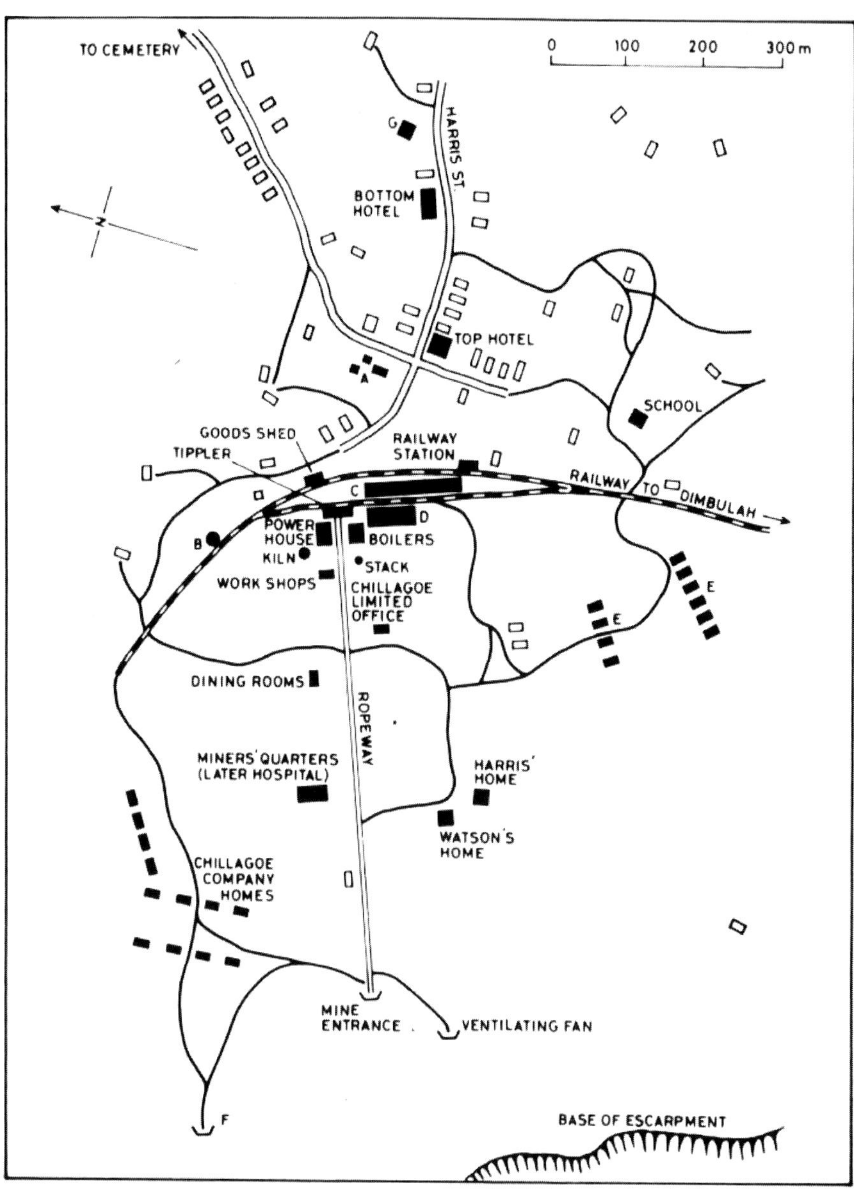

009 Plan of Mount Mulligan town and mine surface workings. Features named on the plan existed at the time of the disaster. Some of later date are identified by letters: A Police Station (1922), B Turntable, C Coal Bin (1923), D Coke Ovens (1923), E State Miners' Houses (1923), F Number Five Adit (1937), G Community Hospital (1936 - still standing)

010 Mount Mulligan State School about 1920, looking northwest (Mary Wardle)

011 Older pupils of Mount Mulligan State School, 21 August 1921. The teachers are Neil Smith and Nellie Hourston. At least 12 of these children lost fathers or brothers in the explosion 29 days later. (Jim McColm)

2.
THE DISASTER

"You'd better all go home. I hold out no hope for any man."

(James Watson, 19 September 1921)

Monday, 19 September 1921, was the beginning of a new cavil at Mount Mulligan. The cavil is an old coalmining practice, intended to equalise every miner's opportunity to improve his earnings. As Mount Mulligan miners were paid by piece-work, that is by weight of coal produced per man, the working conditions in different areas of the mine could greatly affect the miner's income. In areas where the coal was shotty - full of stone pieces, which had to be picked or washed out - or lay in broken strata, less coal could be produced in a working day than in areas where a clean seam of coal lay horizontally. The distance of the working coal-face from the ropeway was another consideration, as the time spent in wheeling a full coal-skip to the ropeway was obviously time not available for extracting coal.

Accordingly, four times each year the miners cavilled, or balloted, for their positions in the mine.[1] Dividing themselves into working pairs, a hewer and a wheeler, the men placed their names in a hat. In the

1 Cavilling Rules, coalmining State Award, *Q.I.G.* 10 November 1919, pp.721-22.

presence of the Underground Manager and two union scrutineers, the pairs of names were drawn in an order corresponding to numbered positions in the mine workings. Not all miners were cavilled. Coal-cutting machine operators were a specially qualified group who could only rotate among a limited number of machine working positions, and some other underground workers such as electricians, carpenters and clippers - who attached the skips to the endless rope - did work not directly involved with coal extraction and were paid a day rate.

The beginning of a new cavil is a time of confusion. Men have to become accustomed to a new working place and often a new workmate. There is usually an abandoned mess to clean up in the new area, since the previous occupants' last day's work there has rarely been conscientiously completed. An unfamiliar environment is confusing in any circumstances, but in the black labyrinth of a coal mine a change of scene induces a fumbling period of disorientation even among veteran miners. Confusion is exacerbated, too, by the absence of men from the cavil or from the first working day. Mount Mulligan had a reputation as a difficult mine because of its relatively thin, shotty coal-seams and its isolation, and the end of a cavil was a likely time for restless miners to seek more congenial conditions in the South, with or without informing the management.[2] An influenza epidemic was affecting Mount Mulligan in 1921, and a number of miners were at home or hospitalised in Mareeba, thus contributing further to the uncertainty of the new cavil.

Fifty-two names were cavilled at Mount Mulligan on Friday, 16 September, and about 74 miners reported to the mine on the following Monday morning. Mostly carrying their own tools, they picked up carbide lamps at the mine entrance, collected the explosives they needed from the store a short distance inside the tunnel, and dispersed into the workings to find their new places.

There were four main working areas in the mine. The Middle or Number Two seam was most fully developed, with roadways extending north and south from the central axis of the mine, the main dip, where the endless ropeway ran. North of the dip was Beattie's Machine Wall, where a Sullivan longwall machine was operating. Thirteen men were to work in this section. South of the dip were two longwall faces, Fitzpatrick's Machine Wall, where the other longwall machine and sixteen men were working, and the Bottom or South Section, which was developed for longwall working, but was being cut by hand in

2 Interview with Jock Clarke, Ipswich, 17 December 1976.

22

Long + Camm ✓	2 + 10 FW
O Halloran + Fogarty ✓	7 + 8 T.S.
Fisher + Seymour ✓	9
Mansfield + Lawson ✓	5 + 6 T.S
Templeton + Loughrie ✓	6 + 9 FW
Jarr + Butler ✓	15
Pattinson + Thompson ✓	11
Drier + Son ✓	14
Hutton + Leary ✓	3 + 11 T.Ste
McColm + Morrissey ✓	19
Jackson + Nixon ✓	20
Regan + Whelan ✓	16
Hawes + Risley ✓	4 + 12 FW
Pattinson + Morrison ✓	1 + 9 FW
Harrison + Johnson ✓	17
Stevens + Swift ✓	13
Surff + Carney ✓	21
Bell + Oslte ✓	12 FW
O Boyle + Speirs ✓	1 + 2 TS
Hall + Smithson ✓	Blank 1
Morgan + Cassloff ✓	8 + 11 FW
Henry + Martin ✓	7 + 10 FW.
Adams + Joachimyik ✓	Blank 2
Cunningham + McIntyre ✓	18
Lomax + Hynes ✓ ✓	3 + 4 Top.h
Bollen + Minogue ✓	Blank 3.

012 Cavil sheet for 19 September 1921, found among George Hawes' effects. (*R.C.* Exhibit 19, p. 173) The numbers refer to positions within the mine; TS and FW stand for Top Seam and Fitzpatrick's Wall.

September 1921. Sixteen men were working on the straight longwall pick-face there, and another eight on the stepped pick-face immediately east of it.

013 The mine entrance about 1919, looking west (Mary Wardle)

The Top or Number One seam workings were of smaller extent and developed on an irregular bord-and-pillar plan. Thirteen men worked there with a shortwall coal-cutting machine. Another eight men were employed in or around the main dip, in the middle seam.[3]

The use of carbide lamps with their exposed flame was potentially hazardous in a coal mine, but was accepted in Mount Mulligan by both management and miners as involving a very remote risk whose alternatives were undesirable. Carbide lamps gave a bright white light, far more comfortable for vision than the dim orange glow of the gauze-enclosed safety lamp, little changed from Sir Humphry Davy's prototype of 1815; and the Queensland miner's preference for convenience over safety has been amply documented.[4] The Queensland Colliery Employees' Union opposed the use of Davy-type safety lamps for mining, as after long periods of working by their poor light, men developed a condition known as Miners' Nystagmus, an involuntary rapid flickering movement of the eyes which severely impaired vision.[5] From Chillagoe Limited's point of view the use of safety lamps was distinctly

3 *R.C.* pp. xxxii-xxxii; plans of mine workings, exhibits 9 and 10; and cavil sheets, exhibits 3, p.164 and 19, p.173.

4 J. Stoodley, 'Queensland Miners' Attitudes Towards the Need for Safety Regulations in the Late Nineteenth Century', *Labour History*, No.14, 1968, pp.23-33.

5 *R.C.* p.96.

undesirable, because a court decision was expected on a 25% loading to be paid to employees working with them.[6]

In any case, flammable gas had never been encountered in the Mount Mulligan mine, a circumstance rare in coal mines, and one which partly explains the disregard of Mount Mulligan miners for a number of safety precautions which were observed as a matter of course by miners elsewhere.

As the mine had been closed since the previous Friday,[7] the Underground Deputy, Frank Grant, with another miner had passed along the working faces and wheeling roads an hour earlier with a safety lamp to check for traces of gas. As usual, none was encountered.[8] Shortly after 8 a.m. all the miners had entered the mine to commence work, and were joined by Tom Evans, the Underground Manager, who began the administrative work attendant on the new cavil in his cabin, about a hundred metres inside the entrance.

Apparently only one person in the town of Mount Mulligan saw the explosion occur. At 9.25 a.m. the children of the Mount Mulligan school were standing on the parade ground before the commencement of lessons, listening to the headmaster, Neil Smith, as he conducted the morning devotional and patriotic ritual. His assistant teacher Nellie Hourston, her attention wandering, was gazing into the distance. Suddenly she was startled by a cloud of black dust erupting half a mile away at the foot of the mountain. Behind the rows of upturned children's faces, in plain view from the school verandah, she could see pieces of timber and sheets of roofing iron, tumbling end over end high in the air. She interrupted Smith to draw his attention to this unusual sight, and as she did so the sound of a violent explosion reached them. Something was seriously wrong. Smith ran immediately to the mine, leaving her to care for the newly-orphaned children of Mount Mulligan in the days that followed.[9]

6 Coalmining State Award, *op. cit.*, p.714. This loading was referred to a later hearing of the court for decision when the 1919 award was handed down, but no later reference to it appears in the *Q.I.G.*: apparently the claim was dropped.

7 Mount Mulligan worked only one shift each weekday.

8 This inspection was required under the Mines Regulation Acts 1910-1920, whenever a mine had been left unoccupied between shifts. (*General Rules: Collieries*, Brisbane 1920, pp.2-3). The Davy safety lamp was a simple oil lamp with two layers of fine copper mesh enclosing the flame to absorb heat and prevent ignition of gas in the atmosphere. It served as a crude indicator of the presence of flammable gas, which burned safely within the gauze, causing a characteristic coloured "cap" to appear on the flame.

9 Interview with Nellie Franklin, *née* Hourston, Malanda, 13 August 1976.

Some witnesses present that morning told of hearing a single large explosion; other people remembered hearing two, the second one much louder. The explosion at Mount Mulligan was clearly heard in Kingsborough, twenty kilometres from the coal mine. North Queensland folklore has the sound carrying much further. Perhaps it was heard in Dimbulah, and Mareeba, and Herberton, but it seems improbable. In any case, the sound of a distant explosion was common in the metalliferous mining areas of North Queensland, unlikely to attract comment at the time, and easy to confuse after the event with many others in memory. In a coalmining community, however, an explosion of the magnitude heard in Mount Mulligan that morning had only one possible cause. The response to it was the instinctive one which has occurred in every coal town where the sound has been heard: the women and surviving men of the town forgot everything else and in a single collective movement converged on the point where the ropeway entered the mountain face.

The first runners met a dazed and coal-blackened man stumbling down the ropeway from the mine. George Morrison was employed by Chillagoe Limited as a blacksmith and tool sharpener. He occupied a small wooden hut only a few paces from the mine entrance, where he maintained picks and other tools for the men working below. Near the blacksmith's hut stood the junction box which regulated electrical current to the coal-cutting machines, and Morrison had frequently complained about the flashes and bangs from the fuses blowing in the mysterious equipment beside him. Preoccupied with his own ordeal, he mumbled to the rescuers who bore him away: "I told them that bloody thing would blow up one day."[10] The hut had been destroyed around him by the blast, but miraculously Morrison escaped nearly unscathed, although badly shocked. He had almost no recollection of the explosion when questioned by the Royal Commissioners a fortnight later.[11]

Watson, the Superintending Engineer, was inspecting the work of the bricklayers on the cokeworks foundations when the explosion occurred, and reached the mine entrance before the crowd gathered around it. The violence of the explosion was obvious in a glance at the surroundings. The steel winding drums, two tonnes in weight, which had worked the old haulage system, had been blasted from their timber framework

10 Interview with Les Weatherston, Brisbane, 22 November 1975.

11 *R.C.* p.1.

014 View up ropeway to the mine entrance after the explosion.
(*Q.G.M.J.* 15 November 1921, p. 442)

above the mine entrance, and lay twenty metres down the ropeway. Steel telegraph poles were bent, leaning away from the mine entrance. A mound of stone, earth and broken timber blocked the mouth of the adit, and it appeared that a massive collapse had occurred in the mine. Heavy black smoke rolled from the mine's two openings. The ventilating fan had been ejected from its shattered concrete housing and lay twisted among the trees, 40 metres in front of the upcast adit. The whole area before the mine entrance had been blackened by a layer of fine coal dust and seared by flame - grass was burning 60 metres from the entrance. Watson was the only person present who had previous experience in the aftermath of a coal dust explosion. He could envisage very accurately from this scene at the surface what conditions must be like in the mine. Watson climbed onto a shale dump near the mine entrance, and told the gathering crowd: "You'd better all go home. I hold out no hope for any man."[12]

---

12 Interview with Bruce Mackey, Cairns, 4 January 1976. Watson's action must have made a vivid impression, because two other witnesses independently described the scene, particularly Watson's statement, in almost identical words, over 50 years after the event. Mary Wardle also recalled him saying, "I'm telling you there's no-one alive in there now." A few minutes earlier, Watson had sent his daughter (later Doris Smith, interviewed Brisbane, 14 May 1976) to wire to the Mines Department: "Explosion in mine this morning 9.30. Hold out no hope recovering any man alive. Mine wrecked." (*Brisbane Courier*, 20 September 1921) Watson's oral statement repeated the phraseology he had composed for the telegram.

The origin of the Mount Mulligan explosion has never been established beyond doubt, but the principal theories all postulate some neglect of elementary safety precautions. The means of propagation of the explosion was undoubtedly the presence of coal dust in the mine. In other words, someone in the mine made a careless mistake which might perhaps have injured one or two miners. The circumstances prevailing in the mine at the time instantaneously transformed this error into a huge explosion involving the very dust particles on the floor, walls and roof, which killed every man who had the misfortune to have cavilled a place that morning in the miles of tunnels which made up the mine.

Explosions have occurred in many coal mines since the Industrial Revolution commenced the modern demand for coal as fuel - explosions which have varied widely in their origins, their means of propagation and their cost in human life. In 1921, popular belief among coal miners was that all colliery explosions were caused by the ignition of flammable gas in the mine atmosphere.

A number of gases are encountered in coal mines, all traditionally referred to by miners as "damps".[13] "Blackdamp" or carbon dioxide (CO_2) is non-flammable and non-toxic, but can cause death by suffocation. It exists naturally in some mines, and is also produced by the combustion of coal in an atmosphere of abundant oxygen. Combustion of coal with insufficient oxygen generates "Whitedamp" or carbon monoxide (CO), usually the product of the slow smouldering which results from spontaneous combustion of the coal in goaf packs, a fairly common occurrence. Whitedamp is both flammable and highly toxic, but rarely exists in a mine in sufficient quantity to be dangerous in either respect. A fire or explosion in a mine leaves large amounts of blackdamp and whitedamp in the atmosphere, and this combined highly-dangerous product is termed "Afterdamp", both toxic and asphyxiating, but rarely flammable.

The most feared mine gas is "Firedamp" or methane (CH_4). Present in most coal mines as a by-product of the geological process of coal formation, firedamp is non-toxic and undetectable by the human senses. Lighter than air, it rises to the roof of mine workings, and in concentrations of between 4 and 15%, forms an explosive mixture with air, its presence until recent years identifiable only by the flickering

13 From German *dampf*: a vapour or fume. (T.J. Beard, *Mine Gases and Explosions*, New York 1908, p.99). Beard is the source of the following description of coal mine gases.

cap on a safety lamp flame.[14] Since firedamp occurs almost everywhere coal is mined, and was known to be potentially explosive when simply exposed to a naked flame, it was long assumed that firedamp accounted for all colliery explosions. This belief was still common among Australian coal miners in 1921, and is reflected in the Mount Mulligan miners' choice of an open flame for illumination in their confident awareness that the mine was free of methane.

However, during the nineteenth century a body of research had grown which suggested that another substance present in all coal mines, the dust of the coal itself, might provide both an origin and means of propagation for an explosion. This suggestion was first raised as early as 1845 in a report on the Haswell colliery explosion in the previous year:

> In considering the extent of the fire from the moment of the explosion, it is not to be supposed that firedamp was its only fuel; the coal dust swept from the floor, roof and walls of the works would instantly take fire and burn if there were oxygen enough present in the air to support its combustion.[15]

This suspicion of the role of coal dust as a fuel additional to firedamp grew by the 1870s to a speculation that it might constitute the origin of an explosion. A French report on an explosion in 1874 found:

> ...the absence of firedamp having been well verified, we believe that in order to explain this accident it is necessary to admit the combustion of the coal dust raised by the explosion of the shot.[16]

Forty years were to elapse before this theory that coal dust could originate an explosion in the absence of firedamp was verified experimentally, and it was much longer before it became orthodox belief among miners. Serious research into coal dust explosions began in Britain after the Seaham Colliery disaster of September 1880, where it was found that the magnitude of the explosion, in which 164 men and boys and 181 draught animals died,[17] could not be explained by the known behaviour of firedamp. Work proceeded slowly, however, and further disasters, culminating in the Courrieres explosion of 1906 in which 1,099 died, were required to prompt a Royal Commission into coal dust explosions. As a result of the Royal Commission's report

14 Strictly speaking, firedamp is a methane-air mixture at an explosive concentration, but the term is used loosely to refer to methane itself.

15 Quoted in Beard, *op. cit.*, p.165, and see D. Hunter, *Diseases of Occupations*, London 1975, pp. 1101-2.

16 Quoted in E. Mason (ed.), *Practical Coal Mining for Miners, Vol. I*, London 1951, p.267.

17 W.N. & J.B. Atkinson, *Explosions in Coal Mines*, London 1886, p.29.

in 1908, experimental stations were established at Altofts in 1910 and Eskmeals in 1911 to simulate mine conditions for the study of coal dust explosibility.[18] The United States in 1911 established a similar experimental mine at Bruceton, Pennsylvania, as a direct result of two mine explosions in December 1907 with a combined death toll of 600 men.[19]

Preliminary findings of explosion tests at Eskmeals and Bruceton were published well before 1921, and anyone following the technical literature could understand the hazards of coal dust and also gain practical advice on how to minimise them. However, not much attention had been paid to these matters in Australia, and nothing had been done to protect the Mount Mulligan mine from the greatest horror known to the coal industry. James Watson's evidence before the Mount Mulligan disaster Royal Commission shows that he was vaguely aware of the explosibility of coal dust, but quite mistaken as to the means of its ignition, and that he considered the circumstances favouring a coal dust explosion to be too complex and rare to be forestalled by mine management.[20] Experience in both Britain and the United States had shown that recourse to theoretical findings on mine safety measures is made only on the impetus of a major disaster: in Australia, that impetus was provided at Mount Mulligan.

Among the first to arrive at the Mount Mulligan mine entrance in the minutes after the explosion were the engineer, Jim Harris and his brother Jack, a carpenter, together with the brothers Plunkett, both surface workers. With them was a group of men unknown to the local people, who had recently arrived in Mount Mulligan to seek work. Watson would allow only a small group of experienced men to investigate the smoking mine, so, posting others to guard the entrance, he, Jim Harris and one of the new men climbed over the debris at the mouth and entered the tunnel. They carried two safety lamps and an electric light.[21]

Inside the adit, much of the timber had been dislodged by the blast and piles of stone from the roof obstructed the ropeway. The atmosphere was heavy with afterdamp and smoke obstructed vision. A clipper, Neville Ruming, lay dead beside a skip a short distance inside

18 Mason, *op. cit.*, pp.269-270.

19 G.S. Rice, *et. al.*, *Coal Dust Explosion Tests in the Experimental Mine*, Washington 1922, p.2.

20 *R.C.* pp.48 and 111.

21 The events of the first rescue attempt in the hours following the explosion are reconstructed from the Royal Commission evidence, *R.C.* pp.2-13 and p.157.

the mine. At the entrance to the Underground Manager's cabin, the party found two more men, alive, but barely conscious. Evans was lying in the doorway, badly burnt, with a piece of timber driven into his chest, its end protruding above his collar. The books and papers in his office were flung into a scorched pile in a corner. Near Evans lay a miner, Martin O'Grady, obviously severely injured and extensively burned. Stretcher parties were called into the mine to remove the two men, and Evans, lucid at times as he was carried out, tried to recite from his memory of the cavil sheet the positions of the men in the workings. O'Grady died within a few hours.

The first party continued a few hundred metres further and found a fourth man, Robert Thompson. He was dead. All were now feeling the effects of carbon monoxide poisoning, and as a stretcher party returned for Thompson's body a heavy fall of stone was heard not far ahead of them, and a wave of afterdamp rolled up the dip. Watson ordered the entire group from the mine, convinced by now that no-one else could be found alive and that further exploration must await adequate ventilation of the mine.

Harris set to work restoring the mine air current by rigging a small fan, first exhausting the ventilating tunnel with little effect, then blowing air into the main entrance. The work took hours, and the inadequate fan made no perceptible difference to the mine atmosphere until well into the night. It was early on Tuesday morning before the bodies of Thompson and a clipper, George Hawes, were recovered, and then the stretcher bearers were severely affected by afterdamp. While they were at work Northern District Inspector of Mines Ernest Laun arrived at the mine with rescue workers from the Chillagoe smelters, and assisted in directing the rescue operation.[22] Watson, ill with influenza before the explosion and poisoned by gas in the rescue attempt, returned to his home and was incapacitated during the days that followed.

The disaster in the Mount Mulligan mine was caused by a small, probably accidental, explosion occurring in the combination of circumstances required to initiate a coal dust explosion. An explosion is simply rapid combustion, that is, the chemical reaction of a substance with oxygen, generating heat and gaseous products. Any substance such as coal which burns can cause an explosion, if enabled to burn sufficiently rapidly. The dust which constitutes a danger in coal mines

22 Laun was based at Charters Towers, but was in Chillagoe on the day of the explosion, and rushed to Mount Mulligan by train with a party of volunteers. (*R.C.* p.22)

015 Mine entrance temporarily repaired after the explosion. (*Q.G.M.J.* 15 October 1921, p. 399)

is not made up of particles which are always present in the mine atmosphere, since to sustain an explosion these would have to be present in such quantities as to prevent miners breathing. The hazard consists in the dust resting on the floor and other surfaces in the mine, often inches deep, but not susceptible to ignition by a naked flame.

If an explosion occurs in contact with this dust, as for example by the premature firing of a blasting shot before it is placed in the drill hole, it raises the dust particles in a cloud which travels outwards from the explosion centre with the resultant shock wave at the speed of sound. Depending on the ratio of carbon to oxygen molecules present in the raised coal dust cloud, it may form an explosive mixture. If this moving cloud of suspended particles, called the "pioneering wave", is ignited by the flame of the originating explosion it may itself explode, and a coal dust explosion is underway. The explosion of the dust is self-perpetuating, raising before itself a pioneering wave of dust particles, which instantly explode. For a distance of about 100 metres from the origin, the following explosion wave travels relatively slowly and does little violence, but if conditions permit, it may then accelerate and overtake the pioneering wave. The result is what films made in the

016 The wreckage of the blacksmith's hut near the mine entrance.
(*Q.G.M.J.* 15 October 1921, p. 399)

Eskmeals experimental mine show as a wall of flame hurtling through the mine at velocities which may exceed 1,000 metres per second.[23]

Velocity, temperature, direction and violence of the explosion vary quite unpredictably in the complex conditions of a coal mine. Shock waves called retonation waves may travel backward from the advancing explosion front, throwing loose objects towards the origin and creating effects which on later inspection can give a false impression as to the direction in which the explosion moved. The temperature at the explosion front may reach 900°C, but coal dust explosions also have the inexplicable capacity to leave areas of a mine quite unaffected by heat and blast, only to regenerate their temperature and violence some distance further on.[24] A coal dust explosion can be sustained by a layer of 150 grams of coal dust per square metre,[25] a barely perceptible coating:

23 A film entitled *Coal Dust Explosions* was prepared in 1923 from demonstrations at the Eskmeals experimental mine. (*Q.G.M.J.*, 15 August 1923, p.301.) Mine explosion footage, probably from this source, was used by ABC-TV in 1971 to dramatise a documentary program on the Mount Mulligan disaster. A maximum explosion velocity of 4,000 feet per second and maximum pressure of 150 lbs per square inch at the explosion front were recorded in the Bruceton tests. (Rice, *et. al.*, pp.17 and 63)

24 This description of coal dust explosion effects is from Rice, *et. al.*, *op. cit.*, *passim*, and Mason, *op. cit.*, pp.273-274.

25 Rice, *et. al.*, *op. cit.*, p.66.

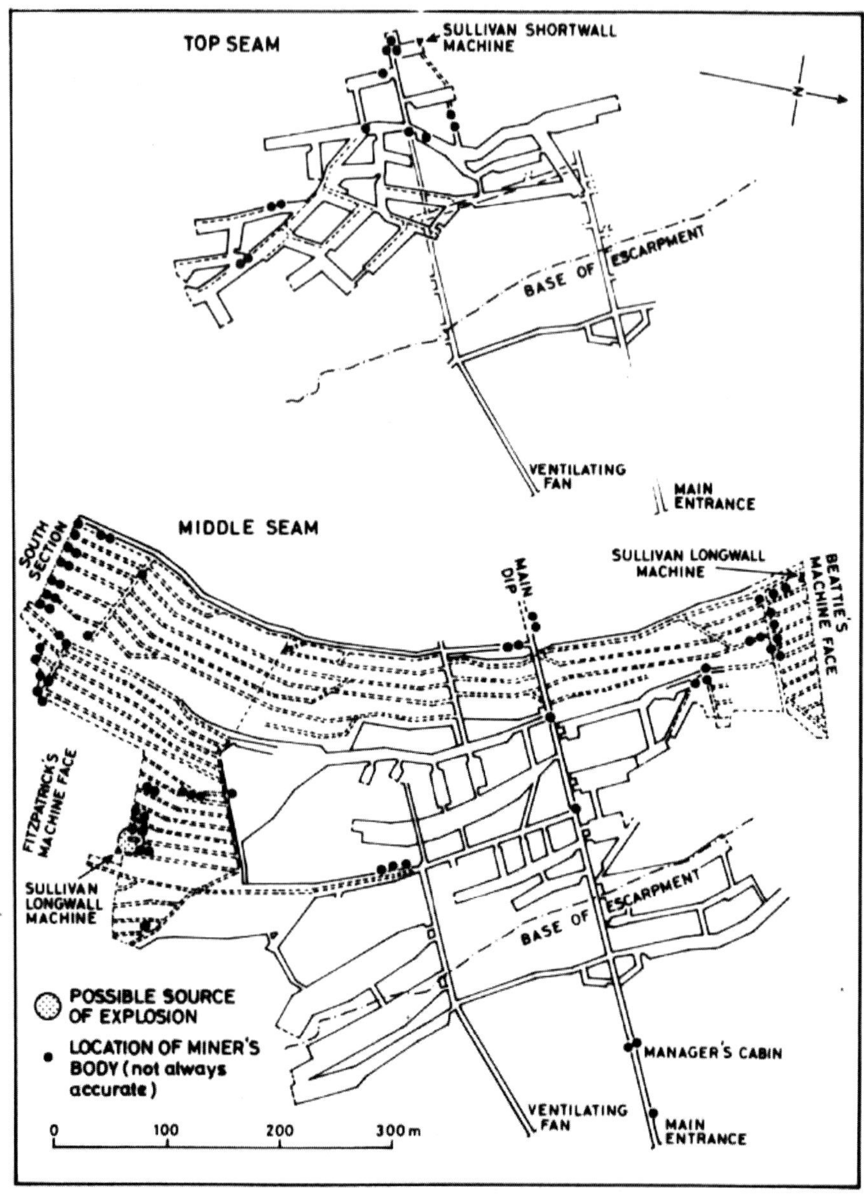

017 Plan of the Mount Mulligan underground workings at the time of the disaster.

It is not, perhaps, generally realised that an infinitesimally small quantity of coal dust is sufficient to generate a disastrous explosion, one-tenth of an ounce per cubic foot in the air, or a layer one two-hundred-and-fiftieth

> of an inch, about the thickness of a newspaper page on the floor, roof, and sides, given the initiating flame, being sufficient to wreck any mine.[26]

The dust on the roof and walls, while less conspicuous than the dust on the floor, is particularly susceptible to explosion, being both more finely divided, and more easily dislodged from its position by a shock wave. A coal dust explosion is inhibited, however, by moisture, which acts as an adhesive, preventing the dust being effectively dispersed into the air by a shock wave; and by the presence of stone dust amongst the coal dust. Finely powdered rock is produced as an inevitable by-product of coalmining and is dispersed throughout the mine with coal dust. Since this stone dust is inert, its presence in sufficient quantity may serve to smother a coal dust explosion as it is thrown into the air by the advancing shock wave. Experiments at Bruceton had shown that the deliberate distribution of stone dust in a mine served as an effective deterrent to coal dust explosions, and the practice was already being adopted in some Australian coal mines by 1921. But because of the cost of stone-dusting, the deep-seated belief that coal dust could only propagate an explosion, not initiate it, and Watson's personal aversion to the practice, stone-dusting had not been adopted at Mount Mulligan.

A miner caught in the path of a coal dust explosion could be affected in three possible ways: the blast wave can lift loose objects in the mine such as tools, skips, timber and loose rock or coal, and hurl them before it as projectiles; it may also transform men into projectiles, throwing them against stationary objects. Either process obviously may cause serious injury. The high temperatures of the flame front may cause burning of the skin, or if the miner is inhaling, of the surface of the lungs. All but four or five of the men killed at Mount Mulligan had been extensively burned.[27] Anyone who survives both blast and flame will be left in an atmosphere in which a great part of the oxygen has been removed and replaced by afterdamp. Death by suffocation or poisoning will almost certainly follow, although not necessarily immediately. After the 1880 disaster in the Seaham Colliery, written messages and guttered lamps were found with several of the dead, demonstrating that they had lived for some time after the explosion.[28] At Mount Mulligan, several miners survived the explosion's immediate effects for a short time, and in the remaining minutes of his life, one created a puzzle for investigators which was not solved for some months after the disaster.

26 Report of N.S.W. Committee of Inquiry into Coal Dust in Collieries, quoted in *R.C.* p. XL.

27 *R.C.* p.29.

28 Atkinson, *op. cit.*, p.37.

The helplessness of those at the Mount Mulligan mine entrance was made apparent in their first attempt at entering the mine. The mine was damaged and thus mechanically dangerous to an unknown degree, and was filled with toxic gas. The cause of the explosion, and thus the likelihood of further explosions, were also unknown, and a fire was believed to be burning somewhere in the mine, its effect observable in the air current from the ventilating tunnel.[29] Apart from a handful of ill or newly-arrived miners, the men surviving in Mount Mulligan were surface workers, clerks and shopkeepers, ill-equipped to explore a coal mine under the most benign circumstances, and forbidden entry by Watson in the face of the known and unknown hazards.

Mount Mulligan had none of the rescue devices which might have facilitated a further reconnaissance. Queensland had a Mines Life Saving Brigade, equipped and trained for just such an emergency as a mine explosion, but it was in Ipswich, several days' journey by rail and sea from Mount Mulligan. Communication with Mount Mulligan, even from Cairns, was possible only by train and telegraph:

> Mount Mulligan is not the easiest place from which to get full news at any time, and it can be easily understood that on an occasion such as this residents there must be fully occupied, and have but little time for sending details, either to the Press or to private persons.[30]

In the hours following the disaster, the telegraph lines became overloaded with competing messages to police, mines, medical and company officials, relaying garbled accounts of the explosion and requesting assistance. The railway telegraph system, connecting Mount Mulligan Stationmaster Franklin with Cairns Traffic Manager Hooper, provided one of the more reliable means of communication. One of the first messages received outside Mount Mulligan was from Franklin:

> Explosion throughout the whole of the mine, presumably caused by gas. The mine is wrecked, and there is much debris to clear before an entry can be effected. About 100 men in the mine are entombed, and there is little hope of their recovery alive. One body has been recovered. Two persons are injured seriously, and are unconscious. Relief workers are proceeding from Dimbulah, also railway lengthsmen. The explosion was heard 14 miles away.[31]

29 A fire in a mine causes air movement by convection. A primitive mine ventilating technique utilised the up-draught from an underground furnace.
30 *Brisbane Courier*, 20 September 1921.
31 *Ibid.*

Volunteers poured into Mount Mulligan as word of the disaster spread by direct observation, telegraph and rumour. First to arrive were a group of miners from the Tyrconnell gold mine at Kingsborough, who came by pump-car from Thornborough. A train from Mareeba brought doctors, nurses, ambulance bearers and volunteer rescue workers, and returned in the late afternoon with the mortally injured Evans and the body of Ruming. The most useful piece of equipment with the Mareeba party was a ten-inch electric ventilating fan from the Biboohra meatworks,[32] which Harris rigged at the mine entrance during the night.

At about 10.30 p.m. a train from Cairns brought more doctors, a police party and a group of twenty volunteers, many of whom were Cairns waterside workers. A Cairns undertaker, H.M. Svendsen, had been requested by telegraph to provide 60 coffins for Mount Mulligan, but only six were available. A further 25 coffins, apparently hastily constructed, followed on a later train, as did five more fans, six oxygen cylinders and some unexpected equipment: a diving suit and pumping apparatus provided by the Cairns Harbour Board, complete with diver.[33] This ingenious but quite useless improvisation was probably inspired by memories of the heroic rescue of miner Modesto Varischetti from a flooded gold mine in Western Australia by a hardhat diver 14 years earlier.[34]

Forty miners from the Chillagoe district arrived with Laun at 2 a.m. on Tuesday, bringing more electric fans and gasmasks provided by Peter Goddard from the State Smelters. In all, about 300 volunteers reached Mount Mulligan. Only skilled miners were permitted to enter the mine, and the remainder were employed in grave-digging and other surface work.

By 5 a.m. on Tuesday, the mine atmosphere was considered safe for the entry of rescue workers. Harris and Laun formed two parties, and dividing the underground workings into districts, commenced a systematic search of the mine. This task would involve days of walking and digging, for in seven years of production the Mount Mulligan mine had expanded into miles of tunnels on two levels, and progress was impeded in many places by falls of rock and timber. The majority of the miners assisting in the search were from small metalliferous mines and few had ever seen a mine as extensive and complex as the Mount Mulligan workings, or previously encountered the ill-defined slowly

32 *Cairns Post*, 20 September 1921.
33 *Ibid.*, 21 September 1921.
34 T. Austen, *The Entombed Miner*, Perth 1986.

018 The steel cable drums from above the mine entrance, blown twenty metres down the ropeway by the explosion. (*Q.G.M.J.* 15 October 1921, p. 399)

crushing goaf areas of a coal mine. Bewildered by their surroundings, and numbed by the horror of their task, they could do little more than stay together as a group, ready to provide labour when a body was found or some temporary repair had to be made:

> ... in a coal mine you go down the mine by a long tunnel not like a metal mine in a cage down a shaft. Of course I was strange to the coal mine. I would not work in one thats all I know. The drives are only about 2'6" to 3' in places. How they filled trucks I can't imagine. Cross cuts they called boards and twists are gates and gigways. I was puzzled. We just kept in sight of one another so as not to get lost. I tell you its a maze to a stranger.[35]

Effectively only two men, Harris and Laun, were searching the entire mine. Pockets of gas were encountered throughout the workings. To provide warning against blackdamp, miners have traditionally carried caged canaries which succumb to quite small concentrations of gas. No canaries were available in Mount Mulligan, but Jim Harris provided a family pet, a painted finch, which served as a gas indicator in the days of the search. There were insufficient safety and electric lamps

35 Walter Filer to his sister Kate, 25 September 1921. Letter in the possession of Kate Antcliff, née Filer, Brisbane. Filer was a Mungana miner who participated in the Mount Mulligan search. His letter is reproduced in full in Appendix A. Obvious minor errors in the letter have been left uncorrected.

019 The ventilating fan motor, blown from the return airway (Number Three Adit) by the explosion. (*Q.G.M.J.* 15 October 1921, p. 399)

for large bodies of men, and once the atmosphere seemed proven free of firedamp, the searchers began to use carbide lamps. The mine electrician, Norman Fraser, rigged electric lights along the main dip, but there were not enough of them to light more than a small part of the workings.

The search teams were confined to the adequately ventilated areas and thus the slow improvement of the air dictated the progress of the search. The air current through the mine was directed by means of temporary screens or brattices into a single section of the workings at a time, and the workers concentrated their efforts there. On entering a heading, the searchers marked the wall with a vertical chalk line, and added a horizontal line to form a cross when it had been cleared, thus avoiding duplication of effort.[36]

The few respirators available were of little use, as they impeded movement and vision, had a life of only a few hours, and were not available in sufficient numbers to equip the body of men needed for digging away falls and carrying the dead. The overall rate of progress of a small number of men proceeding into gassy areas with respirators

36 *R.C.* p.25.

would have been no faster than that of a larger group waiting for adequate ventilation.[37]

On Tuesday, the main dip was cleared of dead, and the air current was directed into Beattie's Wall, to the north. By Tuesday night, 22 bodies had been removed from the mine. The men on Beattie's Wall had apparently had some warning of the explosion's approach, for most were found some distance from their workplaces, in the direction of the main dip, as though running for the mine entrance at the time they died.[38] Two more were found on Wednesday when the much larger South Section was ventilated, but the air improved only slowly there, so the searchers climbed to the top seam and removed the 13 dead from the bord-and-pillar workings. At this time, Laun and Harris were joined in the search operation by Robert Dunlop, the Chillagoe district mining warden. Dunlop had returned from business in Brisbane by the S.S. *Kuranda*, which arrived in Cairns on Tuesday afternoon; hearing of the disaster, he rushed to Mount Mulligan by train.[39]

As the air improved in the South Section, the searchers moved in late on Wednesday and had removed a total of 56 bodies by Wednesday night. On Thursday all the dead were taken from the pick-faces and the search teams were able to enter the remaining section, Fitzpatrick's Wall, later that day. The 74th man was taken out on Friday morning, and the entire mine workings were searched repeatedly. There were no more to be found.[40] A tally man stood at the mine entrance, recording the name of every man who entered or left the mine, as a precaution against the very real possibility of searchers becoming lost in the workings. It is remarkable, when the experience of similar operations elsewhere is considered, that not one of the rescue workers was lost or seriously injured during the search operation.

The conditions that confronted the searchers were probably more horrifying than dangerous. Many of the dead were grossly mutilated and most were burned. By the time the search was well underway on Tuesday morning, the men in the mine had been dead for 24 hours. The temperature of the mine, raised by the explosion, remained sufficiently high throughout the search to affect many of the volunteers with heat exhaustion, and decomposition of the bodies at that temperature

37 *Ibid.*, p.37.

38 Laun's description of rescue work, *Q.G.M.J.*, 15 October 1921, p.428.

39 *Cairns Post*, 21 September 1921 and *Q.G.M.J.*, *ibid.*

40 The events of the search are reconstructed from *R.C.* pp. xxxii-xxxiii and pp.158-63, and the *Cairns Post*, 21-24 September 1921.

proceeded very rapidly. By Tuesday afternoon, all those engaged in handling the bodies were forced to wear eucalyptus-soaked masks:

> ...the corpses bore the appearance of having been suddenly struck by a terrific heat flame. The surface of the bodies was carbonised, the skin peeling off in flakes. All the hair was black and frizzled, and a number of the men's heads had been crushed by falling stones. One victim apparently had been pushing a truck, which upset, and, in falling down, crushed his head. Another victim was found to be practically standing on his head, propped up by fallen timber.[41]

The effect of days of searching, digging and carrying bodies in such a state exacted a heavy physical and psychological toll on the volunteers. We cannot ignore the example that must have been in their minds; they were re-enacting the experiences of stretcher teams three years earlier on the Western Front:

> It's was an awful job, Kate going along the boards picking up dead corpses. The last were simply awful...We used to use plenty of phenol and had masks but I tell you after a few hours below one was glad to return to the mouth.[42]

The bodies when found were disinfected with phenol, carried from the mine on stretchers, loaded into skips on the ropeway and wheeled to the goods shed beside the railway, where Tom Fitchett and Neil Smith took charge of them. There each body was numbered and identified if possible. When the workmen were unable to identify a man, the wives of missing miners were brought from the mine entrance to view the body.[43] A number of the dead were identified only by means of some physical peculiarity, such as James Cairney who had lost a thumb, amputated after an accident in the Girofla mine five months earlier,[44] or by some distinctive item of dress, as in the case of the miner who used copper wire for bootlaces. A Mount Mulligan woman, Mrs Hunt, proved to have an unusual memory for details of dress:

41 *Brisbane Courier*, 22 September 1921.
42 Walter Filer letter.
43 *R.C.* pp.29 and 30.
44 *A.R.* 1921, pp. 113 and 131.

> She is a regular cyclopaedia of information concerning boots, belts and hats, and many men have been thus identified who otherwise would be buried unknown.[45]

Even so, twelve of the dead were buried as 'unidentified',[46] and many of the identifications made were highly tenuous, some being based on the body's location in the assumption that it was the man cavilled to work at that place. This was an unreliable method, as it was not unusual for miners to change positions with others, either singly or in pairs, after the cavil was drawn. Many of the identifiable dead were found in areas other than their workplace, some in quite inexplicable places.[47] In several cases, identifiable bodies were found after another had circumstantially been identified as that person, and in some cases buried under that name.

A few of the bodies were given a cursory medical examination, but no autopsies were performed. All but two of the doctors, nurses and ambulancemen who arrived by Tuesday morning left the same day when it was obvious there was no need for their services. Dr Nye of Atherton, who operated on Evans at Mareeba Hospital, had not travelled to Mount Mulligan when news of the disaster arrived on the Monday morning. "He expressed the opinion that the work there was for clergymen and not doctors."[48] Dr Clarke of Cairns remained in Mount Mulligan until Wednesday, when he too left the work there to the clergymen and a Dr McClean, who was retained by Chillagoe Limited to inspect the dead in the days that followed, but not in sufficient detail to form an opinion on causes of death: "...they were too decomposed to examine them much."[49]

The first funeral ever held in Mount Mulligan took place at 3 p.m. on Tuesday as six of the dead were buried in the cemetery reserve, about a kilometre north of the town. The cemetery had been established only months earlier, and working bees of miners had been clearing and fencing it as recently as the weekend before the explosion. Previously the very few people who had died in the town had been taken to

45 *Cairns Post*, 23 September 1921. Mrs Hunt's knowledge of the miners' clothing is not explained. She was not on the electoral roll, but appears in the company ledger as receiving relief payments after the disaster, although she was not an employee or a miner's dependant. Mrs Wardle identified her as the Aboriginal woman walking beside a coffin in one of the press photographs. She was clearly a respectable resident, as her role was publicly acknowledged. Probably she worked in the single mens' barracks, paid by the miners to do washing and domestic tasks.

46 *R.C.* p.166.

47 *Ibid.*, p.144.

48 *Cairns Post*, 20 September 1921.

49 *R.C.* p.128, and Chillagoe Limited ledger.

020 Recovery workers emerging from the mine entrance with a body on a stretcher (*N.Q.R.* 3 October 1921)

Mareeba for burial.[50] Funerals continued through the week, and the grave-diggers found the cemetery site most unsuitable for hasty digging. At most times, more men were employed as grave-diggers than in exploring the mine, and the non-miners among the volunteers found their work more arduous, if less horrible, than that of their miner comrades. Eventually holes were drilled and mine explosives used to blast holes into the stony ground.[51] The sound of exploding dynamite did nothing for the emotional state of those who had lost husbands and fathers in Monday's explosion.

The work of burial accelerated as the week passed. Dr McClean had stopped even his cursory inspection of the dead as their decomposition advanced, and the work of identification became both more difficult and more hideous. After Wednesday, the volunteer carpenters were

50 One miner had died in a mining accident at Mount Mulligan before the disaster. On 24 February 1919 Herbert Bussey "slipped accidentally into the rotating picks of a coal cutter and sustained terrible injuries". He died on the way to Mareeba hospital. (*A.R.* 1919, p.123).

51 *Cairns Post*, 23 September 1921.

instructed to increase the size of the coffins, as the bodies recovered became increasingly swollen.[52]

On Friday, the work seemed to be done, and the town of Mount Mulligan emptied for the second time in its short life as rescue workers and residents boarded trains and abandoned the mine to a small group of workers engaged on its reconstruction. Frank Grant, Underground Deputy and Secretary of the Mount Mulligan School Committee, was among the last to be recovered from the mine, lying under a fall of rock, and one of the least disfigured of the dead. He was buried shortly before the last train left on Friday evening.[53]

At 9 a.m. on Monday, 26 September, Tom Evans died in Mareeba.[54] Almost exactly a week after the explosion, all those who had been in the mine were dead. With Evans' death, the number of known dead in the Mount Mulligan disaster rose to 75. But a careful count of the bodies removed from the mine, including O'Grady and Evans, came to 74. It was some days before this discrepancy was noticed, as the number of men in the mine was not known, even to the nearest ten, for some time.

The earliest messages from Mount Mulligan on the day of the disaster gave estimates of the number of men in the mine which varied between 70 and 100, as different observers gave different counts based on their own observations of the number normally in the mine, less the number they knew to be absent from it that morning.[55] Tom Fitchett wired to the Mareeba ambulance brigade that he and Evans were the only survivors of 80 miners. Incredibly, Chillagoe Limited did not seem to have any record of who was working in the mine. The only reliable figures available were from the company's August paysheet which listed 83 men employed underground,[56] and the cavil sheet of 16 September, found among union secretary George Hawes' belongings, with its 52 names.[57] Both documents were known to be outdated or incomplete, as the paysheet was three weeks old, and the cavil listed only the paired contract miners, but they provided at least a basis for calculation.

52 *Ibid.*, 22 September 1921.

53 *Ibid.*, 27 September 1921.

54 *Ibid.*

55 *Ibid.*, 20 September 1921. In the chaotic jumble of cabled reports in the *Cairns Post* on this date alone, estimates of 70, 78, 79, 83, 100 and 101 are given. Note also that 60 coffins were ordered.

56 *Ibid.*, 21 September 1921.

57 *R.C.* p.173. One man named on Hawes' cavil sheet - Morrison - was not in the mine. If this is George Morrison, the blacksmith, it is difficult to understand why he was cavilled. However, an examination of the cavil list of dubious origin printed elsewhere in the Royal Commission report (p.159) and the names of the dead, suggests that Hawes simply wrote the wrong name - the man he named Morrison was Thomas Hutton, who was among the dead.

Six men who should have been in the mine at the time of the explosion were absent. Three miners, A. Larsen, W. Westbury and Alf Leary, were ill with influenza and stayed home. Three more, Bill Matthews, Albert Jones and Arthur Griffiths, were in Mareeba Hospital, ill or injured.[58] Around these six men have grown up a number of legends concerning the "sole survivor" who had a premonition of disaster on the morning of 19 September and did not go to the mine. Most of the six participated in the rescue work after the explosion and later returned to work in the mine. Some of them seem to have been afflicted afterwards with feelings of intense guilt, as though culpably absent.[59] The legends of miraculous survival are counterbalanced by those who should have been absent that morning and were not. Sam McColm, married with seven children, had been absent through illness for some time previously, and returned to work on the morning of the explosion. Bill Cole, an elderly retired miner, was standing in that morning for one of the absent men. Both were killed.

Such random absences and attendances complicated the task of counting the likely dead. Numbering the known dead was also complicated by the horrendous conditions under which the searchers worked, the unfamiliarity of most of them with the mine and its occupants, and the difficulty of identifying many of those killed. Despite methodical precautions to ensure an accurate body count, mistakes were made in the confusion of the search:

> ...the bodies of J. Fogarty and J. O'Halloran had been discovered the day before, but not reported through oversight.[60]

When the last group of bodies recovered from Fitzpatrick's Wall was found to include two men who had been thought positively identified and already buried, the repetition of their names in the casualty reports was questioned by the Railway Traffic Manager in Cairns, and Franklin replied:

> Names given this morning are correct. Previous advice was due to bodies being wrongly identified, the graves of which have been marked "unknown".[61]

As a result of these known sources of inaccuracy in the body count, the apparent discrepancy between the number killed and the number

58 *Cairns Post*, 21 and 23 September 1921.
59 Interview with a former Mount Mulligan miner.
60 *Cairns Post*, 23 September 1921.
61 *Ibid.*, 24 September 1921.

021 Recovery workers wheeling a coffin down the ropeway.
The woman on the left is Mrs Hunt. (Q.N.)

recovered was explained as an error in recording the number of bodies buried:

> It is ascertained that the reason it was not known that one body was still remaining was owing to a miscount. The coffins were numbered accurately, but seventy-five bodies should have been brought out, in addition to Evans, instead of 74. Those in charge say they now know where the body is, but there has been a heavy fall of earth there...the body might be removed when the mine is being repaired.[62]

This report is apparently itself in error. If the correct total of dead was 75, then only 73 had been "brought out, in addition to Evans" at this time. The figure of 74 must include Evans, who died three days after this report was written. The true count is further obfuscated by a telegram from Watson to Chillagoe Limited on 26 September, informing them a miscount had been corrected: 75 bodies had been taken from the mine, and the death of Evans brought the total to 76.[63]

At one place in the mine workings, there was a strong smell of decomposition coming from an extensive fall of rock. For some reason, the missing man under this fall was thought to be Donald Butler,

62 *Ibid.*
63 *Q.G.M.J.*, 15 October 1921, p.429.

022 Mount Mulligan cemetery shortly after the disaster (Jim McColm)

although how this could be determined when twelve of the dead were unidentified is not clear. On 7 October, a party of miners began to remove this fall, but found only tools, a skip and a damp patch where one of the last bodies recovered had lain. The fall of rock had obviously occurred after the body was removed. Three days' further search found no more bodies:

> No likely place in the mine now remains unexplored, and whether further search will be made, including unlikely places, is a matter as yet undecided. The evidence tendered at the enquiry shows that 75 men entered the pit on the morning of the accident, and 74 bodies were recovered. The question now presenting itself is whether it is possible some mistake occurred in either tally. The only other alternative is that the body remains unrecovered. It is commonly believed, however, that one man still remains in the mine.[64]

The people of Mount Mulligan had faith in the records kept by Fitchett and Smith. In the months while the town was re-occupied and the mine re-opened for production, the belief survived that a man had unaccountably disappeared in the explosion. Out of this belief grew the story of "Morgan's Ghost". Edward Morgan was one of the miners killed in the disaster, and although his body was listed as identified, popular legend made Morgan the missing man. Most Mount Mulligan miners were clean-shaven, but Morgan had an impressively long black beard,

64 *Cairns Post*, 11 October 1921.

which is how his body had been identified. He was also a teetotaller, a Methodist lay preacher, and a loner.[65] His distinctiveness made him memorable, and the story of Morgan's Ghost flourished, told as a source of wonder by the new miners in 1922 and heard as a source of terror by the boys working in the mine.[66]

On 9 February 1922, Jim Harris and two other men were exploring rarely-used passages in the Fitzpatrick's Wall section in order to plan a ventilating path before expanding the workings. While climbing a monkey-shaft - a narrow, nearly vertical shaft connecting the two levels of the mine - they found their path obstructed by a pair of boots. Wearing them was the body of George Turriff, the missing man, who had been listed among the unidentified five months earlier.[67] Turriff's body, buried in Mount Mulligan the same day, was quite recognisable, apparently preserved and mummified by the conditions prevailing in the shaft after the explosion. The body was unmarked and unburned, and since there was no conceivable reason why Turriff's work would take him into a place so unlikely that no-one had thought to look there for five months, it seems clear that he survived the disaster's first effects, only to seek refuge in the monkey-shaft, where he died of "suffocation by gas, the result of an explosion".[68] But whether the discovery of Turriff's body brought the final count to 75 or 76 dead remains uncertain.

Turriff's cavil mate, Cairney, had been found not far from their cavilled position in the Beattie's Wall section, at the opposite end of the workings. Turriff most probably changed his position before the explosion, or had been on the south side on some unknown errand. If, on the other hand, he was at his workplace when the explosion occurred, he afterwards travelled nearly a kilometre in complete darkness before he died. While this seems unlikely, there was evidence that others had had a short while in which to respond to the explosion. In the top seam, the searchers found:

65 Interview with Mark Morgan, Chillagoe, 27 June 1978.

66 Interview with Jim McColm, Ipswich, 17 December 1976. McColm went to work in the mine as a boy of fourteen after the disaster. The legend was no doubt reinforced by the Royal Commission's suggestion that some action of Morgan's may have initiated the explosion - a point which is discussed in the next chapter.

67 Interview with Mary Wardle, Ravenshoe, 13 August 1976, and *Cairns Post*, 13 February 1922.

68 Entry 2728 : 2706 in Register of Deaths, General Registry Office, Brisbane. Turriff's date of burial, 9 February 1922, has been written over an erased entry in the register, without any explanatory annotation.

> ... the men here had travelled over 100 yards, and in one case a man had been so slightly injured, if at all, by the initial disturbance that he had carried his water-bag with him.[69]

With the exception of Turriff's posthumous mystery, the human wreckage of the Mount Mulligan disaster was disposed of within four days, and the inanimate wreckage was steadily attended to in the weeks that followed. Popular and institutional reaction to the disaster was one of horrified incredulity, summed up in the question, "How did it happen?" From the first day, the newspapers had speculated freely. The Queensland government set out almost immediately to answer the question.

69 *Q.G.M.J.*, 15 October 1921, p.429.

3.
THE ROYAL COMMISSION

"Regulations are not always sensible."

(James Watson to the Royal Commission)

E.G. Theodore, Premier of Queensland since Ryan's departure from state politics in October 1919, set up a Royal Commission to inquire into the Mount Mulligan disaster. The Commissioners were Robert Dunlop, mining warden at Chillagoe (Chairman), William Want, manager of the Box Flat colliery at Bundamba, and Charles Kilpatrick, M.L.C., President of the Queensland Colliery Employees' Union.[1] Dunlop and Kilpatrick were both personal friends of Theodore. On 23 September, while the work of burial at Mount Mulligan was finishing, the commissioners were appointed to:

> Inquire into and Report upon the Recent Disaster at Mount Mulligan Coal Mine, and also into the Methods of Mining carried on at such Mine, and, further, to make such Recommendations as may tend to Prevent the Recurrence of Accidents of a like nature.[2]

1 *Q.G.G.* 23 September 1921, Vol. CXVII, No.112, p.851. Kilpatrick was one of the Labor members appointed to the Legislative Council between 1917 and 1921 as a prelude to its abolition.
2 *R.C.* title page.

Before describing the Royal Commission's proceedings it may be useful to put the enquiry in context by looking briefly at the legal framework of coal mine safety in Queensland in 1921. There was no legislation specifically governing safety in coal mines; they had simply been mentioned in a section of the general legislation covering safety in mines, starting with the *Mines Regulation Acts* of 1881 and 1889, later consolidated into the *Mining Act* 1898, which covered mines of all kinds. Further *Mines Regulation Acts* between 1910 and 1916 expanded the safety provisions, but said very little about coal mining. There were provisions specifying ventilation standards and multiple mine entrances, and requiring pre-shift inspections, all of which were taken directly from the British *Coal Mining Act* 1872, but there was little else relevant to the safety issues peculiar to coal mines.[3]

The first serious coal-related accident in Queensland was a methane explosion which killed five miners at Torbanlea in 1900. A Royal Commission produced a very thorough report which demonstrated that the management of coal mines in Queensland was lagging well behind international practice. It recommended enactment of separate legislation, improved certification of managers, more stringent inspections, better ventilation, and mandatory use of safety lamps in gassy mines.[4] The report was ignored completely for a decade, when the *Mines Regulation Act* 1910 was passed, principally in response to accidents at the Mount Morgan copper mine. The new legislation essentially repeated the colliery provisions in the *Mining Act*, with the addition of a watered-down version of one of the Torbanlea recommendations about safety lamps.

Then, for no apparent reason, new colliery regulations were issued in 1920, with an odd assortment of amendments increasing the power of inspectors, improving ventilation specifications, and for the first time mentioning coal dust in a vague and ineffectual regulation. This was the situation in Queensland coal mine regulation when the Mount Mulligan Royal Commission convened a week after the disaster.

Dunlop was already in Mount Mulligan when the Royal Commission was appointed, and was joined there by Want and Kilpatrick on 28 September. Watson was still too ill to assist them, but in company with Jim Harris, the commissioners carried out a number of inspections of the

3 P. Bell, Coal Mine Safety Legislation in Queensland, 1985.

4 *Report of the Royal Commission into the Torbanlea Colliery Accident*, Brisbane 1900.

023 Members of the Royal Commission into the Mount Mulligan disaster.
From left: J.T.H. Bird (Secretary), Charles Kilpatrick M.L.C. (President, Queensland Colliery Employees' Union), William Want (Manager, Box Flat Colliery) and Robert Dunlop (Mining Warden, Chillagoe) (Q.N.)

mine in the following days, and before taking any evidence, quickly came to:

> ... complete agreement as to the locality of the origin of the explosion, its probable cause, and also to the direction of the forces through the mine workings before escaping to the surface.[5]

These are complex technical matters, and it is rather disturbing that the commissioners believed they could arrive at such conclusions before hearing from any expert witnesses. Evidence was taken in Mount Mulligan from 4 October until 8 October, then in Chillagoe, Mareeba and Cairns before the commissioners travelled to Brisbane, meeting there on 31 October, and producing their report on 2 December 1921, after just 65 days of proceedings.[6] The report stated the cause of the explosion as the commissioners had determined it, and was highly critical of the disregard for safety shown in the administration of the mine.

Debate on the cause of the disaster dominated the proceedings of the Royal Commission and generated considerable acrimony during the

5 *R.C.*, p. XXI.
6 *Ibid.*, Proceedings of the Commission, pp. VII-XIX.

taking of evidence. It was clear that a massive explosion of coal dust had occurred in the mine, but it was necessary to establish how the coal dust explosion had been initiated. The commissioners and some of the expert witnesses were agreed on the source of the explosion, although there are grounds for questioning their opinion in the light of subsequent research findings. It appeared to have originated at Fitzpatrick's Machine Face, not far from where the Sullivan machine was standing, and to have travelled from there throughout the workings. Precisely how it had been initiated, though, was the subject of several distinct theories.

Methane was never seriously entertained as a cause, because the entire weight of evidence produced no suggestion that the gas had ever been encountered at Mount Mulligan. A Government geologist, E.C. Saint-Smith, stated quite categorically that firedamp could never have existed in the mine.[7] This claim was not uncommonly made of a mine where an explosion had occurred. The Mount Kembla mine in New South Wales, which exploded in 1902, killing 96 miners, had also had a reputation as a gas-free mine, and naked lights were in use there before the disaster.[8] The inquest held after the Mount Kembla disaster, however, soon elicited from witnesses a number of reports of firedamp in the mine prior to the explosion, indicating that its reputation for safety had rested on some form of wishful folklore rather than on available evidence.[9] At Mount Mulligan no such suggestion emerged at any time during the Royal Commission, nor was firedamp ever subsequently encountered in the mine workings during the mine's later decades of operation. Methane can safely be dismissed as a possible cause of the explosion.

In its absence, there must have been some other form of detonation in the open to initiate an explosion of coal dust. The electrical installations were initially suspect, but these were of a type designed for use in gassy mines - an instance of the progressive standard set at Mount Mulligan during its early development - and were protected against any possibility of arcing or explosion. The mine electrician, Norman Fraser, gave evidence that there was no sign of any malfunction having occurred in the electrical installations beyond those resulting from the explosion. The circuit breakers had opened when the fan was blown from its motor and the shortwall coal-cutting machine stalled when its operator

7 *Ibid.*, p.131.

8 *Sydney Morning Herald*, 1 August 1902.

9 *Mount Kembla Colliery Disaster: Report of the Royal Commission*, N.S.W. *V. & P.*, 1903, Vol.5, pp.25-30.

died.[10] The longwall machine on Fitzpatrick's Wall, where the explosion apparently originated, had not operated on the morning of the disaster.

The possibility of a carbide lamp having exploded was considered after the discovery of the upper half of a miner's lamp near Fitzpatrick's Wall,[11] but the lamp showed no sign of deformation or scorching, and this theory too was discarded.[12] The witnesses seemed unsure whether a carbide lamp had ever actually been known to explode. Explosives and detonators were found strewn about many parts of the mine after the explosion, showing that there had been ample opportunity for an accidental discharge, but there was no sign that this had occurred. While adversely commenting at some length on the careless handling of explosives throughout the workings, the Royal Commission concentrated on a reconstruction of events immediately preceding the disaster at Number Eleven Bord on Fitzpatrick's Wall, a few metres west of the Sullivan machine.

When a coal-cutting machine separated the coal from the floor, the crush of the roof was often sufficient to break off the coal in large blocks after the machine had passed. Sometimes it was necessary to drill a hole horizontally into the coal near the roof and fire a charge deep in the coal to dislodge it. The resulting blocks of coal were broken up with picks and wedges so that they could be loaded into skips. Further charges could be used to break the coal blocks, but this did not normally justify the effort and inconvenience that drilling and firing demanded.

The process of firing a shot involved drilling a hole about an inch in diameter to a depth of four to six feet into the coal. One or more sticks of explosive were placed in the hole, the last containing a detonator crimped onto a safety fuse, and the hole was then tamped with clay or sand rolled into paper cylinders and rammed into place with a wooden tamping rod. After tools and other items were removed from the area, and men in nearby places warned, the shot firer lit the fuse and took cover a good distance away.

If the charge was properly set and tamped, the result should not have been violent. A block of coal should have been dislodged, shattered into large fragments, and dropped onto the mine floor immediately below the shot hole. One of the principal sources of danger in shot firing was a premature discharge which could result from careless handling of

10 *R.C.* pp. 50-51.
11 *Ibid.*, pp. 80 and 83.
12 *Ibid.*, p. XLIII.

the detonator, accidental lighting of the fuse before the shot was set, or from a defective fuse "jumping" and exploding the shot before the firer had taken cover. Another hazard, a "blown-out shot" occurred either when a weakness in the coal permitted the explosion to discharge into the air, when a hole was excessively charged, or when a charge had been inadequately tamped, and the shot took the line of least resistance, blowing the tamping material out of the drill hole like a bullet, usually without shattering the coal.

At the point where Number Eleven Bord opened onto Fitzpatrick's Machine Face, near the explosion's apparent source, the commissioners found a large block of coal detached from the machine-cut wall, with some roof stone fallen on and around it. In the entrance to the bord sat a half-filled skip, partly derailed from the tramway laid in the bord. The body of Edward Morgan was found lying against the end of the skip. Mining tools were lying on the floor between Morgan and the machine face, and a tamping rod lay beside his body. The body of Alick Casloff, Morgan's cavil mate at that working place, was in the bord, 40 metres north of Morgan's. In the coal-seam above the coal-block was a drill hole, only about fifteen centimetres deep, which did not appear to have been fired. On top of the coal-block there may have been - there is reason for doubt - a shallow depression containing a quantity of comminuted (finely-divided) coal.[13]

This scene provided material for a considerable part of the Royal Commission's examinations and deliberations, for it seemed to provide an origin for the explosion, but that origin was open to several interpretations. The presence of the tamping rod and the shallow drill hole suggested that Morgan had been in the act of preparing a shot immediately before the disaster. A blown-out shot seemed improbable, in view of the shallowness of the drill hole and its unused appearance. The very existence of the hole seems odd. There was no reason to drill into the wall behind a newly-fallen block of coal, and no drill was found near the scene. No evidence in the Royal Commission mentions any examination of the coal block to determine whether the hole in the coalface was simply the end of an unused hole drilled into the wall before the block fell. This would shed light on the situation, but the evidence is silent on the matter.

A premature discharge could have occurred while Morgan was preparing a shot, and Watson devoted a considerable time while giving

13 *Ibid.*, exhibits 6 and 18.

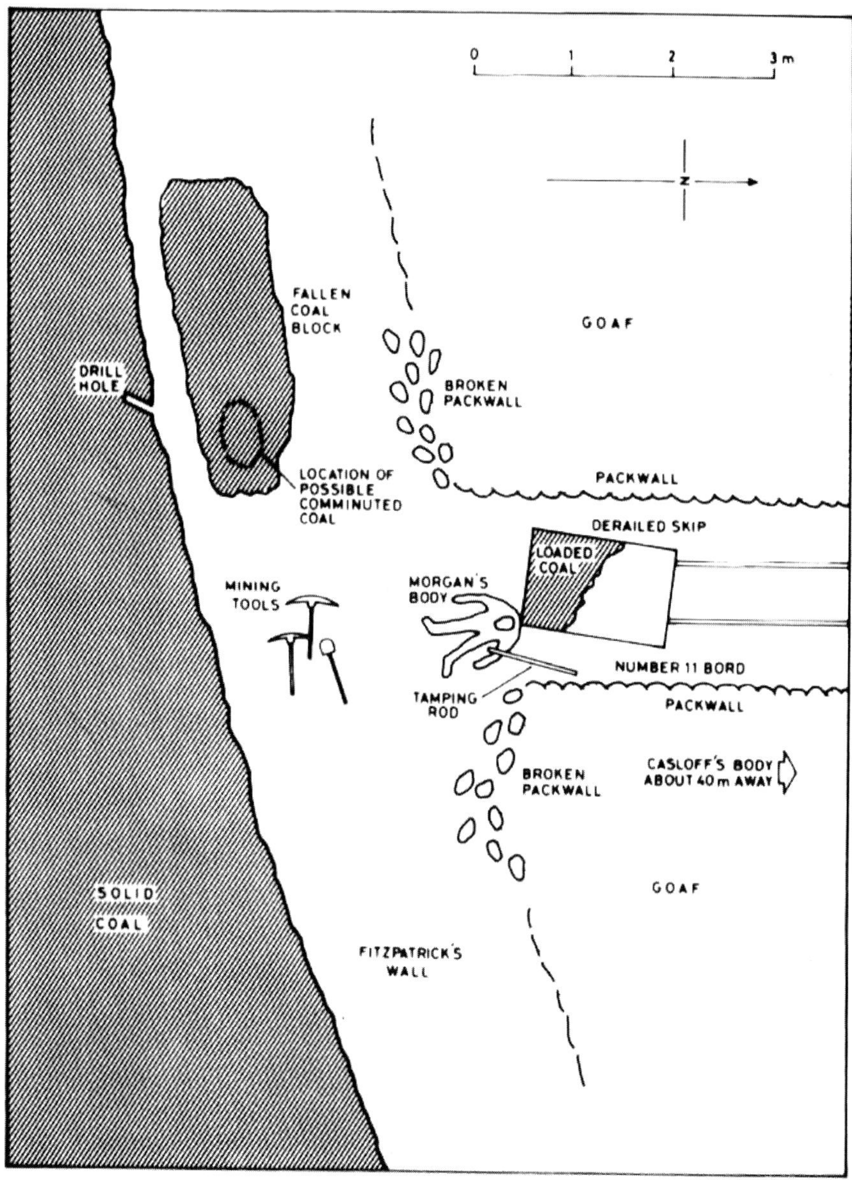

024 Plan of the situation at the explosion's suspected origin after the disaster (Based on *R.C.* Exhibits 6 and 18)

evidence to arguing that this had been the case. However, the absence of a deep drill hole seemed to obviate any reason why Morgan should have been engaged in priming a charge. One possible explanation, and the one at which the Royal Commission finally arrived was:

> ... the firing of an explosive, either accidently or otherwise, on the top of a large block of fallen machine-cut coal, such explosive not having been placed in a shot hole.
>
> It is difficult to understand how explosives, being used in the ordinary way, could be fired in this spot. Alternatively the conclusion that obtrudes itself is that a plaster shot was placed on this block of coal to break it, so as to facilitate handling, and it exploded prematurely, either because of defect in the fuse or from some other cause, such as a fall of roof stone.[14]

A plaster shot, or "lay-on" (or "gruncher" at Mount Mulligan),[15] was a charge laid on the surface of a block of coal to shatter it. No hole was drilled and tamping was not possible, but the charge was loosely stemmed by piling sand or other material around it. Obviously the temptation to lay plasters would be strongest in piece-work miners seeking to avoid the time-consuming process of drilling; but the practice was resorted to by only the most indolent of miners, and was utterly reprehensible, for besides being a highly inefficient way to use explosives, it was appallingly dangerous. Whether the magnitude of this danger would be clear to miners who believed the initiation of a major mine explosion to depend on the presence of methane, however, is not certain. Saint-Smith stated before the Royal Commission that he considered a plaster shot to have caused the disaster and defended this position later under cross-examination.[16] Most of the miners and officials connected with the Mount Mulligan mine denied that plastering had ever been practised there and asserted that no coal miner would ever do such a thing.

> 1649. [Questions by Want] You don't think there would be any necessity to use "lay-ons" or "plasters"? - No.
>
> 1650. Do you think that the men were aware that the practice was prohibited? - I never heard anything mentioned in connection with it at all in the top seam.
>
> 1651. You don't know if the management had any difficulty in that direction? - I never heard it mentioned in any shape or form. The word "plasters" was never mentioned there.[17]

It is difficult to imagine a coal miner, confronted by three coalmining experts, giving any other answers to such questions in the atmosphere that must have prevailed at the Mount Morgan Royal Commission

14 *Ibid.*, p. XLIII.

15 Interview with Les Weatherston, New Farm, 22 November 1975.

16 *R.C.*, p. 133.

17 *Ibid.*, p. 60. Evidence of Bill Matthews, miner.

hearings, while aware of the barrage of questions that an affirmative answer would provoke. Some witnesses, however, conceded that the practice of plastering, although condemned, could occur:

> 1163. [Watson questioned by Kilpatrick] Have you any knowledge of what has been said to be the practice here of using plasters or lay-ons in the mine? - The only time I knew it was done was about three years ago. I happened to be in the mine and I found a man in the act of preparing one of those plasters, and I ordered him to stop it. I threatened him with immediate dismissal if I heard of him doing it again. I also instructed Evans to put a stop to that practice.
>
> 1164. You certainly consider such a practice was dangerous? - Yes. I would not allow a man to stay in the mine two minutes if I saw him using a plaster.[18]

Another miner admitted hearsay knowledge of the practice: "I have heard that it was plastered sometimes".[19] Obviously the possibility of a plaster shot having been fired or prepared cannot be dismissed. The commissioners, particularly Want, seem to have seized on that possibility early in their inspection of the mine workings, and allowed it to colour their treatment of the evidence given by witnesses. Much of the case for a plaster shot rests on the existence of a depression filled with comminuted coal on top of the coal-block at Morgan and Casloff's work place, a circumstance which would be consistent with an exposed charge having been fired at that point, and Want repeatedly raised this detail in his examination of witnesses. In the consideration of evidence leading to its conclusion on the origin of the disaster, the Royal Commission report referred to "the comminution of coal on top of the fall noticed by so many witnesses as singular".[20]

In fact, the witnesses were conspicuously divided on this point. Of the six witnesses who had inspected the mine after the explosion, and who responded to Want's patently leading questions on the comminuted coal, three said they had not seen it:

> 2266. [Questions by Want] Did you see a large block of coal in the road in Fitzpatrick's machine district, and did you notice that it had a comminuted surface? - I saw the coal there, but I did not notice the feature about it that you mention.

18 *Ibid.*, p. 46. Kilpatrick's mention of "what has been said to be the practice here" must refer to conversation outside the hearings. No previous acknowledgment of plastering having occurred at Mount Mulligan appears in the printed evidence.
19 *Ibid.*, p.59. Evidence of George Williams, miner, questioned by Want.
20 *Ibid.*, p. XXXVII.

2267. You did not notice it was comminuted in one particular place? - No

....

2269. If you had seen a comminuted surface on that block of coal, would it have suggested anything to you? - I would have made a careful examination if there was a suggestion of anything of that kind.[21]

These three witnesses included two coal mine inspectors and a coal miner, all of whom had had opportunity to inspect the place minutely in the knowledge that it was the suspected origin of the disaster, and that they would be required subsequently to give evidence at an enquiry into the disaster's cause. Saint-Smith and Laun agreed with Want on the presence of the comminuted coal,[22] but it must be noted that Saint-Smith held, sometimes quite aggressively, to the plaster theory throughout his evidence, and Laun had no experience in coal mines. Watson had noticed the comminuted coal, but disagreed flatly with Dunlop and Want on its extent and significance:

3705. [Question by Dunlop] Laun, in his evidence, said he felt this coal, and it was sitting in a hole in the block of coal about 3 or 4 in. deep, as if it were at one time part of the block of coal. - I do not agree with that.

3706. *By Mr Want*: Is the top of the coal comminuted to a depth of 4 in., with an area of 3 or 4 ft.? - It is nothing of the kind.[23]

Thus the comminuted coal patch, a central piece of evidence in the Royal Commission's finding on the cause of the disaster, must be treated with reserve. Certainly the conclusion that a plaster shot was fired does not in itself suffice as an explanation consistent with the evidence. Morgan, if he had laid a plaster, would not have been within four metres of the spot when it fired, nor would he have left his tools lying on the ground nearby. The presence of the tamping rod beside Morgan's body was referred to at several places in the Royal Commission's proceedings as evidence that Morgan had been in the act of preparing a shot when he died. But a plaster shot would not have required a tamping rod. If, as Watson argued, Morgan had accidentally lit the fuse from his lamp flame while preparing a legitimate shot, it is difficult to understand why a man would be holding a primed charge, a lamp and a tamping rod all at one time, nor indeed, how he could. The location of Morgan's tamping rod is difficult to fit into any theory about the initiation of the disaster. Perhaps it is best dismissed as an incidental result of the explosion.

21 *Ibid.*, p.86. Evidence of C.F.V. Jackson, State Mining Engineer and Chief Inspector of Mines. In general agreement with this was the evidence of J. Stafford, Inspector of Mines (p.90), and G. Williams, miner (p.101).

22 *Ibid.*, pp.124 and 133.

23 *Ibid.*

It was never established that the block of coal had fallen from the seam prior to the disaster. The plaster-origin proponents assumed it to be a legacy of the previous cavil, which Morgan and Casloff had to break up on Monday morning. It may just as probably have been undercut previously, but dislodged by the explosion, negating any reason to fire a plaster shot at that place at the time of the disaster.

The evidence at Number Eleven Bord is not satisfactorily explained by any comprehensible mining practice, responsible or otherwise, on the part of Morgan and Casloff. If the explosion in fact originated at their workplace, some accidental element must have intruded into their actions. A premature discharge from an accidental short lighting by a carbide lamp flame, a jumped fuse, or jarring of the detonator while a plaster shot was in preparation could have produced the circumstances found after the disaster, and the Royal Commission's finding does include this possibility, although rather grudgingly.

A premature discharge would be likely to cause mutilation of the man holding the charge at the time, but this leads to no helpful evidence. Morgan and Casloff's bodies were removed from the mine four days after the explosion, in a state of advanced decomposition:

> I do not think the body [Morgan's] was examined closely enough for anybody to tell. The fingers on the hand might have been badly shattered. It has to be remembered that when that man was found, decomposition had set in and he was not closely examined. I do not think the doctors made any detailed examination either. As far as I know, they did not.[24]

One more comment must be made on the events at Number Eleven Bord before the disaster. Casloff had been injured in mine accidents on three occasions in the previous two years - once in 1920 at Mount Mulligan and twice in the Tyrconnel mine at Kingsborough in 1919 - an extraordinarily bad safety record. One of the Tyrconnell accidents involved a prematurely exploding shot.[25]

The argument that the disaster's origin was in Fitzpatrick's Wall rests on the commissioners' and witnesses' observations of the direction in which the explosion exerted its force on objects within the mine

24 *Ibid.*, pp.146-147. Evidence by Watson.

25 *A.R.* 1919, pp.141-142 and 1920, p.127. Casloff's name is spelled variously Kazloff and Kozloff in these reports, but his identity is established in the proceedings of the Royal Commission (p.147). Note that his name is also mis-spelled Cassloff on Hawes' cavil sheet. Watson in evidence described Morgan as "one of the best men in the mine and one of the most careful" (p.147), and said elsewhere, "Casloff was always more or less frightened [of shot-firing]. Morgan was the recognised leader of the two men" (p.150).

workings. While the virtual unanimity of their conclusions seems to confirm the matter, it must be observed that there is a subsequently established flaw in the assumption underlying these observations, thus leaving open the possibility that the Royal Commission was in error about the location of the explosion's origin, and rendering irrelevant its deliberations on the interpretation to be placed upon the ambiguous evidence found there.

It was frequently stated before the Royal Commission that the explosion's source could be defined by the direction indicated in the effects of the radiating blast wave, and the deposition of coked coal dust on surfaces in the mine. However, there were inconsistencies in these signs. At one place in the mine workings a wooden door had been blown some distance along the bord in one direction, and its hinges in the other.[26] Elsewhere, a dead horse lay facing the skip it had been pulling, with its collar and harness lying several metres away in opposite directions. Witnesses could come to no agreement on the implications of this scene,[27] but it should have served warning that it was not sufficient to assume that because an object lay some distance from the point where it was presumed to have been before the explosion, its location pointed to the direction in which the main shock wave had travelled. The complex behaviour of retonation waves, and their effect both on subjects in their path and the deposition of coked dust in their wake, is noted in a report on the Bruceton experimental mine explosions:

> Because of the uncertainty as to the manner in which coke dust is deposited in relation to the path of an explosion, observation of the deposits with a view to fixing the point of origin is of doubtful value.[28]

Further confusion in the interpretation of forces in the mine is demonstrated in Watson's evidence. Watson claimed that the explosion's origin could be determined by observing where the blast appeared to have been most violent, in the belief that the force would diminish as the shock wave travelled outward: "in the case of any explosion it naturally must follow that it decreases in intensity as it radiates from the centre."[29] No one present at the hearing disagreed with this statement, which is a fair description of an explosion with a single point of origin and with no means of propagation after the instant of ignition. But in the case of a

26 *R.C.* p.79.
27 *Ibid.*, pp.22, 95 and 108.
28 Rice *et al.*, *op.cit.*, p.135.
29 *R.C.* p.109.

self-propagating coal dust explosion, Watson's belief is false, and indeed the reverse of what actually occurs:

> ... the explosion starts with low velocity...and low pressures...both the velocity and the pressure increase slowly for several hundred feet and then more rapidly until at the end of a zone 350 or more feet long the explosion is travelling at a very high velocity, with great pressures.[30]

It seems likely that Watson, and possibly other witnesses, were quite mistaken in their inference of an origin by evidence of the signs of violence observed in the mine workings.

James Watson's evidence occupied more time than that of any other witness, and he was clearly and understandably defensive in his position in charge of a mine where a major disaster had occurred.[31] However, the exact nature of that position was the subject of some dispute at the Royal Commission. Since at least 1910, the Queensland *Mines Regulation Act* had required that every mine must have a Manager, and had made mine safety the responsibility of that person:

> 15.1 Every mine while being worked shall be under a manager, who shall be personally in charge of the mine and the performance of the work done therein and shall be responsible for the control, management and direction of the mine.
>
> The owner or agent of every mine shall appoint himself or some other person to be manager of such mine, and shall within fourteen days of such appointment send written notice to the warden of the manager's name and address.[32]

Despite these provisions, the Mount Mulligan mine appears never to have had a Manager. In 1914, Watson had been appointed Superintending Engineer (sometimes Superintendent Engineer) to supervise development at the Chillagoe company's new coal mine. The title Superintending Engineer was not recognised in Queensland mining law. Watson had stayed on after the mine was in production, clearly in a very senior position, but was never appointed Manager. There was an Underground Manager, Tom Evans, but his position had never been

30 Rice *et al., op.cit.*, pp.16-17.

31 The widow of a miner killed in the Mount Mulligan disaster, when interviewed, said of Watson: "He was involved in two disasters in New South Wales before he came to Mount Mulligan, you know". This implicit calumny must be refuted. Watson became manager of the Stockton Colliery two years after the 1896 disaster there and was sent as an inspector to Mount Kembla after the 1902 explosion. (*R.C.* pp.4 and 5). He had thus had previous experience in a mine disaster's aftermath, but was in no way connected with either mine before their respective explosions.

32 Queensland *Mines Regulation Acts* 1910-1916, Sec 15.

reported to the warden either. Legally, there was no-one in charge of safety at Mount Mulligan as the act required.

Watson protested that he had not been responsible for safety in the mine, but the royal commissioners did not accept his denial. While their report repeatedly referred to Tom Evans by the title of "Manager", it stated, "The mine and business are under the control of Mr J.T. Watson"[33], and spent several pages critically dissecting his evidence. Curiously, the Royal Commission did not comment on the fact that no manager had been formally appointed, although that would appear to have some bearing on the mine's safety standards. Such a comment would have implied negligence on the part of Chillagoe Limited and the Mines Department, and the commissioners consistently avoided criticism of both those bodies throughout their report. (The Warden to whom the Manager's name should have been reported was Dunlop, who chaired the Royal Commission.) Mine disasters need a scapegoat, and Watson was the only senior person at Mount Mulligan who was still alive.

All of this created a dreadful irony in Watson's position. In 1902, at the age of thirty, he had been an inspector of coal mines in the Wollongong district of New South Wales. He had a reputation for recommending stern punishment of safety breaches, and after the Mount Kembla disaster was one of the witnesses whose evidence resulted in the prosecution of William Rogers the mine manager, a process that historians Stuart Piggin and Henry Lee have described as "scapegoating".[34] Watson also played a part in drafting more satisfactory legislation afterward.

In defending himself at the Mount Mulligan enquiry, Watson disagreed with the evidence of other witnesses, sometimes to the point of outright obstructiveness, and publicly criticised aspects of the Royal Commission's findings on several occasions after its report appeared. At the time he gave evidence in Mount Mulligan, Watson had not closely examined the mine workings, having been ill since the day of the disaster.[35] Watson's incapacitation during this time may not have been entirely physical: he was described as 'raving somewhat' when visited on the Friday following the disaster.[36]

33 *R.C.* p. xxiv.

34 S. Piggin and H. Lee, *The Mt Kembla Disaster*, Sydney 1992, p. 205.

35 *R.C.* p.112.

36 *Ibid.*, p.131. By Saint-Smith, whose evidence was consistently hostile towards Watson.

Watson appeared in a very bad light during the Royal Commission hearings for it became evident during the taking of evidence that many aspects of the management of the mine, including some predisposing the apparent cause of the disaster, were highly unsatisfactory. Several of the provisions of the General Rules for Collieries under the *Mines Regulation Acts* (1910-1920) had been neglected. The Royal Commission reported:

> EXPLOSIVES
>
> 4. Explosives were distributed, carried, used and stored underground in a careless manner, without regard to the regulations.
>
> ENTRIES IN RECORD BOOK
>
> 5. Entries in the Record Book were not made as prescribed by regulation.
>
> DEPUTY
>
> 6. An uncertified Deputy was employed in the mine, contrary to the regulations.
>
> CONDITION OF THE MINE
>
> 7. The mine was dusty and extremely dry, and no adequate means were adopted to render dust innocuous, as prescribed by the regulations.
>
> DEPARTMENTAL INSPECTIONS
>
> 8. We find that departmental inspections were made by men without colliery experience, without the necessary equipment, and were not made as frequently as necessary.[37]

How Watson must have squirmed in embarrassment as he recalled his own damning evidence at Mount Kembla nineteen years earlier! On the first of these charges, the careless handling of explosives, the regulations in force in 1921 stated, *inter alia*:

> Explosives shall not be taken for use into the workings except in quantities actually required during the shift, nor except in securely covered cases or canisters;...
>
> The person responsible for the safe storage of explosives shall not issue detonators except to shot firers or other persons specially authorised....
>
> Detonators shall be stored apart from other explosives. Detonators shall not be placed dangerously near any passage or road or working face....
>
> No person other than a shot firer appointed aforesaid shall be allowed to charge or fire explosives [or]...to have explosives in his possession....
>
> No tool consisting wholly or in part of metal shall be used in charging, tamping, or ramming....

---

37 *R.C.* pp. XLIII-XLIV.

> Coal or coal dust shall not be used for tamping or stemming.[38]

It was clear that miners at Mount Mulligan were in the habit of drawing explosives and detonators at the same time from the magazine, often in excessive quantities, and carrying and storing them in whatever manner they found convenient. After the disaster, the searchers found loose explosives and detonators scattered in profusion about the mine: on the floor, loose in skips with metal tools, close to tramways.[39] Registered shot-firers had been appointed at Mount Mulligan, but their appointments seemed to have been a formality not dependent on any qualification, and in practice, explosives and detonators were issued to any man who requested them. Copper-tipped tamping rods were in use, but this drew no comment from the Royal Commission when mentioned in evidence.[40] The proscription of "metal" in the regulations was apparently generally interpreted as applying only to harder metals such as iron, more prone to striking a spark. The colliery regulations acknowledged the existence of coal dust in three brief and vaguely worded sentences:

> In every colliery the roads shall be examined daily and a report on their condition as to coal-dust shall be recorded in the record book.
>
> Systematic steps shall be taken either by watering or spreading stone dust or other means to prevent coal dust being carried along any road.
>
> The floor, roof and sides of all roads shall be kept clean and free from dust.[41]

There is more than a little irony in the fact that Queensland's first coal dust explosion followed just a year after the enactment of the first regulation designed to prevent it. It is not clear from the context of the regulations whether coal dust was regarded as a hazard or simply as a nuisance: the token form of the second regulation neither specifies the "systematic steps" to be taken, nor invites strict observance. The third is, on the face of it, an impossibility. No action had been taken to lessen the explosive potential of coal dust at Mount Mulligan; like other safety precautions, this was considered unnecessary in a gas-free mine. Watering could not have been employed in any case since in the dry heat of the spring and summer months, the quantity of water required would have exceeded the mine's meagre supply, and the stone used for pack-

38 *General Rules: Collieries*, pp.10-12.

39 *R.C.* pp.54, 61 and 70.

40 *Ibid.*, p.56. Evidence of Arthur Griffiths.

41 *General Rules: Collieries*, p.3. The regulation concerning coal dust is an undated amendment to the original 1910 regulations, probably added in March 1920.

walls in the middle seam was a fireclay which rapidly crumbled when wet.[42]

The use of stone dust had been a major concern in the Bruceton experiments and by 1915, criteria were established for the effective distribution of shale or limestone dust in mines to render coal dust inert.[43] Watson, however, was clearly opposed to the use of stone dust, which he described as "a mere palliative and of no value, in my opinion, in the prevention of explosions."[44]

In supporting this opinion, he showed some familiarity with recent research in stone-dusting, but seriously misinterpreted it, apparently confusing the practice of stone-dusting throughout the mine with the altogether different technique of establishing "preventive zones" or erecting stone dust "barriers" at selected positions in the workings.[45] Reading to the Royal Commission from a technical report which criticised the use of preventive zones in coal mines, Watson expanded the criticism to embrace the entire use of stone dust.[46] Watson also expressed concern for the health of miners with stone dust in the atmosphere of the mine. Some forms of stone dust were known to induce lung diseases, notably phthisis, and this was frequently advanced as an argument against stone-dusting. However, research had already established that certain types of stone were quite innocuous when inhaled, and this objection was no longer sustainable in 1921.[47]

The use of coal dust for tamping was potentially one of the more hazardous of the common breaches of safety regulations at Mount Mulligan. The circumstances required to initiate a coal dust explosion - the firing of a charge in contact with a quantity of coal dust in the open - would be fulfilled if coal dust were the tamping material of a blown-out shot, or the stemming for a plaster. Yet the evidence of witnesses showed that coal dust was almost universally used for tamping charges, and would thus undoubtedly be used for stemming an illegal plaster shot. One miner, aware of the danger of the practice, claimed he had

42 *R.C.* p.42.

43 In 1921, the definitive work on the subject was G.S. Rice and L.M. Jones, *Methods of Preventing and Limiting Explosions in Coal Mines*, Washington 1915, cited in Rice *et al.*, *op.cit.*, p.29.

44 *R.C.*, p.113.

45 The stone dust barriers developed at Bruceton consisted of large boxes, suspended from the mine roof on delicately balanced supports, and filled with stone dust. They were designed to upset on the passage of a shockwave, filling the tunnel with a cloud of inert stone dust. (Rice *et al.*, *op.cit.*)

46 *R.C.* p.113.

47 "Stone Dust and Coal Dust Explosions", *Engineering*, 2 August 1912, p.164. Phthisis is a form of tuberculosis induced by breathing sharp-edged dust particles such as coal (Miner's Phthisis) or silica (Grinder's Phthisis). The article cited recommends shale dust as non-injurious.

requested safer tamping material as required by the regulations and had been refused it by the management:

> 1572. *By Mr Kilpatrick*: Did you ask any of the officials for sand? - Yes. I approached the officials here.
>
> 1573. Did you bring to their notice that sand should be sent into the mine for tamping purposes? - Yes.
>
> 1574. Did you ask Mr Evans, the manager, particularly about the sand? - Yes, and I asked Grant....
>
> 1576. What did Evans say? - He said I was always after something and if I wanted sand I would have to carry it in....
>
> 1579. What did Grant answer you? - He said it was not the practice at Mount Mulligan to send sand into the mine....
>
> 1581. Did you ask Parkinson about the sand? - Yes.
>
> 1582. What did he tell you? - He said, "I know you should be supplied with sand. I do not know why you don't get it." That finished it, and I always used to carry it in myself.[48]

Parkinson, the underground deputy named in this evidence, was unqualified for the position, contrary to the regulations governing the duties of deputies:

> No person shall be deemed to be competent for the purposes of this rule unless he holds a Certificate of Fitness as Deputy issued in accordance with the provisions of this act.[49]

And, as the Royal Commission noted in its findings, Parkinson was not the only official connected with the mine who was ill-equipped to perform his duties there. It seemed clear that the underground manager and his deputies tolerated gross breaches of colliery regulations in the mine workings, but the fact that these breaches were not detected during the inspections of the mine by Mines Department officers was even more disturbing. The mine had been inspected frequently, if not always thoroughly, at irregular intervals. The last inspection had been by Laun, only five days before the disaster.[50]

The Queensland Department of Mines employed three inspectors in the Northern District, which included Mount Mulligan: S. Horsley, the senior inspector, was based at Herberton; O.M. Williams, ordinarily

---

48 *Ibid.*, p.58. Evidence of George Williams, *inter alia*. Les Weatherston, interviewed New Farm 22 November 1975, said that when he went to work at Mount Mulligan in 1926, coal dust was still routinely used by miners for tamping shots, although registered shot-firers used clay.

49 Amendment gazetted 19 April 1919, in *General Rules: Collieries*, p.3.

50 *R.C.* p.65.

based at Mareeba, was relieving in Charters Towers at the time of the disaster; and Laun, normally in Charters Towers, had been for some months based at Kidston, near Einasleigh, supervising the construction of a state battery. All three inspectors had at times visited the Mount Mulligan mine, but none of them had any previous experience in coal mines.[51]

Horsley, in overall charge of mine safety in the Northern District since 1905, was cross-examined in detail by the commissioners on his knowledge of the colliery safety regulations. He admitted almost total ignorance:

> To what class of permitted explosive does monobel belong? - I do not know. I never looked it up....
>
> Except in the case of a long wall, what is the maximum number of men to be employed in any ventilating district? - I do not know.[52]

This ignorance is understandable, if not excusable. The Northern District consisted principally of a great number of metalliferous workings producing gold, tin and copper, mostly small and widely separated. An inspector was required to familiarise himself with safety regulations and working conditions in a large number of mines. In 1921, coal mine safety regulations were published in a separate and obscure pamphlet arising from the Mines Regulation Acts which covered mines of all kinds; and there was only one coal mine in the whole of the Northern District. Many of the safety breaches at Mount Mulligan, for example, tamping with coal dust - a practice horrendously dangerous in a coal mine, but only recently known to be so - would in all probability not attract the attention of a mines inspector preoccupied with more familiar and universal problems such as timbering, ventilation, sanitary installations and worn haulage cables. In every North Queensland mine but Mount Mulligan, after all, a miner could safely tamp his shots with any material that came to hand.

The use of gelignite for blasting coal was a practice which demonstrates the gap that existed in 1921 between theoretical opinion on mine safety and legislative provision to ensure it. Gelignite was known to be potentially dangerous for colliery use, as its flame temperature and shattering effect were both very high, increasing the likelihood of a blown-out shot. The preferred explosive was Monobel. Watson stated before the Royal Commission that because of its

51 *Ibid.*, pp.62-72.

52 *Ibid.*, pp.63-64 *inter alia*. Evidence of Horsley, questioned by Want.

dangerous properties, gelignite "should not be permitted underground at all".[53] Chief Inspector Jackson stressed the danger of using different types of explosives together, thus inviting quite unpredictable effects in shot-firing.[54]

After the disaster, however, both gelignite and Monobel were found in the mine, sometimes together.[55] Watson admitted that in the past, he had ordered gelignite "on occasions when there was no other explosive available" and seemed surprised to learn that both were in use at the time of the explosion.[56] There was, however, no statutory order prohibiting the use of gelignite nor the combined use of different explosives, in Queensland coal mines at the time, despite the fact that Watson, the Chief Inspector and the commissioners, and thus presumably general informed opinion of the time, agreed that these practices were hazardous.

Watson defended himself before the Royal Commission by pleading ignorance of the state of affairs in the mine. His evidence placed responsibility for activities underground squarely on Evans:

> 1155. [Questions by Kilpatrick] Have you any knowledge of the provisions of ... the [Mines Regulation] Act relating to collieries? - In a general way, I have.
>
> 1156. You don't know, as superintending engineer of the mine, whether those provisions were carried out or not? - I did not interfere in any way with the management of the mine....
>
> 1172. Did you ever examine the Record Book to see if there were any records of inspections there? - I never examined the Record Book for a long while....
>
> 1179. Generally speaking, do you think that all matters in connection with the Mines Regulation Act...were carried out by those in charge? So far as I know....Usually I did not interfere with Evans at all; in fact, he resented any interference with matters for which he was responsible.[57]

This evidence seeks to absolve Watson from responsibility for the unsafe state of the mine at the time of the disaster. Evans was dead before the date of this hearing; his evidence could have clarified many of the doubtful areas left by the Royal Commission's report. It is clear that a degree of antipathy existed between Watson and Evans in administrative

53 *Ibid.*, p.118.
54 *Ibid.*, p.85.
55 *Ibid.*, pp.75 and 100.
56 *Ibid.*, p.44.
57 *Ibid.*, pp.45-46 *inter alia*. Evidence of Watson.

matters, but it seems extraordinary that Watson, with his high qualifications and decades of experience in mine management could say: "I have been in the mine very little during the last twelve months".[58] There was also apparent ill-feeling between Evans and Grant:

> 3086. *By Mr Kilpatrick.* Do you think there was any rivalry existing between Evans and Grant which might make for ineffectual management? - There was certainly always a feeling between them. I hate to have to say it now, but I must tell you what I know.
>
> 3087. We quite understand that? - You understand that. There was not always the good feeling between them that there might have been. I would not like to say too much on the point, because the men cannot answer for themselves.[59]

When George Williams' evidence on Evans' reaction to his request for safe tamping material is added, a picture emerges of Evans as an abrupt, dogmatic man, quick to take offence when his authority in matters of mine management was questioned. But O.M. Williams, the inspector most familiar with Mount Mulligan, said of Evans: "He was very strict with the men, and would not tolerate any dangerous practices".[60] Evans' omnipotence in underground affairs is questionable in the light of other evidence from Watson, who took personal credit, for example, for detecting the man preparing the plaster shot and threatening him with dismissal. Watson also claimed to have insisted on the use of Monobel in the mine because of the danger inherent in the use of other explosives. As the commissioners pointed out, this undermines Watson's other position of ignorance of underground matters.[61] If he was aware of the need for, and expected to enforce compliance with, some safety requirements, the plausibility of his plea of ignorance and helplessness elsewhere is reduced.

Watson, later in the Royal Commission hearings, forced himself into the unsupportable position of demanding stronger safety regulations, in the face of the manifest laxity at Mount Mulligan in enforcing the existing ones. He read to the Royal Commission a list of suggestions for more stringent regulation of coalmining practices: standardisation of

58 *Ibid.*, p.45. In the twelve months before the disaster, Watson may have been preoccupied with surface work, notably the construction of the cokeworks, but he himself made no such claim.

59 *Ibid.*, p.116. Evidence of Watson. Elsewhere Inspector Williams stated that Evans had been on holiday, possibly from July until September 1921, and that Grant had been underground manager in his absence (p.69). Although this seems to have an important bearing on the management of the mine, the Royal Commission did not seek corroboration of Williams' vague statement.

60 *Ibid.*, p.69.

61 *Ibid.*, p. XXIX.

permitted explosives, registration of shot-firers, mandatory electrical detonation of charges, the use of electric lamps, improvement of inspection records, and firing of shots after the mine was vacated by the shift.[62] These suggestions have an air of prophecy - every one of them is in use in Queensland coal mines now - but they must have had a casuistic ring, coming from the man who six days earlier had said "I did not interfere in any way with the management of the mine".[63]

Watson expressed contempt both for the safety regulations in force in Queensland: "Regulations are not always sensible", and for coal miners who disregarded them: "the miners are primarily responsible".[64] Having inspected the mine in greater detail after the Royal Commission had returned to Brisbane, he developed the theory that the disaster's origin lay in an accidental discharge while Morgan was preparing a shot for the shallow drill hole at Number Eleven Bord, and travelled to Brisbane to give further evidence on 10 November. Clearly incensed at the evidence previously heard on the careless handling of explosives in the mine and on the probability of a plaster shot having been fired, Watson obtained the commissioner's permission to examine his principal critic, Saint-Smith:

> According to the newspaper reports in the North, Mr Saint-Smith expressed the opinion that from what he saw he considered that there had been a good deal of carelessness in the handling of explosives underground, and I would like to ask him one or two questions bearing on that....
>
> *The Chairman*: Very well, Mr Watson, you may question Mr Saint-Smith.[65]

A witness cross-examining another witness was a dramatic departure from a Royal Commission's normal procedures. In a sometimes heated exchange, Watson challenged Saint-Smith on his earlier evidence, forcing the geologist to admit that he, too, was unfamiliar with mine regulations, but that in his opinion, if the use of explosives at Mount Mulligan was not in breach of them, "it is time the regulations were amended to make it a breach".[66] But Watson's questioning was limited to the fruitless pursuit of redress for Saint-Smith's earlier comments on the handling of explosives, by attempting to establish that the situation found in the mine was the result of the explosion's violence, and not a reflection of normal practice. Watson did not use the opportunity to probe other

62 *Ibid.*, pp.117-120.
63 *Ibid.*, p.45.
64 *Ibid.*, pp.152 and 153.
65 *Ibid.*, p.154.
66 *Ibid.*, p.154.

weak points in the evidence supporting what was clearly going to be the Royal Commission's finding. Their report was most damaging to Watson:

> ...his evidence is not satisfactory, and open to question in some particulars. His statement that Mr Evans was wholly responsible for the management of the mine, in view of his own statements that he was Agent for the owners and Superintending Engineer, is doubtful....
>
> It is regrettable that the expressed contempt for, and ignorance of, important mandatory regulations dealing with safety and general conditions, by the Superintending Engineer, should have had its reflex in the conduct of the mine.[67]

Ten days after the publication of the Royal Commission's findings, extracts from a lengthy rejoinder by Watson appeared in a Brisbane newspaper. Watson found the commissioners' conclusion "absurd", and reiterated his contention that an accidental discharge had occurred while a legitimate shot was in preparation. More seriously, he attacked the commissioners and their methods of investigation:

> The investigations by the members of the Commission were not carried out in a manner which would cause any competent observer to view their opinion with respect.
>
> In the first place the personnel of the Commission left much to be desired.... The investigations were carried out with most indecent haste, and no right of cross-examination of witnesses was allowed. The whole of the responsible officers of the mine were killed, and no first-hand evidence was available....
>
> The plan prepared under the direction of the chairman is grossly inaccurate in many important details, and particularly so in regard to the position of the men referred to.[68]

Watson also claimed, as he had done in evidence, that the mines regulations were so ineffective that the common practice in coal mines was to ignore them:

> As a matter of cold fact, the regulations governing mining conditions in Queensland are in such a chaotic state that no one, not even the officers of the Mines Department themselves, know where they stand.[69]

---

67 *Ibid.*, p. XXXVI.

68 Brisbane *Daily Mail*, 12 December 1921. Watson's reference to cross-examination seems strange, because he had been permitted to cross-examine Saint-Smith. He must have been refused this right on other occasions not recorded in evidence. No other cross-examination occurred, but no request for it is recorded. His criticism of the published plans is justified - they are inaccurate in a number of respects.

69 *Ibid.*

The colliery regulations in force in 1921 were a patch-work of provisions drawn from the general mining regulations, and contained relatively few references which applied specifically to coal mines. About half the length of the regulations dealt with aspects of safety in vertical shafts and winding gear, which had no relevance at Mount Mulligan and many other Queensland coal mines, which were entered by adits, not shafts. Other sections of the regulations dealt with ventilation, inspections, lighting, sanitation and explosives, and while specific procedures were laid down for the use of explosives in gassy mines, the only acknowledgment of the danger of coal dust appeared in the three rules inserted as an amendment less than five lines in length.[70] This is presumably the section of the regulations to which Watson referred when claiming:

> In regard to the regulations of March 1920, regarding dust in mines, it appears as if few if any of the persons concerned in the management and inspection of mines even knew of their existence.[71]

Whatever means had been adopted to promulgate the coal dust amendment, inadequate as it was, it is clear that Watson had not heard of it, and that if Evans had, he had done nothing to implement it at Mount Mulligan. It is not possible to determine the extent to which the regulations were observed in coal mines in other parts of Queensland, although it is likely that the presence of firedamp in most other mines would have predisposed a healthier respect for safe mining practices than was the case at Mount Mulligan. The total ignorance of the colliery regulations expressed by all three Northern District mines inspectors at the Royal Commission suggests that Watson may not have overstated his case in claiming: "there is not a single mine in the State where they are fully carried out".[72] The regulations seem hardly to have been in a "chaotic" state, as Watson claimed, but they were certainly inadequate and not well-known, and this inadequacy and unfamiliarity increased the likelihood of their being ignored.

To this extent, Watson was supporting the recommendations of the Royal Commission which suggested sweeping changes in legislation and

---

70 *General Rules: Collieries, passim*. The Royal Commission Report also refers to 'Special Rules issued under "The Mines Regulation Act of 1910" for the Conduct and Guidance of Officials and all Persons Employed in or about Mount Mulligan Colliery'. (*R.C.* p. VII). No copy of these special rules appears to have survived.

71 *Daily Mail*, 12 December 1921.

72 *Ibid.*

regulations governing coalmining in Queensland.[73] His aim, of course, was not to demand reform, but to justify the disregard of regulations at Mount Mulligan as a reflection of universal practice. His attack on the Royal Commission's findings ridiculed the plaster shot theory, pointing out that the proximity of Morgan's body to the explosion's suspected origin had been unknown to the commissioners when the theory was developed, and that this seriously undermined any attempt to attribute the explosion to a deliberate action on Morgan's part:

> When the members of the Commission, or, rather, one of them, originally formed the opinion that a "plaster" shot had been fired on top of the fallen coal, they did not know that one of the men had been found within a few feet of the place where the alleged "plaster" was fired....[74]

Watson also pointed out something which appears not to have arisen in the Royal Commission's proceedings: that no trace of burnt or unburnt fuse was found at Number Eleven Bord. If correct, this brings into question any theory involving the proper or improper use of explosives at that place. The firing of a charge, whether accidentally or otherwise, must be initiated by a detonator, and the detonator is crimped onto the fuse before it is placed in the charge. If no fuse was present, Morgan's actions before the explosion are completely uncertain, and it becomes very difficult to attribute the explosion's origin to his workplace. Watson's new evidence appears to have elicited no official response and his entire attack on the qualifications, procedures and findings of the Royal Commission was ignored.

In a less dignified vein, Watson had earlier written to the *Queensland Government Mining Journal*, apparently seeking to deflate Laun's claim to having led the rescue operation. The *Journal* had previously published a report by Laun on the disaster which contained the statement:

> Messrs Watson and Harris, whose trying experiences on the Monday had greatly exhausted them, were after difficulty prevailed upon by myself to retire for rest, and I then took charge of the rescue operations.[75]

That Laun had no intention of belittling the efforts of Watson and Harris seems clear enough and is demonstrated in a report he submitted to the Chief Secretary's office, stating: "the greatest amount of courage was required by those who entered the mine first and did the exploratory

73 Changes in Queensland mining regulations and legislation following the Mount Mulligan disaster are treated in the next chapter.
74 *Daily Mail*, 12 December 1921.
75 *Q.G.M.J.* 15 October 1921, p.428.

work in the early stages".[76] But, piqued at Laun's unfortunate use of the phrase "took charge", Watson informed the *Journal* editor:

> The facts are that when the writer collapsed on Tuesday night he asked Mr Laun to assist Mr Harris, the company's mechanical engineer, in the conduct of the rescue operations...Mr Laun ably assisted in the work, but was not at any time in full charge of operations.[77]

The letter is a petty quibble, serving only to illustrate the bitterness Watson felt after the Royal Commission hearings. Seizing on any opportunity to defend himself publicly, he succeeded only in adding an air of spitefulness to the Mount Mulligan aftermath. In a strange footnote to this correspondence, Watson, three years later, seems to have changed his opinion completely on the origin of the Mount Mulligan disaster. In a learned paper read at Newcastle in 1924, he informed his audience of engineers that the Mount Mulligan disaster was caused by the explosion of an acetylene lamp. In carefully but rather equivocally reconstructing the event, Watson did not identify the position in the mine clearly, but his description obviously refers to somewhere other than Fitzpatrick's Machine Wall, although he said: "All the evidence of forces in the mine point to the place in question as the site of the initial explosion".[78]

Watson's theory of 1924 is quite incompatible with the evidence given by himself and others, and with his own expressed conclusion, before the Royal Commission of 1921. Either he subsequently discovered evidence in the mine which the Royal Commission had overlooked, or his later theory arose from his own distortion of the evidence with the passage of time.

It is difficult to evaluate Watson in the light of events surrounding the 1921 disaster. Was he responsible for safety at Mount Mulligan or not? He is an almost tragic figure when one considers his undoubted expertise in colliery management, his courage in the hours following the disaster, and the slighting and somewhat prejudiced treatment he received from the Royal Commission. Ironically, having been implicitly allotted a major part of the blame for the disaster by the Royal Commission, he was subsequently decorated for his part in the rescue attempt. But in the light of his petulant and futile reactions to criticism,

76 Laun to Under-Secretary, Chief Secretary's Office, 19 November 1921. Q.S.A. PRE A848 25/7633, 21/10115.

77 *Q.G.M.J.* 15 November 1921, p.475.

78 J.T. Watson, "Explosions and Fires in Mines", Institution of Engineers of Australia *Transactions*, Vol.5, 1924, p.28.

his earlier failure to exert whatever authority he had in the safe conduct of mining operations, and his wild attempts to seek explanations for the disaster in chance events not involving his own failings, much of the sympathy he would otherwise deserve is lost. Watson left Mount Mulligan and the mining industry early in 1923 and worked in a number of civil engineering positions with the Queensland Irrigation and Water Supply Commission and Main Roads Department until his death in 1938.[79]

Watson's complaints that "the personnel of the Commission left much to be desired" and that its "investigations were carried out with most indecent haste" cannot simply be dismissed as an angry rejoinder. The Royal Commission's procedures and findings are open to considerable criticism. One disturbing aspect of the commissioners' report is their statement that they had reached a conclusion on the cause of the explosion before they commenced taking evidence, a conclusion based in part on invalid reasoning arising from their observations in the mine. Their subsequent questioning shows a distinct tendency to lead witnesses in the direction of that preconceived conclusion and their summing up of evidence in places disregards or distorts information not helpful to that conclusion: the existence of the comminuted coal, the ambiguous significance of the tamping rod, the presence or absence of fuse, the position of Morgan's body and the nature of his injuries.

The commissioners themselves can hardly be regarded as impartial. Dunlop was an employee of the Mines Department, and as Warden had been responsible for matters of mine administration, including safety, at Mount Mulligan before the disaster. He was also a personal friend of Premier Theodore, and at the time of the Royal Commission would have been actively involved in negotiations for the State purchase of the Mungana mines from another friend, Fred Reid, a transaction that would later become the subject of another Royal Commission. He knew that the State also wanted to buy Mount Mulligan from the Chillagoe company. Fitzpatrick wore two hats to the Royal Commission. As Union President, he had visited Mount Mulligan only a few weeks before the explosion, and had routinely certified working conditions to be safe. As a Labor MLC, he too was a close friend of Theodore. Clearly there were constraints on the findings these two would make; both bore a degree of personal responsibility for the disaster, and neither would be too critical of Chillagoe Limited, the Mines Department, or the State. Want was an

79 Interview with Jack Watson, Slade Point, 6 March 1977; and Chillagoe Limited ledger, entry 23 March 1923.

experienced mine manager with no known hidden agenda, but he was completely unfamiliar with Mount Mulligan and conditions in the north. Dunlop was rewarded with a transfer as Warden and Police Magistrate to the Cloncurry Mineral Field in November while the Royal Commission was winding up.

An examination of the questions asked by each of the commissioners shows clear trends in their thinking. Dunlop, as Chairman, asked the greatest number of questions and showed obvious familiarity with mining procedures and regulations, and was almost invariably fair and calm in his approach to witnesses. Want pressed some of the witnesses rather aggressively and consistently pursued the theme of the plaster shot in questions on the disaster's cause. Saint-Smith, the principal expert witness, was highly amenable to this line of questioning and provided much ammunition for the Royal Commission's criticism of the Mount Mulligan mine's management.

Kilpatrick, as might be expected, concerned himself with working and safety conditions and on several occasions took over the questioning of miners who seemed confused, trying quite gently to bring some order out of their answers. Kilpatrick undoubtedly knew the surviving miners better than did Want or Dunlop, and during the Royal Commission's investigations he held a meeting of the Mount Mulligan branch of the union to elect new office-bearers. Fifteen members attended.[80] Kilpatrick also moved from the role of Royal Commissioner to that of Union President on two occasions when confronted by Mines Department officials during the taking of evidence: once to lecture Inspector Stafford on the causes of Miners' Nystagmus,[81] and once to harangue Chief Inspector Jackson on the inadequacy of the Ipswich Mines Life-Saving Brigade:

> Are you aware that the trainees themselves, the advisory committee, the mining officials themselves, and the organization I represent...are thoroughly disgusted with the whole thing...?[82]

The Royal Commission report contains findings which are demonstrably inaccurate. The plans of the mine workings showing the locations of the miners' bodies, prepared by Dunlop, are quite irreconcilable with the evidence given on the positions of Morgan and Casloff, both orally, and in two other plans of their workplace tendered as exhibits. This is

80 *Worker*, 6 October 1921.
81 *R.C.* p.96.
82 *Ibid.*, p.74.

an extraordinary anomaly, in view of the weight placed on Morgan and Casloff's actions in the findings of the Royal Commission. The plans also show the locations of 75 bodies - at least one must be in error, or fabricated, because Turriff's body, supposedly one of that 75, was not found until two months after the Royal Commission reported. Indeed, there is such a weight of contradictory evidence on this point that it seems quite likely that 76 miners were killed at Mount Mulligan. The report repeated the statement that a body still lay in the mine, identifying its location:

> If the cavil sheets available are correct, there is still one body unrecovered, which was thought to be under a fall of earth in the second pick place off No.12 South.[83]

Apart from whatever is implied by the word "was", this statement glosses over the fact that the missing man was long known not to be at that place. The reference to the cavil sheets gives an unwarranted air of precision to the body-count. A purported cavil sheet appears as part of Exhibit Three in the Royal Commission report, and it contains the names of all 75 believed to have been killed.[84] But this cavil sheet was clearly created after the disaster, once the number of dead had been established from the number of men found to be missing from the community, and is thus derived from knowledge of the number killed, although the Royal Commission attempted to present it as a basis for that knowledge. The man to whom it is attributed, C.V. Lewis, Chillagoe Limited accountant at Mount Mulligan, did not know the cavil when he gave evidence before the Royal Commission:

> 784. Would the cavilling list come into your possession? - It was not supplied to me as a rule.
>
> 785. But you would have to have a list of men working in the mine? - Yes. I have made out a list, which I will tender in evidence.[85]

The Royal Commission was extremely casual toward the whole question of establishing the number of dead and of determining their causes of death. This question was not specified in their commission, but is an important one, as no inquest was held into the deaths of the 75 miners, no death certificates were supplied by the doctors in attendance after

83 *Ibid.*, p. XXXIII. This apparently reflects the belief that Donald Butler's body was buried under a fall of earth - a theory which had been disproved nearly two months earlier - see *Cairns Post*, 11 October 1921.

84 *Ibid.*, p.164.

85 *Ibid.*, p.28. Evidence of C.V. Lewis, questioned by Dunlop, 4 October 1921. Note that Chillagoe Limited had been unable to produce a list of men working in the mine immediately after the disaster - only the August pay sheet was available.

the disaster, and the Royal Commission thus appears to have been acting in place of both a coroner's court hearing and a warden's enquiry.[86]

In previous major coal mine disasters, inquests had been held almost immediately afterward, usually into the deaths of a token number of miners, the findings afterwards being applied to the deaths of all. At Bulli, after the 1887 disaster, an inquest into the death of one miner sat three days after the explosion,[87] and was later followed by a Royal Commission.[88] At Mount Kembla in 1902, a Coronial Enquiry into the deaths of three miners convened on the day following the disaster and remained in session for six weeks to establish the cause of death of the 96 miners. This Enquiry was followed by an even more exhaustive Royal Commission, whose published report occupied over a thousand pages, and a separate enquiry into the conduct of the mine manager.[89]

At Mount Mulligan the Royal Commissioners met for 65 days and took evidence from 29 witnesses. The Torbanlea Royal Commission, investigating a mere five deaths in simpler circumstances 21 years earlier, had sat for 73 days and interviewed 53 witnesses.[90] The Mount Mulligan Royal Commission was hasty and superficial by comparison with others held in similar circumstances, and neither the number of dead nor the way they died was satisfactorily established by any official enquiry after the Mount Mulligan disaster.

The Royal Commission's efforts were of considerable value: at the very least, the proceedings of the commission provide a wealth of information on conditions at Mount Mulligan in 1921, the disaster and its immediate aftermath. In reporting on the deficiencies that existed in the operation of the mine, the Royal Commission was to initiate a series of rather tardy reforms in the regulation of coalmining in Queensland. The findings of the Royal Commission, however, must be regarded with some caution, in view of the extent to which they clearly

86 None of the miners killed in the Mount Mulligan disaster is named in the Inquest Deposition Register, 2 February 1921-18 August 1922, Q.S.A. JUS R15. Burial of the miners appears to have been ordered by Dunlop as mining warden, although no warden's enquiry was held. Apparently formalities in the issuing of death certificates were waived to expedite the payment of funeral benefits: see reply by Home Secretary W. McCormack to a question by T.R. Roberts, M.L.A.; *Q.P.D.* Vol.137, 1921, p.966.

87 *Sydney Morning Herald*, 26 March 1887.

88 *Bulli Colliery Accident: Report of the Royal Commission*, N.S.W. *V. & P.*, 2nd Session 1887, Vol.4, pp.271-459.

89 *Mount Kembla Colliery Disaster: Report of the Royal Commission*, N.S.W. *V. & P.*, 1903, Vol.5, pp.1-1050; and *Conduct of Mr Rogers, as Manager, Mount Kembla Colliery, ibid.*, pp.1051-1226. Both the Bulli and Mount Kembla Royal Commissions came to conclusions broadly similar to those at Mount Mulligan, attributing the disasters to disregard of safety regulations and lax management.

90 *Report of the Royal Commission into the Torbanlea Colliery Accident.*

rely on unpublished evidence, and the selective manner in which they treat the evidence published in support of their conclusions. The Royal Commission conspicuously avoided comment on Chillagoe Limited in its conduct of the mine's operations, very lightly chided the Mines Department inspectors who had confessed total ignorance of the colliery regulations which it was their job to uphold, and sought only to investigate and attribute blame amongst individuals present at Mount Mulligan.[91] With the single exception of their principal scapegoat James Watson, everyone the commissioners blamed was dead.

In forming an opinion on the cause of the disaster, the Mount Mulligan Royal Commission merely narrowed the range of possibilities without conclusively determining which of the several remaining must be accepted. The commissioners seem to have been preoccupied with averting bad publicity, and did not provide a satisfactory explanation for the cause of the disaster. While their report went to some lengths to blame Watson, the evidence does not convincingly establish his culpability. Since it is no longer possible to come to a conclusive decision on the cause of the explosion from the surviving evidence, the question must remain open. It is reasonably certain that the immediate cause of the disaster, whether at Number Eleven Bord or elsewhere, lay in some neglect of safety precautions: some unknown, probably habitual practice which in most other coal mines would have been detected and forbidden long before.

Beyond the immediate cause of the explosion there lay a host of circumstances most of which cannot be established as direct causes of the disaster, but which contributed in some way to the likelihood of its occurrence. Some of these circumstances are common to all coal mines. Coalmining is an inherently dangerous occupation, and the constant threat of violent death induces in miners a form of cynical fatalism: a deterministic outlook which may at times outweigh caution in the handling of dangerous conditions. Even in highly dangerous mines there are extraordinary accounts of miners coldly flirting with disaster. Miners working underground at Bulli in 1887 casually walked a few paces away

91 Chillagoe Limited played no formal part in the Commission's proceedings, but retained the Cairns law firm McDonnell & Hamlyn Harris in some connection with the hearings. (Chillagoe Limited ledger, entry 29 November 1921.)

from known sources of escaping firedamp before lighting their pipes![92] Mount Mulligan was regarded as a safe mine, and thus men there felt free to exercise more licence in matters of safety than in a gassy mine.

The men mining at Mount Mulligan in 1921 came from two sources. Those from coal mines elsewhere were almost certainly confronted at Mount Mulligan with working conditions safer than those they had previously encountered. Alongside them were men previously experienced in metalliferous mines, who, uneducated in the coalmining tradition, were quite possibly unaware of the dangers inherent in their new surroundings. Whether familiar with conditions more dangerous or less so, either class of miner might bring to Mount Mulligan potentially disastrous attitudes and practices. The tradition of piece-work mining, common to most coal mines, further predisposed a state of mine in which the saving of time was of more value than the observance of safety regulations.

At Mount Mulligan there were more specific circumstances not common to all coal mines, which increased the likelihood of the explosion. The climate, hot and dry throughout the spring and summer months, facilitated the dispersal of fine, dry coal dust throughout the workings, increasing its capacity to propagate an explosion.[93]

The Chillagoe Company had for two decades consistently demonstrated its inability to supervise the operation of its northern mines. Financial adversity led the company into penny-pinching habits at Mount Mulligan, such as the refusal to supply safe tamping material in the mine, and possibly the disregard of the coal dust regulation; paradoxically, loose management permitted the profligate distribution of costly explosives to unqualified miners. Both circumstances contributed to danger in the mine.

The isolation of Mount Mulligan led to chronic labour shortage, and hence to the use of coal-cutting machines which contributed to the quantity of coal dust dispersed in mining. The same isolation also probably helped to maintain a frontier ethos in which disregard of

92 *Sydney Morning Herald*, 2 April 1887. Some British coal miners in the nineteenth century were in the habit of 'puffing out a fiery stream' by filling their mouths with firedamp at the coal-seam, and igniting it while exhaling. (R.L. Galloway, *Annals of Coal Mining and the Coal Trade*, 2nd Series, London 1904, p.38). Such behaviour among experienced miners cannot be attributed to ignorance of the possible consequences - the only other explanation is fatalistic bravado.

93 In September, the Mareeba district has an average maximum temperature of 82.3°F, and average relative humidity at 9 a.m. of 64%. (*Resources and Industry of Far North Queensland, op.cit.*, pp.26-27). Conditions in the mine would be both hotter and drier than those recorded at the surface.

mining regulations was seen as a demonstration of hardy masculine individualism. Certainly the uniqueness of Mount Mulligan's industry led to unfamiliarity of the visiting mining inspectors with the regulations and procedures of the mine, making them blind to dangerous practices.

In addition, there were purely random circumstances, whose contribution to the disaster is indefinable, but which increased its likelihood by tending to lower safety standards. The transfers of mining inspectors in the months preceding the disaster confused their areas of responsibility and reduced their already poor collective familiarity with procedures at Mount Mulligan. The new cavil led to confusion and clumsiness in the mine on the morning of the disaster, and perhaps the influenza epidemic added to this uncertainty. Personal antipathy dividing those in authority at the mine made for a social climate in which supervision of mining operations was relaxed, and Evans' absence on leave in the months before the explosion raises questions about the maintenance of this supervision in his absence, and on his return.

The use of gelignite, unprotected detonators and carbide lamps in the mine can not be shown to have helped in any way to cause the explosion, but each served to reduce the mine's safety. Casloff cannot be ignored in considering the disaster's possible causes. The Royal Commission's case for establishing his workplace as the explosion's origin is a poor one, but his previous safety record, and particularly the incident involving an accidental explosion at Kingsborough, cannot be dismissed as irrelevant.

Probably more than any other cause, the absence of the miner's bane - firedamp - allowed careless practices to recur until the morning when the laws of probability operated to initiate a coal dust explosion:

> The only trouble with the mine, it appears to me, was that it was so safe that recklessness was possible. The mine was, if anything, too safe.[94]

94 *R.C.* p.139. Evidence of Saint-Smith. In interviews on the disaster, the theory was twice advanced that the explosion was initiated by an accidental detonation of explosives in a skip. Jim McColm (interviewed Ipswich, 17 December 1976) referred to the discovery in the mine of a skip which had been destroyed by a violent local explosion, and Coal Mine Inspector J.T. Taylor is said to have held the same theory. (Interview with Inspector R.N. Hardie, Ipswich, 22 December 1976). Neither the theory nor the evidence for it is mentioned in the Royal Commission proceedings, although reference is made at one point to loose explosives with metal tools, indicating the potential for such an accident. (*R.C.* p.76). As neither McColm nor Taylor inspected the mine immediately after the disaster, the theory appears to have no foundation in first-hand evidence and has not been discussed elsewhere in this study; however, it cannot be dismissed as implausible.

4.
THE AFTERMATH

"Was it this morning, one short day back,
He kissed her goodbye and smiled?"

(J.C. Gasking, *The World's News*, 1 October 1921)

The Mount Mulligan disaster was not the greatest of its kind in Australia when measured in absolute terms of cost in human life. Both the Bulli and Mount Kembla explosions killed more miners. But both these earlier disasters occurred within a few miles of Wollongong, in sizeable communities in close contact with other coalmining towns. In its impact on the local community, the Mount Mulligan disaster was incomparably greater because of the completeness of the death toll, the isolation of the township and the size of the community.

At both Bulli and Mount Kembla there were survivors: at Mount Kembla at least 160 miners escaped alive from distant parts of the mine.[1] Some of these were not even aware of the explosion until they emerged at the end of their shift. No-one in the Mount Mulligan mine at the time of the explosion survived. The totality of the loss of life at

1 *Mount Kembla Colliery Disaster, op.cit.*, pp. xvi-xvii.

Mount Mulligan, evident in the early stages of the rescue attempt, gave an air of hopelessness to the search for the dead that followed, and yet the operation continued for four days at considerable risk to the searchers.

More recent practice, when it has been established that a mine contains no survivors after an explosion, is to seal the mine entrances rather than risk further loss of life in recovering the dead. Three Queensland coal mine disasters in recent decades demonstrate this difference in approach: on 31 July 1972 an explosion at Box Flat colliery, Ipswich, killed three men a short distance inside the mine entrance and entombed another fourteen, eight of them members of the Mines Rescue Squad who had been called in to deal with a fire in the mine. Within six hours, all entrances to the mine were sealed in order to extinguish underground fires; the violence of the explosion demonstrated that none of the fourteen men underground could have survived.[2] Similarly, after the explosion of 20 September 1975 in the Kianga mine which trapped thirteen men underground, the mine was sealed after drill-hole samples of the mine atmosphere established that fires were burning in the mine, and that the utterly remote possibility of men having survived did not justify the risk to rescuers' lives that entry to the mine would entail.[3] Neither mine has been reopened.

The explosion at the Moura No. 4 mine on 16 July 1986 had a different outcome. Twelve miners in one section of the underground workings were killed, but eight others survived. The bodies of the dead were retrieved within the next week.[4] But when Moura No. 2 exploded on 7 August 1994, ten miners escaped while eleven others who had been working together never emerged. Cautious rescue attempts began, but 36 hours later a second and larger explosion occurred in the mine, and it was then sealed.[5] Even more recently, on 19 November 2010 a series of explosions in the Pike River coal mine near Greymouth in New Zealand entombed 29 miners. The outcome remains in doubt, but it seems unlikely the mine will be re-opened.

2 *Courier Mail*, 1 August 1972. A new section of the Box Flat mine was abandoned and flooded in March 1977 when it began to heat, presumably from spontaneous combustion of coal. After the Kianga disaster, the Q.C.E.U. had instructed its members to remove themselves from any underground mine in the event of heating or fire. (*Q.P.D.* Vol.272, 1976-77, p.1986).

3 *Report of an Accident at Kianga No.1 Underground Mine*, (Queensland Department of Mines, 1976) p.23, and *A.R.* 1975, p.79. The Mines Rescue Squad was at Kianga hours before the mine was sealed, but, probably as a result of the Box Flat experience, no attempt was made to enter the mine.

4 *Report on an Accident at Moura No. 4 Underground Mine*, Brisbane 1987.

5 *Report on an Accident at Moura No.:2 Underground Mine*, Brisbane 1996.

Had the Mount Mulligan disaster occurred in recent decades, expert opinion would almost certainly have demanded that the mine be permanently sealed and another mine be opened for production elsewhere on the coal-seam. But at Mount Mulligan in 1921, such decisions were not immediately in the hands of remote authority, nor were the possible consequences of a rescue attempt as clearly understood. The decision to re-enter the mine was made spontaneously by the Mount Mulligan community, and even when it was apparent that no survivors would be found, the work of recovery was maintained. There is no evidence of even passing thought having been given to abandoning the mine; the surviving community clearly assumed from the first moments that the mine would re-open, and that the first step in recovery must obviously be the removal and burial of the dead. Community pressure would probably have defeated any attempt at sealing the mine.

The isolation of Mount Mulligan made the disaster a private thing, involving only the immediate members of the close-knit community in the first hours after the explosion. The labour and resources of the town itself provided the only means of coping with the disaster, and the bereaved of the community had only their equally-afflicted neighbours for solace during the first day. The number personally involved in the aftermath grew progressively as volunteers came from steadily increasing distances: first miners from close communities such as Kingsborough and Wolfram, then people of more diverse backgrounds from distant towns. The Mount Mulligan residents were increasingly isolated in a large body of strangers. In the Wollongong area, where the 1887 and 1902 disasters occurred, there was a large district of coalmining communities with an established coal-based tradition; Mount Mulligan was an isolated town, its coalmining lore and the ethos that arose from it quite alien to the surrounding district. The residents of the town were united in a private cataclysm which outsiders could not fully share.

The isolation and unique industry of Mount Mulligan also created practical difficulties in the aftermath. On 19 September, Mines Minister A.J. Jones wired to Mount Mulligan, offering to send the Ipswich Life Saving Brigade with rescue equipment. The journey Jones envisaged from Ipswich to Mount Mulligan in 1921 would have involved a series of alternate railway and motor vehicle stages along the route of the unfinished coastal railway, a nine hour launch trip from Lucinda to Mourilyan, and a special train from there to Mount Mulligan. He believed it could be done in only three days, pointing out that "men had been entombed for a longer period than that ... and had been recovered alive".[6] The rescue of Modesto Varischetti cast its shadow over many people's reactions to the Mount Mulligan explosion.

Laun naturally declined this incredible offer,[7] realizing as Jones did not that the only work to be done at Mount Mulligan was removal of the dead, which could be done with the resources at hand. Even had there been men trapped alive in the mine, their rescue would have been accomplished sooner at the arduous pace that was being achieved than by the rescue odyssey proposed by Jones.

Mount Mulligan's isolation thus rendered useless the State's only means of coping with a coal mine explosion, and also contributed to the impact of the disaster on the community; of incomparable magnitude relative to the population of the town. There is no accurate record of the number of people in Mount Mulligan in 1921 but a careful examination of available figures suggests a population of about 350.[8] About a third of the adults in Mount Mulligan died in the disaster.

About 40 of the dead were married - 21 of their wives lived in Mount Mulligan - and 35 of them were survived by dependent children - 83 children in all.[9] Several of the miners killed were very young: in 1921 a boy could be employed alone in the mine at sixteen and was allowed underground at fourteen, if accompanied by his father.[10] Only 33 of the miners killed had relatives living in Mount Mulligan. Three had left wives in Broken Hill on going to find work in North Queensland, six were recent arrivals from Wonthaggi, and thirteen others were from outside Queensland. Seven had their only known relatives in Britain. The identities of some of the dead remain mysterious; for reasons of their own, two of the miners killed were known in Mount Mulligan by false names, and 11 more were listed with their relatives and sometimes even their place of origin unknown.[11]

There are stories of terrible human grief summed up in the report on the distribution of relief funds; some families suffered multiple casualties that day, as many of the dead were relatives. There were the

6 *Brisbane Courier*, 20 September 1921.
7 *Ibid.*, 22 September 1921.
8 See Appendix D.
9 *R.C.* pp.165-166 and *Report on the Mount Mulligan Relief Funds*, pp.2-4.
10 Interview with Jim McColm, Ipswich, 17 December 1976.
11 *R.C.*, *op.cit.* See also Public Curator to Under-Secretary, Chief Secretary's Office, 24 July 1922, Q.S.A. PRE A848, 22/06834; and *Relief Funds*, *op.cit.*, pp.1-4.

brothers Thomas and Edward Hutton, Thomas and Wilfred Thompson, Robert and Frederick Pattinson, Cecil Hawes and his adult son Thomas. George James and his fifteen-year-old son Robert were killed together, and so were John Drier and his seventeen-year-old son Jonathon. The Drier boy's case has an extra poignancy, for when he died his teenage girlfriend was pregnant; the girl's brother also died in the mine.

Of course, none of these details were known in the first minutes after the explosion. The immediate response of the survivors was to rush to the mine entrance to seek news of relatives, but some instinctive, disciplined recognition of the boundary of the underground miner's domain halted the movement at that point. Watson had no difficulty in controlling entry into the mine, and during the ensuing days no attempt to enter was made by those unqualified to carry out rescue work. There were still recognised leaders in authority at the mine entrance after the explosion, and the community was prepared to accept decisions handed down from their accepted position of expertise. Possibly if James Watson and Jim Harris had died in the mine, the situation at the entrance might have been different.[12]

Interviews with those present, and photographs of the scene, suggest that the majority of the adult relatives of the miners killed remained at the mine entrance until a recognisable member of their family was carried out, or otherwise until the search operation finished on the Friday following the explosion:

> The women folk were stationed on a little rise a fair distance from the mouth of the tunnel....They refused food, saying it would choke them, and would not hear of going to their homes. Their usual reply was, "Oh, no, my man may be brought out, and even if he does not live he may have life enough to say a parting word to me; I would not like to miss the chance of a word before he died".[13]

The atmosphere at the mine entrance during those four days alternated between hours of silent waiting and short periods of hasty activity. The women, dressed in the customary long white dresses and straw hats of the time, sat together on the shale-dump beside the ropeway. When stretcher bearers emerged with a body, the group rose and moved forward, some of them going to inspect the man if he was not readily

12 One witness claimed that the women at the mine entrance threatened to take picks and shovels and enter the mine immediately after Watson forbade entry. All other accounts, however, suggest resigned acceptance on the part of those present.

13 *Cairns Post*, 22 September 1921.

identified.[14] Some of the women refused food and remained awake for the entire period; and toward the end the psychological strain they underwent was reflected in a change of mood from silent commiseration to seemingly callous black humour. Two witnesses recall sudden eerie peals of hysterical laughter erupting from the group of women, to be followed abruptly by total silence.

The complete disruption of the normal functioning of the community, and the influx of rescue workers during the days following the disaster demanded some emergency measures. Men were billeted in the hotels, the hall and private homes. The two hotels provided meals, cooked by volunteers and served to the rescue workers and miners' relatives at the mine entrance:

> Mrs Pearce, a grand old lady, and her daughter, Mrs MacDonald...have never left their post at the mouth of the pit, where they are supplying tea to the rescuers.[15]

Practical assistance was received from outside Mount Mulligan: the women of Gordonvale, a sugar-milling town south of Cairns, provided pre-cooked meals by train.[16] Even so, the supply of food was short and meat was requisitioned from nearby pastoralists. There may have been attempts at profiteering - one witness recalls a mob action against a butcher who raised his price after the influx of volunteers[17] - but some of those who supplied food to the town did so free of charge.[18]

The children of Mount Mulligan presented a problem. The school closed on the day of the disaster and remained closed for over two weeks.[19] There were 74 children enrolled at the time. They had to be kept away from the mine and the goods shed, entertained, fed and comforted in a town where most of the adults were numbed with grief or utterly preoccupied with the task of searching the mine. The town's projector was set up in the blacked-out hall, and the meagre supply of films on hand was shown repeatedly for days in an attempt to keep the children occupied. Nellie Hourston was given charge of them, but could

14 Interview with Mary Wardle, Ravenshoe, 13 August 1976; and see Taylor photographs of the mine entrance, taken about the afternoon of Thursday, 22 September.

15 *Brisbane Courier*, 23 September 1921. Chillagoe Limited met the expense of accommodation and provisions for rescue workers. (Chillagoe Limited ledger, entries 26 October and 29 November 1921).

16 *Ibid.*, 24 September 1921.

17 Interview with Jack Watson, Slade Point, 6 March 1977.

18 Letter from W.P. Crowley, Hodgkinson pastoralist, in *Cairns Post*, 18 October 1921.

19 Smith to Under-Secretary, Public Instruction, telegram 19 September 1921: 'Explosion at mine parents of nearly all children entombed school closed', Q.S.A. EDU Z1930 38/1893, 21/43660; and telegram 27 September, *ibid.*, 21/44825.

025 Women and recovery workers near the mine entrance after the explosion. This image is a retouched assemblage of two photographs from different positions (Q.N.)

do very little single-handed. The distress and novelty of the situation lured those who could escape toward the mine, where harassed volunteers maintained watch to keep them at a distance.[20]

Apart from the few brief instances of hysteria at the mine entrance late in the week, the response of the Mount Mulligan community was calm acceptance of the disaster and orderly attempts to restore the mine. There appears to have been little irrational behaviour or breakdown in social organization. The first rescue attempts were conducted intelligently, despite the inadequate resources available, and there was then an easy transition to external authority in the organization of the relief work and the running of the disrupted community, despite the sudden influx of strangers. Part of this response can be attributed to the disciplined collective spirit commonly observed in coalmining communities:

> Mine-workers...develop both a strong locality and a strong craft consciousness. Mining communities live in relative isolation, even in big towns....This in itself tends to strengthen exclusiveness and self-consciousness....The individual mine-worker, indeed, is never free from the dominance of mass ideas and mass feeling. These contribute an unconscious bias to his judgments, so that whatever individuality he does express is limited to the range set by the collective over-mind. This is a

20 Interviews with Ivy O'Gorman, Cairns, 3 & 5 January 1976; and Jack Watson, Slade Point, 6 March 1977.

> key to the understanding of much of the behaviour which is a perpetual enigma to those unfamiliar with mining.[21]

Within this ethos, the response to disaster was conditioned by awareness that an event such as a mine explosion is a risk inherent in the craft: "I wondered every morning when I said goodbye whether I would see him that night".[22]

The behaviour of the Mount Mulligan relief workers was almost entirely exemplary, and the appreciation of the community for their efforts created a sense of common purpose among townspeople and strangers for the few days of the rescue effort. There is no doubt of the courage and endurance displayed by the majority of volunteers. The press published stirring accounts of individual dedication,[23] and generalised with excessive metaphors:

> When the history of our young island-country comes to be written, names of the men and women who took part in the Mount Mulligan disaster rescue work will be emblazoned for ever on the forefront scroll of fame.[24]

Among the Mount Mulligan people, however, there was some resentment toward those attracted by the spectacle, who came to Mount Mulligan without intending to work. News reporters were regarded as undesirable intruders; one resident said, "The journalists *flocked* in!"[25] Even among the volunteers there were the sight-seers and the work-shy:

> When the need for help became known along the railway from Cairns inland, the response was most generous. Most of the volunteers did their best with no thought of payment or reward. They simply looked upon it as duty. There were a few however who showed a very poor spirit, apparently coming to the mine out of idle curiosity and not to work. Another small section, who came later could not face the horrid sights and smells and

21 F.R.E. Mauldon, *The Economics of Australian Coal*, Melbourne 1929, pp.160-161. Mauldon's observation precedes a description of the industrial tradition among Australian coal miners.

22 Miner's wife interviewed after Springhill (Nova Scotia) coal mine disaster, 1958, quoted in R.A. Lucas, *Men in Crisis*, New York 1969, p.4. Lucas also comments on the miners' need to suppress their fears in order to remain at the work, quoting for example: "If you really thought about it, you wouldn't work in it, would you?" *ibid.*, p.33.

23 See anecdotes in *Brisbane Courier*, 21 September 1921.

24 *Cairns Post*, 23 September 1921.

25 Interview with Mary Wardle, Ravenshoe, 13 August 1976. The sameness of the reports in most newspapers suggests that in fact the number of journalists was very small, but perhaps limited access to telegraph facilities forced them to combine their reports. Only one photographer, Arthur Taylor of Cairns, visited the disaster scene, and his surviving photographs all appear to have been taken within a period of a few hours, at most.

> quietly drifted away. This was easily understood when a number of strong men had their stomachs turned.[26]

This element of "very poor spirit" included someone who turned the confusion of the time to advantage by systematically looting the relief workers' lodgings while they were absent at the mine. Among the victims were Laun and Dunlop who had possessions stolen from their room at O'Brien's Hotel.[27]

The time of confusion was relatively short. Since the first objective in the crisis was the recovery of the dead, the volunteers were sent home after the majority of the bodies had been removed. About 100 whom the *Cairns Post* described as "rescue workers" left Mount Mulligan by train on Thursday morning, although these may have included many of the superfluous visitors, as the search of the mine continued unabated throughout Thursday. With the last three bodies located, the Mareeba and Cairns volunteers left late on Thursday, leaving the Mungana and Chillagoe volunteers and the local residents to complete the work.[28]

Once past the need for concerted response to the crisis, the Mount Mulligan community collapsed. Many of the townspeople left with the volunteers, and a report from the town on the Friday following the disaster said: 'to-morrow's train will scarcely leave any one at Mount Mulligan".[29] The number who remained is difficult to assess, especially since many of those who left went only to places such as Mareeba or Herberton, to return in the following weeks. Widows and children with no surviving relatives in Mount Mulligan in most cases left within the week and never returned. But the short-term exodus can have been only partial, as surface workers and some miners resumed work immediately after the search operation finished. About 60 men were employed on the cokeworks and "the new tunnel" - presumably Number Four Adit, soon to be abandoned.[30] The school also reopened within a few weeks at a reduced but substantial attendance level.

The impression gained from all sources is of an immediate, major evacuation of the town with a slow reoccupation within three or four weeks. But the temporary exodus from Mount Mulligan was followed by a steady permanent departure: in the months following the explosion

26 Laun to Under-Secretary, Chief Secretary's Office, 19 November 1921. Q.S.A. PRE A848, 21/10115.

27 Interview with Nellie Franklin, Malanda, 13 August 1976.

28 *Cairns Post*, 23 September 1921, and see Filer letter.

29 *Brisbane Courier*, 24 September 1921.

30 *Ibid.*, 30 September 1921.

a great number of the town's residents left, never to return. Not only the miners' families were affected; within months the superintending engineer, both teachers, the station-master, the butcher and the licensee of the top hotel had left, and been replaced.[31]

Initiatives for the relief of the families of the miners killed began immediately after the disaster. Salvation Army Commandant Smith of Cairns began to distribute relief money in Mount Mulligan in the first days after the explosion,[32] and the Colliery Employees' Union provided early sustenance payments: £4,000 was wired to Mareeba on 21 September to cover payments to dependants of Union members.[33] Union President Kilpatrick and Secretary D.A. Gledson, M.L.A., arrived in Mount Mulligan on 28 September and supervised the payment of grants of £50 per man killed.[34]

On the day following the disaster Woothakata Shire Clerk John Rank contacted Watson in Mount Mulligan to ascertain the need for relief, and with the approval of Shire Chairman Atherton, wired to a number of Queensland local authorities soliciting donations for a relief fund to be administered by the shire: "Immediate financial assistance required widows and orphans Mount Mulligan. Kindly open lists forwarding through Woothakata Shire Council Mareeba."[35] Rank also organised accommodation in Mareeba for families of the dead miners, and on Friday, the day the exodus from Mount Mulligan was underway, visited the town, but found that the accommodation was not wanted:

> Mr John Rank, clerk of Woothakata Shire, arrived at Mount Mulligan today. His main mission is as representative of the people of Mareeba, offering homes for housing widows and families from Mount Mulligan. He has personally seen fourteen widows, and none will accept the change just now.[36]

---

31 The turnover in population that followed the disaster was described in interviews with Ivy O'Gorman, Mary Wardle, Doris Smith and Lily Spiers, and is confirmed by changes in the town's listings in business directories and the State Electoral Roll.

32 *Brisbane Courier*, 23 September 1921.

33 *Ibid.*, 22 September 1921. The union paid £3,460 in Sickness and Death Fund payments in the second half of 1921. There is no record of the amount of this paid to Mt Mulligan dependants, but only £680 had been paid from the fund in the first half of the year. (Half-yearly statement and balance sheets, Q.C.E.U. office, Ipswich.)

34 *Ibid.*, 30 September 1921. Chillagoe Limited also made *ad hoc* payments of £5 to £10 to fifteen dependents, apparently according to immediate need (Chillagoe Limited ledger, entries 23 September, 5 October and 9 & 10 November 1921), and paid outstanding local debts of dead miners. (*Ibid.*, 29 November 1921).

35 Rank to Mayor of Brisbane, telegram 20 September 1921, quoted in *Cairns Post*, 22 September 1921.

36 *Ibid.*, 24 September 1921.

This rebuff was the first indication that the relief measures offered by the Woothakata Shire Council did not necessarily meet with the approval of the people of Mount Mulligan. The politics of the looming controversy are fairly transparent. The shire's headquarters was originally at Thornborough, and the council was dominated by the mining community for many years. As the mining settlements declined in population, the pastoralists gained power, and the municipal centre moved to Mareeba in 1919. From 1916 to 1921 the Shire Chairman had been Jim Harris of Mount Mulligan, then early that year the chair had been won by Ernest Atherton, grazier of Chillagoe, later to become Country Party Mines Minister in the Moore Government.[37] This was a confrontation between the Labor-voting Hodgkinson miners and the conservative Mareeba farmers.

Other funds opened throughout the state. Archbishop Duhig sent Watson £173 collected at a fund-raising dinner of Catholic clergy.[38] Local authorities, newspapers, unions and charitable organizations opened their own funds: the Mayor of Brisbane, declining Rank's invitation to contribute to the Shire's fund, chose to open his own appeal at a lunch-hour meeting in the Town Hall on Tuesday, 27 September.[39]

Official succour was also at hand. Under the Ryan government's *Workers' Compensation Acts* 1916-1918, the miners killed at Mount Mulligan were insured in the State Insurance Office for sums of £300 to £600, depending on the extent of dependence on them. Attorney-General J. Mullan estimated the cost of this compensation to the state at £40,000:[40]

> This is one of the most deplorable and terrible disasters which has befallen Queensland," said the Minister for Justice (Mr J. Mullan) yesterday. "It will be some little consolation to know that the dependants of those who are killed will be entitled to compensation up to a maximum sum of £600.[41]

The proliferating local funds began making erratic *ad hoc* payments to the families of the dead, in Mount Mulligan and elsewhere. Payments sent to Watson, Dunlop and the Mount Mulligan police were distributed on the basis of immediate need. Early in October Rank wired a small payment from the shire fund to each widow in a place other than Mount Mulligan, and requested from each a list of dependent children as a

37 M. Thompson and L. Townsend, *Pictorial History of Mareeba*, Mareeba 1981, p. 37.
38 *Brisbane Courier*, 22 & 26 September 1921.
39 *Ibid.*, 23 September 1921.
40 *Cairns Post*, 4 October 1921.
41 *Brisbane Courier*, 21 September 1921.

basis for further payments.[42] Local jealousy over the distribution of relief money soon developed. A meeting of the Cairns Shire Council on 14 October debated the problem that donations had been collected for three weeks, but no-one had yet applied for aid, nor did any organization exist to administer it. Some degree of contention between the Cairns and Woothakata Shires was evident, for the meeting considered passing the money to the State 'to avoid jealousy amongst local administrations', and finally resolved to have Shire Chairman S.H. Warner confer with Councillor Atherton on the formation of a committee to administer the payments.[43]

There was a swift response to the Cairns Shire Council's deliberations. Two days later the Woothakata Shire Council announced that a local committee had been formed in Mount Mulligan to collect information on those needing relief.[44] Rank stated that £20 had been paid to each absent bereaved family, £1000 in all, with £2500 still in hand, and called a meeting of all Cairns Harbour Board region local authorities in Mareeba to administer the fund. The announcement was prompted because:

> The Woothakata Shire Council desires to give the matter of receipt and administration of relief funds every publicity, in order to remove from the public mind the effect of irresponsible statements, some of which have appeared in the press and elsewhere and have been called to the attention of the Chairman and Shire Council.[45]

Some form of coordination of the relief effort was required. On 27 September, Gledson had asked Theodore in the Legislative Assembly:

> Will he take steps to have a trust fund formed for the receipt and the distribution of funds subscribed for the relief of the relatives of the unfortunate victims of the recent colliery disaster at Mount Mulligan?[46]

No action was taken for nearly a month after Gledson's question, but in mid-October, when the Woothakata Shire Council's reluctance to co-operate with other bodies was beginning to attract the attention of the Northern press, legislation was drafted to control the collection and

42 *Cairns Post*, 10 October 1921.

43 *Ibid.*, 15 October 1921. Note that Cairns had both a shire and a Town Council.

44 The Committee consisted of warden Dunlop, stationmaster Franklin, headteacher Smith, storekeeper Grainer and a prospector named Hopkins.

45 *Cairns Post*, 17 October 1921. It is not clear what 'irresponsible statements' have been made, although it is evident from other sources that other local authorities and the people of Mount Mulligan regarded the Woothakata Shire Council's efforts with suspicion. On 25 October, the Cairns Town Council advised Rank that the meeting of local authorities was unnecessary, since the Relief Funds Bill was before parliament. (*Ibid.*, 26 October 1921).

46 *Q.P.D.*, Vol.37, 1921, p.930.

distribution of relief money. The Mount Mulligan Relief Funds Bill was introduced on 24 October, passed all stages in the Assembly with no serious debate, and was passed by the Council the following day.[47]

The Relief Funds Acts provided that all funds paid for the relief of Mount Mulligan dependants were to vest in trustees, who would dispose of them for the dependants' benefit.[48] The three appointed trustees, Public Curator F.W. Mole (Chairman), Brisbane Mayor H.J. Diddams and H.J. Ryan, member for Cook,[49] met on 28 November 1921 and drew up a policy for payments from the relief fund: £100 was to be invested for each dependent child at 4% compound interest, the sum realised to be paid to the child on its 21st birthday; and £14,000 was to be invested to provide an annuity at twelve shillings per week for the maintenance of each child.[50]

However, the Woothakata Shire Council remained intent on administering its own relief program. A meeting of the Council on 7 November resolved to evade the requirements of the Relief Funds Act by distributing the funds they had collected before the trustees could act to restrain them. The people of Mount Mulligan protested vigorously and requested state intervention:

> Meeting Council Mareeba Monday decided distribute entire relief fund held by them approximately three thousand pounds to dependants immediately to avoid government control fear discrimination will not be used and circumstances each case considered local committee and majority dependants here desire government control and distribution.[51]

Now the struggle over the right to distribute relief funds became acrimonious. Woothakata Council sought exemption from the provisions

---

47 *Ibid.*, Vol.138, pp.1723-1724, 1822-1823 and 1864. While the bill was short and contained no measures in any way contentious, debate was probably expedited by the imminence of the Constitution Act amendment Bill which finally succeeded in abolishing the Legislative Council, initiated in the Assembly about an hour after the initiation of the Relief Funds Bill. (*Ibid.*, p.1729).

48 *Queensland Statutes*, Vol.11, pp.9811-9813; and see also the Regulations under the Act, *Q.G.G.* Vol.117, 19 November 1921, p.1635.

49 *Q.G.G., op.cit.*, p.1633.

50 Mole to Under-Secretary, Chief Secretary's Office, 24 July 1922. Q.S.A. PRE A848, 22/06834; and see *Relief Funds*, pp.1-4. £34,624/14/2 had been donated to the fund by the time of Mole's letter. The Annual Report of the Public Curator records the steady diminution of the trust fund until 1931, when £9,423/9/5 remained invested, and 36 children were recipients. The fund is not mentioned after 1933, when Mole retired.

51 Franklin, Secretary Local Committee to Attorney General, telegram 9 November 1921, Q.S.A. PRE A848, 21/09183. The telegram has been annotated 'Urgent' in the Justice Department, and 'Attach to Bill as passed' in the Chief Secretary's Department on the same date. The Act received assent on 7 November 1921.

of the Act which allowed for exemption of established funds.[52] When the request was refused, the Council found a distant but influential ally in the Lord Mayor of Melbourne, J.W. Swanson, who presided over a substantial fund which was beyond the reach of Queensland legislation. At Councillor Atherton's request, Swanson announced his intention to withhold the Victorian funds "until he was satisfied that they were going to the proper authorities" and would not be used "as a means of advertisement for a political party".[53]

Swanson's response confirms that the Woothakata Shire Council's attitude stemmed from party political motivation as well as a parochial attempt at self-aggrandisement. Once the political issue was in the open, the vigorously anti-Labor *Cairns Post* weighed in against the Queensland government:

> So well and truly distrusted and detested is the Minority government of Queensland that the Lord Mayor of Melbourne declines to commit to its keeping the relief funds raised in that city for the sufferers at Mount Mulligan. It is not believed that even in so purely charitable a matter, the Theodorian pledge-breakers can be trusted to act without political bias... Queensland's present ministers would work political bias into a weather forecast if the thing could only be done and there was profit in it to themselves.[54]

The resistance was a futile gesture, however, as all relief money in Queensland came under the provisions of the Act, and while Swanson could retain his money indefinitely, he had no means of distributing it among Mount Mulligan dependants without bringing it under the control of the trustees. The Shire Council surrendered in early December, protesting it "had not received the consideration and courtesy it was entitled to"[55] and submitted over £4,000 to the trustees on 12 January 1922. £6,000 was received from the Lord Mayor of Melbourne on 16 January.[56] The whole vulgar controversy had served only to divert public attention from the situation of the women and children who were left without financial support by the Mount Mulligan disaster.

---

52 *Queensland Statutes, op.cit.*, p.9813; and Rank to Theodore, urgent telegram 12 November 1921, Q.S.A. PRE A848, 21/09367. The request for exemption is annotated 'Mr Gillies [M.L.A. Eacham] has conveyed to Rank the Premier's decision. 14-XI-21.'

53 *Brisbane Courier*, 26 November 1921.

54 *Cairns Post*, 29 November 1921.

55 Rank to Theodore, 13 December 1921, Q.S.A. PRE A848. 21/10724. The letter is annotated 'Don't bother acting'. See also *Cairns Post*, 15 December 1921, reporting the Woothakata Shire Council meeting of 8 December.

56 *Relief Funds*, p.6.

The method of payment adopted by the trustees proved satisfactory to the majority of recipients, although the amount distributed from the relief fund was much smaller than the workers' compensation payment, and so probably attracted less attention. In all, the widow of a Mount Mulligan miner should have received £600 as workers' compensation, £100 from the relief funds, £50 from the union and at least £20 from the shire: a total of £770 from different sources, in addition to a continuing annuity of twelve shillings a week, or £31/4/- per annum, for support of each of her children, who were further provided for at the age of 21. By comparison, most Mount Mulligan wage miners in 1921 earned between four and five pounds a week, or between £200 and £250 in a year.[57]

Complaints about the distribution of compensation and relief payments generally arose from misunderstanding of the methods of payment, or the slowness of the trustees, rather than from the size of the payments eventually made. In 1921, Queensland was quite advanced in its provision for the dependants of victims of industrial accidents. A call from the Sydney Labour Council for action by the Queensland government allowed Attorney-General Mullan to make a well-publicised reply:

> "The Workers' Compensation Act 1916 to 1918," which was passed by the present Queensland Labor Government, copy of which I forward under separate cover, gives the workers in Queensland greater compensation, including death benefits, than any other State in the Commonwealth.[58]

The trustees were hampered by lack of knowledge of the dependents of many of the dead miners. Their published report of July 1922 had 11 men noted "Dependants not at present known", even at that late date.[59] The formula for assessment of payment to dependents assumed a stable home situation, with a miner supporting a wife and children. In fact the domestic arrangements of a number of the Mount Mulligan miners had been rather more complex, and several of them contributed to the support of other relatives, some of them in distant places:

> I received a letter dated 26 June notifying me to call at Bank as the cheque was forwarded £180 but I refused to sign. My dear brothers loss to me is

57 Adult coal miners' wages in the Northern division varied from 17/1 to £1/-/4 a shift, depending on the work done. At Mount Mulligan there were five shifts a week, but the mine was usually closed for part of the year. Piecework miners earned 6/5 per ton in a longwall workings and 9/2_ per ton in the bord-and-pillar workings, probably yielding weekly earnings comparable with those of the better-paid wage men. (*Coalmining State Award, op.cit.*, pp.720-721.)

58 Mullan to President, Sydney Labour Council, 3 October 1921. Q.S.A. JUS G199 (letterbook), p.404.

59 *Relief Funds*, pp.2-4.

> more than all the compensation, my husband died many years ago and left me with three children only babies, and my darling Brother never forgot me or my children....I don't know what ever took him to such a desolate region, up amongst the blacks to lose his life....I would like you to try and get a better compensation as I am very much in need of it and anything but well myself.[60]

It was very difficult for the trustees to assess the degree of dependency of miners' parents and siblings, especially those in the British Isles or remote parts of Australia. However, their report demonstrates a degree of liberality perhaps unusual for the time in granting relief funds to several *de facto* wives and a number of illegitimate children; all such cases seem to have been treated in exactly the same way as *de jure* families.

For some months, the principal sources of complaint among recipients of relief and compensation were three widows at Broken Hill: Elizabeth Cairney, Elsie Bollen and Martha Regan. After the first payments were made in January 1922, each woman wrote to Theodore, complaining of their inadequacy:

> With the combined amounts I have received from the Workers' Compensation Act and the "Mt Mulligan Relief Funds Act 1921, I have received £300....It may appear to be a grand thing to the men who have arranged this matter in this alleged scientific manner, but as far as I am concerned (and I think considering I am the person who will have to do the washing to keep the children) I think that I am the best able to judge which is right and which is wrong....I appeal to you as the head of the great Labor Movement to see that this matter is arranged in such a manner as to allow this money to be drawn to enable women in my position to rear their children as they should be reared.[61]

At the time of these complaints, no final decision had been made on the size of the payments that could be afforded from the growing relief fund, and those complaining seemed unaware of the significance of the money invested for their children, and the fact that part of the compensation payment of £600 was also to be paid in the form of annuities. The "ladies at Broken Hill" were regarded with a degree of suspicion by the trustees, since the wording and typed format of their letters were very similar, and their complaints were not echoed by dependants in other places:

60 Margaret Ruane to Theodore, 4 July 1922, Q.S.A. PRE A848, 22/06405. Mrs Ruane received £125 from the Relief Fund, and £180 compensation, with no provision for her children. (*Relief Funds*, p.3). There is no record of her case having been reviewed.

61 Elizabeth Cairney to Theodore, 16 February 1922, Q.S.A. PRE A848, no file number.

> Until the trustees know exactly what funds they will ultimately have at their disposal, and what beneficiaries will ultimately have to be provided for, they do not deem it prudent, at the present time, to make a more liberal payment than that covered by the abovementioned resolution. It is possible, and very probable, that later on further payments will be made, but I have not deemed it prudent to advise the ladies at Broken Hill to this effect, as the only opposition received by the Trustees is from three widows residing at the one centre, Broken Hill.[62]

When the final form of the payments was decided, their provisions were more generous than had been anticipated. Mrs Cairney, for example, who had complained of receiving only £300 to maintain herself and her three children, was ultimately granted an additional £400 cash compensation, and £1/16/- per week children's maintenance, in addition to the £100 invested for each of her children at 21 years of age.[63] When the full extent of the payments was made known, most of the complaints evaporated. Elizabeth Cairney, whose case has been scrutinised simply because it is among the best documented, ought to be quoted in her gracious final letter to Theodore:

> I am deeply and sincerely grateful to you for the interest you have taken in the matter, and the sensible and effective way you have decided to pay the money to the children, which will be of some use in the rearing of my children.[64]

The compensation and relief ultimately paid seems to have satisfied all recipients. But during the lengthy process of assessing the claims, dissatisfaction arose from the excessive secrecy in which the trustees cloaked their proceedings, and their lack of tact and sympathy in correspondence with dependants. This administrative insensitivity, and the political manoeuvring that surround the collection of relief funds, served to confuse and delay payment, and gave rise to a regrettable public impression of its handling.

The superb spontaneous effort of the Mount Mulligan rescue attempt was only achieved by ignoring normal considerations of expense and

62 Mole to Under-Secretary, Chief Secretary's Office, 2 February 1922, Q.S.A. PRE A848, 22/01023.

63 *Relief Funds*, p.2.

64 Elizabeth Cairney to Theodore, 21 March 1922, Q.S.A. PRE A848, no file number. Theodore's personal prestige in mining areas is evident in the number of cases in which letters from the public were addressed to him, rather than to more appropriate but less familiar officials; and in the tone of the letters.

proper channels. The rescue workers rallied to Mount Mulligan's assistance with little thought to matters such as wages or insurance. Trains were commandeered and equipment borrowed in highly irregular circumstances in the atmosphere of heroic improvisation that followed the arrival of dramatic telegrams requesting help. In the disaster's aftermath, the attempt to sort out these spontaneous measures led to further instances of controversy.

In the question of payment and insurance of the rescue workers, the state government acted magnanimously, if inefficiently. During the rescue operation at Mount Mulligan, Attorney-General Mullan made special provision to guarantee compensation to the volunteer workers, without payment of premiums. In view of the risk normally attendant on coal mine rescue work this seems a generous measure, but it was not made until 22 September, when the hazards of rescue work at Mount Mulligan had greatly diminished.[65] The payment of wages to the rescue workers presented more difficult problems. Chillagoe Limited employees were paid normal wages during the rescue work, but no thought was given at first to the payment of volunteers from other places. During the brief debate in the Legislative Assembly on the Mount Mulligan Relief Funds Bill on 24 October, Theodore erred by stating that "most, if not all, of the men engaged in the actual rescue work were paid their wages".[66] This blunder elicited a number of enquiries from the great majority of rescue workers who had not been paid. In response to a telegram from the Mayor of Cairns, J.G. Hoare, pointing out that none of the Cairns volunteers had received any wages,[67] Theodore replied: "Government will pay rescuers wages lost during absence from ordinary work during rescue operations".[68]

For months afterward, the Chief Secretary's Office received letters from men who claimed to have worked in the Mount Mulligan rescue, and who had afterwards heard that others had been paid for doing so:

> Now Sir I am a working man with wife & 5 Children & the time could hardly be Spared but when a Man in Business in cairns can get Recompensed by Your Government it seems hardly Fair that I who entered and worked side

65 *Q.P.D.* Vol.137, 1921, p.851. Mullan's reply to a question from H.J. Ryan, M.L.A., Cook.

66 *Ibid.*, Vol.138, p.1724.

67 *Cairns Post*, 26 October 1921, and see letter from 'Tramp', *ibid.*, 27 October 1921. A dispute, the details of which are not clear, also arose over Chillagoe Limited's liability for payment of rescue workers: 'Reference Mulligan rescuers pay consider mens efforts belittled unanimous opinion Chillagoe company pay full time'. W. Lynch, Mungana to W.J. Riordan MLC, telegram 10 November 1921. Q.S.A. PRE A848, no file number.

68 Theodore to Hoare, telegram 28 October 1921, quoted in *Cairns Post*, 29 October 1921.

> by side with this man should be ignored had You the tally book You would have been able to see who went in & out of the mine.[69]

There was great difficulty in assessing the validity of these claims. Two tally books showed the names of 129 men who had entered the mine, but these records were not entirely accurate,[70] and there were at least 100 other volunteers who, lacking mining experience, had been put to work at various tasks on the surface. No record whatever had been kept of these men or their contribution to the rescue work, and payment depended on corroboration of a man's presence by others - a process involving the Premier's Department in months of correspondence with witnesses in scattered mining towns.

Beyond monetary considerations, the question of recognition of the rescue workers by means of some form of medal or other decoration generated particularly intense feeling. The first requests from rescue workers to be considered for the award of a medal were written within a fortnight of the disaster.[71] These seemingly grotesque appeals for public recognition must be seen in the context of the time: the Great War had ended only three years previously, and popular feeling created a distinct social gulf between those who were entitled to wear medals and those who were not. Those who requested medals for themselves were no doubt influenced also by the extravagant terms in which the press had described their efforts.

The Royal Humane Society indicated its intention to recognise those who had shown conspicuous qualities in the Mount Mulligan rescue work, and Theodore invited comments from Laun, Watson and Harris on the proper recipients of awards for bravery. They responded with quite different opinions, since each had worked under different circumstances during the search of the mine. Harris provided his comments under protest and disagreed with the whole idea of decorations:

69 H. Lockyer to Theodore, 18 July 1922, Q.S.A. PRE A848, 22/06651, and see also O. Briske to Theodore, 7 April 1922, *ibid.*, 22/03318. Lockyer's letter convincingly establishes that he worked in the mine during the rescue, but his name is not in the tally books.

70 Dunlop to Under-Secretary, Chief Secretary's Department, 14 December 1921, appending list of names abstracted from tally books. Q.S.A. PRE A848, 21/10999. At least nine men who can be shown from other sources to have been in the mine during the rescue, are not named on Dunlop's list.

71 Several letters in Q.S.A. PRE A848, the earliest dated 27 September 1921.

> I consider the matter should be let drop and no one given special praise or credit....it would be foolish to give special recognition to anyone as one and all who entered the mine ran a certain amount of risk.[72]

From these disparate accounts, eleven recipients of decorations were selected. While controversy must inevitably have arisen in such a matter, the selection of those to be recognised appears quite arbitrary, bearing little resemblance to what consensus emerged from consultation with the rescue leaders.[73] The Royal Humane Society awards were presented in Melbourne on 24 July 1922. Watson received the society's highest award, the Clarke Medal. Jim Harris was awarded on Silver Medal, and nine other Mount Mulligan volunteers received Bronze Medals or Certificates of Merit:[74]

> Regret was expressed by the president (Mr G. Lush) that the awards made in connection with the Mount Mulligan mining disaster had not given complete satisfaction to every one, but the society had acted on the best local information available.[75]

The Brisbane *Telegraph* had earlier fanned the coals of resentment by claiming, in a somewhat inaccurate description of the rescue work, that the Society had ignored those who contributed the bulk of the effort:

> ...none of the fine bodies of miners from Thornborough, Chillagoe, or Mungana have received any awards...although they unquestionably did the bulk of the rescue work not one of them is mentioned in the Society's awards on this occasion. People are asking where the Society collects its information.[76]

A later edition of the same paper had reported an interview with Theodore in which he attributed the advice on which the awards were based to Harris and Watson:

> Both the manager of the Mount Mulligan mine (Mr Watson) and the engineer (Mr Harris) who were the first two men to enter the mine after the disaster, made recommendations of individuals for recognition by the Royal Humane Society...The department had no interest in the matter and

72 Harris to Police Constable Dwyer, 8 November 1921, Q.S.A. PRE A848, no file number. See also Laun to Under-Secretary, Chief Secretary's Office, 19 November 1921, *ibid.*, 21/10115; and Watson, 3 January 1922, *ibid.*, 22/00248.

73 Gillies (Acting Premier) to Governor of Queensland, 9 May 1922, Q.S.A. PRE A848, 22/1835. The letter demonstrates that the decision on awards was made in the Chief Secretary's Department on the basis of a rather thoughtless comparison of the advice obtained from those present.

74 *Brisbane Courier*, 8 July 1922.

75 *Ibid.*, 25 July 1922.

76 Brisbane *Telegraph*, 13 July 1922.

> could only be guided by the reports which it received from persons who were qualified to give advice.[77]

As these two men had received the highest awards, Theodore's public response to the controversy was embarrassing and grossly unfair to both of them. While each had "made recommendations", they had done so only at Theodore's invitation; Harris had recommended that no awards be made and neither had recommended himself (or the other) for an award. Theodore also failed to mention the report by Inspector Laun which must have been at least equally influential since it was the longest and fullest of the three reports, and specifically recommended both Watson and Harris for decorations.

Watson was particularly embarrassed by the medals controversy since he had recently undergone public humiliation at the hands of the Mount Mulligan Royal Commission, and was now placed in the totally invidious position of appearing to have recommended himself for the highest honour for rescue work in the aftermath of a disaster for which he had been allocated a large share of blame![78] The situation was created by a casual and arbitrary reading of the rescue reports in the Chief Secretary's Department, and by Theodore's subsequent unprincipled evasion of responsibility for the advice given to the Royal Humane Society.

The response of the press to the Mount Mulligan disaster varied according to the particular newspaper's regional and political outlook. News stories from Mount Mulligan were wired to Cairns and thence to southern papers. As there was only one means of communication, none of the papers could secure exclusive stories from the disaster scene, and the coverage of the disaster and the first week of its aftermath was almost identical in most eastern Australian newspapers. Naturally, the *Cairns Post* and other Northern papers carried longer items, with more details of purely local interest, and had exclusive access to dramatic interviews at the Cairns railway station with returning rescue workers. The Brisbane papers wrote shorter accounts by editing the cable stories, and the coverage then became briefer as the distance from Mount Mulligan increased. The Southern press, however, gave better

77 *Ibid.*, later edition. These clippings are attached to Watson's complaint (see next footnote) in Q.S.A. PRE A848.

78 See complaint by Watson in Chief Secretary's Office minute, no date. Q.S.A. PRE A848, 22/6860.

coverage to Queensland Mines Department and Chillagoe Limited reports on the disaster than did the Northern papers. Most newspapers with photogravure facilities printed full-page layouts of Arthur Taylor's photographs of the damage at the mine entrance and the work of the volunteers.[79]

The news coverage, however, was of short duration. By the end of the first week, most newspapers had lost interest in the story, leaving only the *Cairns Post* to pursue parochial matters such as payment for relief workers and reconstruction of the mine. The Mount Mulligan disaster's eclipse as a news item in distant papers was assisted by an incomparably greater industrial disaster two days later. On 21 September, the Badische aniline dye plant at Oppau in Germany exploded, levelling a large area of the town and killing or injuring close to 3,000 people.[80]

Beyond the almost identical news coverage, editorial comment on Mount Mulligan in the press restricted itself to conventional sentiments of regret and dismay, with an occasional expression of praise for the volunteers:

> It is an industry that has taken heavy toll of human life in all parts of the world, and in face of the Mt Mulligan disaster, which brings the danger and the uncertainty of it home to all of us, we can only give expression to a sense of the deep sorrow which the people of Queensland will feel, and join with them in conveying to the bereaved families of the unfortunate men who are entombed an expression of the sincerest sympathy, while still hoping for news that may substantially alleviate their grief and anxiety.[81]

Poetry, most of it turgidly sentimental, appeared in several newspapers:

> Yet 'neath earth's radiant breast the death fiend lurked;
> Sudden the mine reeked with his poison breath;
> Strong men, who sang for gladness as they worked,

79 See for example, *North Queensland Register*, 3 October 1921; *Sydney Mail*, 5 October 1921; *Queenslander*, 8 October 1921. Taylor's photographs reappeared occasionally for decades afterward to illustrate commemorative stories rewritten from earlier newspaper accounts of the disaster: see *Daily Mirror*, 27 July 1954; Brisbane *Truth*, 15 August 1954; *Sunday Mail*, 18 September 1966; Brisbane *Telegraph*, 13 January 1975 & 23 September 1975.

80 *Brisbane Courier*, 23 September 1921.

81 *Ibid.*, 20 September 1921.

Sank in a moment, grappling hard with death![82]

The *Cairns Post*, preoccupied with industrial trouble in the sugar-growing areas of the Cairns hinterland,[83] feared that because of the disruption of Mount Mulligan's coal production, "the present prevailing depression will be most acutely accentuated"; and turned its editorial comment on the disaster into a plea for industrial harmony:

> Come to terms with your bosses, boys, and let us see that capital and labor can agree to get on one with the other. But while those without recognition to law and order are allowed to "spruik" from public platforms in the centre of the town, what can you expect but that trouble will always be with us?[84]

The labour press, while presenting news of the disaster from the same source as the conservative daily papers, added cartoon and editorial comment on the nature of capitalism and its relation to the disaster:

> Periodically the world is reminded by some great calamity of the risks run by the workers in carrying on the industries without which civilization would be brought to a standstill...Honor boards and statuary are erected to the sacred memory of the soldiers who gave up their lives for their country on the bloody battlefields, but those heroes who died to provide us with life's luxuries and necessities have no such monuments to preserve the memory of their sacrifice.[85]

This metaphor of coalmining as a war in which the miners were soldiers was made most explicit in the Colliery Employees' Union paper, *Common Cause*:

> This is the death roll of industry; a death roll which is a concrete reminder of that war which is ever present - the war between those, on the one hand, who control the machinery of production and use it to grind out profits and ever more profits, and those, on the other hand, who, working the machine, are allowed merely enough to live and to perpetuate their slavery.

82 'A Tribute to our Miners' by Emily Bulcock, Brisbane *Daily Mail*, 22 September 1921. Another, similar poem by Bulcock appeared in the *Brisbane Courier* on the same day. A poem by J.C. Gasking in *The World's News*, 1 October 1921, gives a more personal view of the disaster:

> Was it this morning, one short day back,
> He kissed her goodbye and smiled,
> Turning again, as he climbed the track,
> For a sight of his wife and child?

83 I.W.W. agitators were active at the time in the sugar-milling areas south of Cairns. (*Worker*, 25 August and 1 September 1921)

84 *Cairns Post*, 20 September 1921.

85 *Worker*, 29 September 1921.

> This tragedy at Mount Mulligan, the latest grim, bloody milestone that marks the progress of the coal-mining industry in Australia, is a reminder that the worker pays in industry as in battle; in peace as in war.[86]

Union newspapers were united in accurately pointing out the brief and morbid interest of the popular press in industrial accidents:

> Meanwhile public interest (manufactured by the newspapers) is waning. Already mention of the tragedy has disappeared...The whole process is as transient as the lifting of a hat to a passing hearse.[87]
>
> One word more: let us have no "sympathy" from the capitalist press, whose speciality where the miners are concerned is vituperation. Our constitution is not equal to its hypocrisy.[88]

But the response of the labour press to the disaster was very disappointing. There was much angry rhetoric, but none of the union papers made any constructive criticism of the conduct of coalmining in Queensland, nor suggested any reforms which might lessen the danger of the industry. The general tone of both conservative and labour editorials suggests that such disasters were seen as an abhorrent but inevitable part of the business of mining coal.

The early reports from Mount Mulligan after the explosion emphasised the more spectacular manifestations of damage at the surface and gave rise to a widespread impression of catastrophic damage in the underground workings. The economic implications of cessation or a prolonged reduction in coal production were alarming, and the *Cairns Post*, which had laboured so hard a decade earlier to make the Cairns hinterland dependent on Mount Mulligan coal, now envisaged ruinous commercial stagnation:

> We are told that the power house and other surface requirements necessary to work the mine have been blown practically to atoms. This infers a complete stoppage of supplies of coal to Einasleigh mine, Chillagoe smelters, Cairns railways, and many boats trading to our small ports between Townsville and Port Douglas.[89]

---

86 *Common Cause*, 23 September 1921. The first issue of *Common Cause*, 19 March 1920, had observed: 'How strange would be the headline, "Eleven Stockholders Burn to Death in Mining Disaster".'

87 *Ibid.*, 30 September 1921.

88 *Worker*, 13 October 1921.

89 *Cairns Post*, 20 September 1921. In fact the power house and other surface plant were 600 metres from the mine entrance, and unaffected by the explosion.

The rescue workers soon discovered that the mine workings were "not so much knocked about as was feared at first".[90] Much of the mine timber was dislodged and local falls of rock had occurred, but this damage was not extensive and required only labour rather than capital expenditure.[91] Much of the structural damage to the mine was made good as a necessary part of the search operation, and replacement of the ventilating fan and its housing and repairs to burnt electrical installations constituted the only substantial items of plant expenditure. Many of the skips in the mine were damaged, but these were expected to have a relatively short and violent life in the normal course of mining, and there was little other equipment in the mine which could sustain damage. The fire in the workings was located and ten tons of burning coal were dug from the seam and extinguished on the Saturday following the disaster.[92] In view of the magnitude of the explosion the cost to Chillagoe Limited was relatively slight, although mining was suspended for some months:

> The damage to the underground workings is not nearly as extensive as was expected, and it is anticipated that expenditure on repairs and rescue work will not exceed £4,000. The superintending engineer advises that coal production will be resumed by the end of the year.[93]

Coal production at Mount Mulligan in 1921 was about 6,000 tons less than in the previous year, or about 30% less than the anticipated output for the year.[94]

The mine re-opened for production early in 1922. From late September 1921, 60 men had been employed in and about the mine, making repairs, constructing the coke-works, and developing Number Four Adit and the tramway to it.[95] The work to be done in restoring the mine to production does not explain the delay in resuming mining: either the cost of repairs and lost income had exhausted the company's liquid funds, or labour was diverted to other tasks. All the damage caused by the disaster seems to have been repaired well before the

90 C.V. Lewis to Chillagoe Limited, telegram 21 September 1921, quoted in *Brisbane Courier*, 22 September 1921.

91 Laun's report in *Q.G.M.J.*, 15 October 1921, p.428.

92 *R.C.*, p.132.

93 Chillagoe Limited Directors' Report, 6 December 1921, in *Q.G.M.J.*, 14 January 1922, p.37.

94 Coal production at Mount Mulligan, 1920-1922:

1920	23,642 tons
1921	16,444 tons
1922	22,484 tons

The value of coal in this period was about £1 per ton. (*A.R.*'s 1920-1922, Table B.)

95 *Brisbane Courier*, 30 September 1921 and *Cairns Post*, 19 October 1921.

end of 1921,[96] but Watson apparently concentrated his attention on development of the new mine on the Chillagoe lease for some time after the disaster. Number Four Adit never produced payable coal; when the mine resumed production in February, operations were confined to the original workings. The date of the abandonment of the new mine is not certain, but 23 men were paid off in late November and this was probably due to its closure.[97] The halt in production after the disaster was certainly not due to the normal shortage of labour; the publicity the mine had received in a time of tight employment brought "hundreds of letters" to the Chillagoe Limited office, requesting jobs.[98]

Chillagoe Limited found itself embroiled in petty disputes over payment for labour and equipment employed in the disaster aftermath, and consistently refused to make payment. The District Superintendent of Railways debited the company with the fares of the relief workers who travelled to Mount Mulligan, but Watson disputed the account.[99] Cairns Ambulance Superintendent, J. Hogan, had personally guaranteed payment for the special trains on the day of the disaster, and Chillagoe Limited's refusal to pay left him in an embarrassing position; however, in the event the Railways Department waived the charge.[100]

In a rather ludicrous footnote to the disaster, the Cairns Harbour Board also attempted to extract payment from the company for its diving suit and diver which had not been used at Mount Mulligan. Watson quite properly replied that the company had not asked for any such assistance:

> Yours of 27th October to hand, with account for diving plant and diver's wage &c, £6-18-0. As I never authorised the sending of diving plant and diver, I am returning the account.[101]

---

96 *A.R.* 1921, p.39.

97 *Cairns Post*, 29 November 1921. The same news item records another instance of austere times at Mount Mulligan: the Ambulance Committee resolved to put an end to use of the ambulance rail car for "joy rides".

98 Interview with Doris Smith, Brisbane, 14 May 1976.

99 Commissioner for Railways to Under-Secretary, Chief Secretary's Office, 9 November 1921, Q.S.A. PRE A848 21/9191.

100 *Cairns Post*, 8 November 1921.

101 Watson to Secretary, Cairns Harbour Board, 2 November 1921, quoted in *ibid*. The Board's account was: xxx

Hire of diving plant 3 days 20-22 Sep	£3
Diver's wages, 3 days @ 25/- per day	£3-15-0
Carriage of diving plant	3-0
	£6-18-0

The Harbour Board accordingly sent the account to the unfortunate Hogan, but there is no record of the outcome. This pecuniary quibbling suggests not only intransigence on the part of Chillagoe Limited, but also severe financial straits. In what appeared to be an act of utter meanness, the company also rejected a suggestion to erect a memorial to the miners killed at Mount Mulligan on the grounds of its probable cost:

> I have the honor to acknowledge receipt of your esteemed favor of 15th instant which was duly submitted to my Board, and am desired to convey the assurance of their sincere approval of the proposal to erect a Memorial to those who lost their lives in the Mt Mulligan disaster, but before definitely dealing with the matter they will be glad to learn the estimated cost and also the situation of the Memorial.[102]

In further conversation on the proposal for the memorial, the company secretary was more specific in the matter of finance: "if the cost amounted to say £300 he feared the Company would not be financially in a position to advance their moiety".[103] This inability to raise £300 in cash was not another instance of unspeakable penny-pinching; the company was in desperate trouble. Eking out an existence on mortgages from the Queensland government, Chillagoe Limited was suddenly confronted with a loss of about £10,000 in repairs and lost production at Mount Mulligan,[104] together with the disaster's effect on the value of its shares. In debt to the state, and operating at marginal profitability with small liquid reserves, the company could not absorb such a setback, although the material damage done at Mount Mulligan was only a fraction of what might have occurred. Company Chairman J.S Reid's brother wrote to him eleven days after the disaster:

> The papers have published cables announcing the utter destruction of the Mount Mulligan coal workings and I take it that, if their statements are in accordance with the facts this terrible convulsion which had wrecked all within reach means the end of the Chillagoe Co.[105]

Reid died in January 1922, perhaps the 77th victim of the explosion. Chillagoe Limited was wound up in late 1923. The Mount Mulligan disaster precipitated the financial collapse of the last fragment of the Chillagoe mining empire.

---

102 Hewitt to Under-Secretary, Chief Secretary's Office, 26 July 1922, Q.S.A. PRE A848, 22/06990.

103 Chief Secretary's Office minute, 1 August 1922, attached to *ibid*. The minute notes the number of miners killed as 78. No memorial was built at Mount Mulligan until the 75th anniversary of the disaster in 1996.

104 Previous references note £4,000 estimated cost of repairs, and approximately £6,000 loss in value of coal extracted.

105 K.H. Kennedy, "Sons of the Manse", *Lectures on North Queensland History No. 4*, James Cook University 1984, p. 25.

The last impact of the Mount Mulligan disaster was felt in its effects on the regulation of coalmining in Queensland. The Royal Commission into the disaster had recommended a number of reforms, but these recommendations were confused and piecemeal. Some applied to highly detailed aspects of the mining regulations, such as increasing the length of electrical shot-firing cables from 20 yards to 30,[106] while others demanded sweeping revision of the whole system of regulation in coalmines:

> We recommend as follows:-
>
> SEPARATE COLLIERIES ACT
>
> 1. The passing into law of an Act for collieries, separate and distinct from "*The Mines Regulation Act of 1910*", with a re-enactment of all approved sections of the said Act.[107]

The regulatory amendments recommended by the commissioners involved revision of the means of mine inspection, improvement of record books, greater control of the use of explosives and safety lamps, adoption of British stone-dusting regulations, and the establishment of mines rescue organizations and experimental stations to enquire into the prevention of mine explosions.[108] Some of the recommendations were remarkably similar to those of the Torbanlea Royal Commission 21 years earlier, and reform was almost as slow to follow. Out of the Mount Mulligan recommendations there appeared only two amendments to the Colliery Regulations in the two years following the disaster. In August 1922, the regulations were amended to restrict the use of explosives to a range of safe, permitted types "in any coalmine that is not naturally damp and free from explosive gas"; and to restrict the use of explosives underground to the hands of competent shot-firers.[109] On the second anniversary of the Mount Mulligan disaster, a further amendment required that: "the manager of every coalmine shall provide a supply of clay or other non-inflammable substance for tamping or stemming holes charged with explosives...."[110] No further attention was paid to coal mine safety in Queensland until four years after the disaster, when

106 *R.C.* p. XLV.
107 *Ibid.*, p. XLIV.
108 *Ibid.*, pp. XLIV-XLVII.
109 *General Rules: Collieries*, pp.11-12.
110 *Ibid.*, p.12.

on 15 October 1925 the Coal Mining Bill was initiated in the Legislative Assembly:

> The Bill is a consolidation of the Coal Mining Act and regulations of this State, and there is nothing contentious in it...it simply re-enacts clauses in the present Act and amends the provisions in regard to coalmining in the direction of providing greater safety for those engaged in the industry.[111]

The Coal Mining Bill separated coal mines from the provisions of the Mines Regulation Act, established new and fuller regulations for coal mines, and created the office of Chief Inspector of Coal Mines to oversee their operation. Many of the regulatory recommendations of the Mount Mulligan Royal Commission were contained in the schedules to the bill, which seems a direct response to the commissioners' recommendations for "an Act for collieries" in 1921; but Mines Minister Jones made no reference to the Mount Mulligan disaster or the subsequent Royal Commission in explaining the bill before the house. Whatever decisions had been made in the Mines Department in the meantime, the Mount Mulligan disaster had faded to a distant memory in parliament, hazily recalled at only one point in the debate on the bill:

> Only a few years ago a disaster occurred at Mount Mulligan, and about fifty men were blown into eternity. It is well known by all that that accident was due to carelessness on the part of the management - I do not say on the part of the manager - and we do not want a repetition of such a disaster.[112]

The 1925 legislation, an unacknowledged legacy of the Mount Mulligan explosion, has not prevented the recurrence of similar disasters. Since 1972, five major coal mine disasters have occurred in Australia, killing 67 miners; four of them have been in Queensland, and all of them have involved coal dust explosions. [113]

It seems that lessons from coal mine disasters are learned only very slowly, or that the lessons learned are considered too costly in implementation by those who make profits from the extraction of coal. The numbers of men killed in Queensland coal mine explosions have been trending downward on each occasion since 1921, but this is due more to the mechanised character of the industry and the resulting decline in the numbers employed underground, than to the increased safety of the mines. It would be a fitting conclusion to the Mount

111 Mines Minister A.J. Jones, speaking to the Second Reading, 22 October 1925, *Q.P.D.* Vol.146, 1925, p.1475. Jones was in error in referring to the Coal Mining Act. No such act existed at the time - presumably he meant the Mines Regulation Act.

112 H.F. Walker M.L.A., Cooroora, *ibid.*, p.1476.

113 See Appendix C.

026 *Worker* 29 September 1921

DEATH DECLARES A DIVIDEND.

027 *Australian Worker* 29 September 1921

THE PROFIT AND THE LOSS.

028 *Worker* 29 September 1921

Mulligan disaster to record that the deaths of the 75 had contributed to regulation which had preserved the lives of many others. But it seems possible only to record that underground coalmining remains an inherently dangerous craft, its danger still controlled as much by the self-preservation instincts of the individual miner as by any systematic provision to ensure his safety.

5.
PROSPERITY AND DECLINE

"The Mount Mulligan State Mine is a most uneconomical proposition and continually presents complex problems".

(Mines Minister's submission to Cabinet,
21 March 1951, in Q.S.A. A/8508)

Mount Mulligan continued to produce coal for 36 years after the 1921 disaster, but most of that period was marked by a lingering decline into unprofitability with imminent closure of the mine an almost daily prospect. Mount Mulligan coal became steadily more uneconomical in relative terms as thicker and more extensive seams of better quality coal were discovered in other parts of Queensland. Only the distance of the Cairns hinterland from other coal-producing areas maintained production at Mount Mulligan, at a level that was never a substantial proportion of the state's coal output, and gradually dwindled into insignificance. Finally in the 1950s alternative sources of energy became available in the Cairns district, and the tiny quantity of coal still required no longer justified operating the inefficient and unprofitable Mount Mulligan mine.

When the mine resumed production after the disaster, it did so amid auspicious portents. New developments in mining and surface plant promised greater efficiency in coal extraction and processing: two 80 yards long electric conveyors were installed along the machine-faces to carry coal from the working-face to the wheeling road, thereby centralizing the loading of skips and reducing wheeling distances. Water pipes had been laid in the mine providing water sprays at the faces to lay coal dust.[1] Of most importance was the completion of the cokeworks and the first successful firing in August 1922. Ninety tons of coke had been fired by the end of the month and the first consignment was railed to the Chillagoe smelters in September,[2] thus achieving for the first time the objective sought in developing the mine more than ten years before.

The coke oven consisted of fourteen brick retorts constructed alongside the railway. Coal was prepared for the ovens by mechanically screening, grinding to uniform size and washing, in sophisticated automatic plant. The retorts were individually charged by a travelling hopper on an overhead gantry, and after firing were discharged directly into railway trucks:

> The coking operations, the methods of fuel economy, and the total elimination of waste heat provided by the new plant show that efficiency is the keynote of the whole achievement, and that no pains have been spared to secure the most up-to-date machinery for the performance of the various details in the work.[3]

The cokeworks were designed to incorporate a by-product saving plant - the distilled coal-gas from the retorts was to be piped to the powerhouse furnace to eliminate the consumption of coal in electricity generation.[4] But this system was never installed, and the cokeworks operated only sporadically in 1922 owing to problems in the design of the works and the unsuitability for coking of much of the coal produced.

Despite these hopeful developments at Mount Mulligan, there was never any real possibility of Chillagoe Limited's financial recovery. The company's difficulties were exacerbated by a period of industrial unrest in the mine. After opening in February 1922, the mine was soon closed by a strike which lasted until May;[5] another strike stopped production

1 *A.R.* 1922, pp.13 and 40.
2 *Q.G.M.J.*, 14 October 1922, p.406.
3 *Ibid.*, 15 August 1922, p.300.
4 *A.R.*, *op.cit*, and interview with Jim McColm, Ipswich 17 December 1976.
5 *Ibid.*, p.13.

throughout January and February 1923.[6] The workers involved in these stoppages were new to the mine, and the months in which the strikes occurred suggest that they may have arisen out of wet season working conditions. Not all the men attracted by the mine's publicity mixed easily with the local people - one Mount Mulligan resident recalls: "after the disaster, all the riffraff of Australia came".[7]

The cost of reconstruction of the mine after the disaster, the fruitless development of Number Four Adit, delays in coal production and difficulties in coke manufacture left Chillagoe Limited in an utterly hopeless financial situation. The £90,000 grant to the company in 1919 was long since exhausted, as was a further £50,000 grant in 1921.[8] Now nearly £150,000 in debt, with coal production grossing only some £20,000 per annum and much of the plant installed in the mine a decade earlier nearing replacement, the company approached the Queensland government in June 1923 seeking state acquisition of the Mount Mulligan mine and a small cash payment in return for cancellation of mortgages:

> On 27th June, 1923, the company's offer to sell the equity of redemption and give quiet possession for the sum of £5,500 and the cancellation of all debts was accepted, and on 1st July, 1923, the mine was taken over on behalf of the state by the general manager of the State Smelters at Chillagoe, under whose supervision it is operated.[9]

Chillagoe Limited underwent liquidation immediately and was wound up by November 1923.[10] The state commenced development work at Mount Mulligan: much of the mine's plant was found to be run down, the underground workings were haphazardly organised, and the cokeworks, which had not fired since late 1922, were "in need of extensive repairs".[11]

In response to these conditions, the mine's new manager, Jim Harris, was given a freer hand in expenditure than Chillagoe Limited had been able to afford. The top seam was abandoned as the coal there was of inferior quality. The middle seam workings were extended westward, the main dip being driven a further 120 yards, and new long wall faces

6 *A.R.* 1923, p.37.

7 Interview with Mary Wardle, Ravenshoe, 13 August 1976. Mrs Wardle attributed the strikes of 1922-23 to I.W.W. agitators from South Johnstone. A former I.W.W. member declined an interview in Brisbane in late 1976, but in a telephone conversation disclaimed any I.W.W. involvement at Mount Mulligan.

8 *Auditor-General's Report, 1922-23*, p.108.

9 *Ibid.*, pp.108-109. The company's debt, including interest, was £148,903/6/3 at 21 June 1923.

10 Hewitt to Registrar of Joint Stock Companies, 11 December 1923, Q.S.A. Company Register 23/1913.

11 *A.R.* 1923, p.37.

opened from it to the north and south. An additional Sullivan machine was installed and the wheeling roads were brushed and widened for pony-haulage. The underground conveyors, installed the previous year, were found unsatisfactory and removed.[12]

On the surface there was more conspicuous development. Twelve new four-roomed houses with electric light and piped water were built by the state as miners' homes on the mountain slope to the south of the mine workings. Beside the railway opposite the coke ovens rose a huge timber structure - coal storage bins with a capacity of 3,000 tones. During Chillagoe Limited's period of operation, production had often been halted because of the unavailability of rail transport for the coal. The surface storage bins, capable of holding more than a month's output, were intended to permit continuous production to be maintained:

> Hitherto work in the pit was continually held up waiting for coal trucks, and vice versa, but the completion of the storage bins will obviate all trouble of that nature.[13]

At the foot of the conveyor that raised coal from the tippler to the bins, the state management installed new screens and a mechanical picking table to reduce the amount of stone in the coal.[14] An inspection of the mine shortly after the state acquisition revealed an excessive proportion of shale among the coal, and recommended introduction of penalty rates in the form of fines to be imposed on skips carrying more than 25 pounds of stone:

> It is an absolute necessity to install a "Dirt Scale" at this Mine. The proportion of stone...filled into "Skips" at present is far beyond any consideration for the men. It is often difficult to identify small stone, and some of the Shales below, and I quite realize their difficulties, but at present they deliberately fill both (and boast of their success after hours.)[15]

The renovated coke ovens were fired again in January 1924 and produced coke until 6 May, when the need to maintain a supply of coal to Queensland Railways forced the cessation of coke-firing. Shortage of skilled labour still limited coal production, and nearly half the mine's output for the year - 21,000 tons - was supplied to the state railways.[16]

---

12 *Ibid.*, pp.101-102.

13 *Ibid.*, p.37.

14 *A.R.* 1925, p.35.

15 Charles Baddeley, Report on Mount Mulligan State Coal Mine, 23 July-11 August 1923, Premier's Department office copy, p.3. Q.S.A. PRE A782, 23/10633. A skip held about 15 cwt of coal.

16 *A.R.* 1923, p.101. The Report on the Mount Mulligan State Coal Mine in *A.R.* 1923 (in *Q.P.P.* 1924) reports on the financial year 1923-24. In every other instance the report is on the calendar year, and the 1924 report thus duplicates 6 months of the 1923 report.

1924 was in many ways Mount Mulligan's most promising year. The expanded underground workings and improved surface facilities increased coal production to over 44,000 tons: the highest output Mount Mulligan ever achieved in one year.[17] About 160 men were employed, as the mine had commenced working two shifts,[18] and the population of the town increased accordingly. In that year, too, the cokeworks fired for nearly four months, and the dream of cheap smelting fuel for Chillagoe seemed at last achieved.

But 1924 was not the beginning of a new era of prosperity: it was the peak of Mount Mulligan's achievement, and from that year the mine descended steadily into inefficiency and obscurity. The cokeworks were never fired again after 6 May 1924, and sat idle for the next nine years.[19] The reality was that, despite the optimistic geological reports of ten years earlier, most of the coal under Mount Mulligan was too high in ash to make good coke. The 1924 production figure, never repeated, was less than four percent of the state's coal production, and Mount Mulligan's proportional contribution shrank in succeeding years as local output declined and the state's total production grew.[20] Even in that heady year, the mine operated at a loss to the state of £17,576.[21]

The reasons for this rapid decline in significance are found not at Mount Mulligan, but 500 kilometres south on the Bowen River. Coal had been found there in the 1860s, and in 1919 mining operations had commenced at the Bowen State Coal Mine (now Collinsville) on a 5,000 acre lease taken up by the Ryan government in 1915.[22] The seam initially opened at Bowen River contained over three metres of excellent coking coal with no stone or dirt bands and a promise of vast reserves. As early as 1919, a report on the Bowen State Mine had clearly proposed that its potential coke market would subsume that of Mount Mulligan:

> For years, all smelting operations at Chillagoe, Irvinebank, and Cloncurry have had to be carried out with coke brought at great expense from Newcastle. A considerable saving in smelting operations at these centres

---

17 *A.R.* 1924, Table B; and see Appendix E.

18 *A.R.* 1924 gives no employment figure, but those for 1925 and 1926 were 162 and 161 respectively.

19 A photograph of the coal bins in *Q.G.M.J.* 15 June 1925 shows the disused cokeworks.

20 Queensland coal production in 1924 was 1,123,117 tons. Production at Mount Mulligan was 44,397 tons, or 3.9% of the total. (*A.R.* 1924, Table B).

21 *A.R.* 1923, p.102.

22 *A.R.* 1915, p.41.

> will be effected as soon as the railway to the coalfield is completed and open for traffic.[23]

By 1924, coal production at the Bowen State Mine was more than twice that at Mount Mulligan, although the number of men employed at Bowen was only slightly greater.[24] In that same year the north coast railway, connecting Cairns with Brisbane, was completed. The *Cairns Post*'s 1912 vision of a combination of coal mine, deepwater port and long-distance railway was at last realised; but the port was Bowen, not Cairns, and the coal mine was at Collinsville, not Mount Mulligan. The final blow came in 1933 when the Bowen State Cokeworks were built to supply fuel to the new lead smelter at Mount Isa, and the washing and loading machinery from the Mount Mulligan cokeworks was dismantled and railed to Bowen.[25]

Whatever hope remained of prolonged prosperity at Mount Mulligan was dashed when, on 13 February 1927, the Chillagoe State Smelters closed and production at Mount Mulligan immediately fell "due to the loss of their best customer".[26] The immediate reason for the smelter's closure was explained in varying ways - the smelter manager attributed the shutdown to difficulties in coal production at Mount Mulligan:

> All furnaces ceased operation on the 13th February owing, firstly, to a strike at Mount Mulligan State coal mine, and secondly, to heavy and continuous rain causing considerable damage to the coal mine and railway.[27]

---

23 *A.R.* 1919, p.37. The Bowen River deposits are the northern tip of the large Permian Bowen Basin field, which now produces the bulk of Queensland's coal.

24 Coal production in tons, 1919-24. (*A.R.*'s Table B.)

Year	Mount Mulligan	Bowen River
1919	19,998	306
1920	23,642	3,914
1921	16,444	2,138
1922	22,484	11,806
1923	32,618	91,643
1924	44,397	103,986

25 R. Rees, History of the Bowen Cokeworks, manuscript c. 1985; D. Menghetti, "Bowen Coke Works", 2005.

26 *A.R.* 1927, p.37. Queensland Railways was more probably Mount Mulligan's "best customer", but the closure of the smelters forced coal production down from nearly 37,000 tons in 1926 to just over 20,000 tons in 1927. (See Appendix E.)

27 *Ibid.*, p.85.

029 Coal bin and surface workings from the verandah of the *Mount Mulligan* hotel about 1930, looking west (Mary Wardle)

However, the Supervisor of State Coal Mines put an altogether different interpretation on the situation in reporting that work at Mount Mulligan had been "intermittent" in 1927, because the closure of the smelters had been "responsible for considerable loss of trade", and made no mention in his report of either strike problems or rain, indeed he mentioned that it had been an abnormally dry year.[28] Elsewhere, the smelter manager gave other reasons for the closure: "It can safely be asserted that there is not the remotest possibility of the smelters reopening until the price of lead increases very considerably", and mentioned in passing that "difficulties" had risen "in regard to the management".[29]

When employees of the same department give five different explanations for the same problem, it means that something very embarrassing must have happened. This second closure of the Chillagoe smelters was partly caused by a decline in metal prices and the consequent closure of the small mines of the Mungana-Chillagoe district, but had been brought abruptly to a head by what the new manager referred to as "difficulties" in the smelter's management. The nature of these difficulties was not fully exposed until 1930, when the Mungana

28 *Ibid.*, p.86.
29 *Ibid.*, p.37.

Royal Commission began to probe the activities of the state's mining enterprises in North Queensland.

The "Mungana Scandal", as the whole affair became known, was a complex web of questionable dealings and outright corrupt practices, extending throughout the state's mining and smelting industry, and involving several men in high public office.[30] The Royal Commission of 1930 investigated Goddard's management of the smelters, particularly in relation to preferential treatment extended to a Mungana mine owner, Frederick Reid; and a number of business dealings involving, besides Goddard and Reid, former Premiers Theodore and McCormack and Warden Dunlop.[31] Mount Mulligan played only a minor part in the affairs investigated, but that part, while of small concern to the Royal Commission, gives an important insight into the state's management of the coal mine during the 1920s.

At some time during 1925, Jim Harris left Mount Mulligan and was replaced as manager by James Strang.[32] During that year the main dip at Mount Mulligan apparently developed "creep" - an upward movement of the floor, which required brushing and retimbering, and thus diverted labour from coal extraction into non-productive tasks. Goddard's annual report explained the problem thus:

> The main tunnel between 10 south and 13 district (a distance of 11 chains) was timbered with special timber, and between 12 and 13 districts the main tunnel was brushed and retimbered twice. This state of affairs was brought about by taking all the coal out of each side of the main tunnel and not leaving sufficient support of pillars in to support the overburden.[33]

Goddard's explanation is completely unsatisfactory. A comparison of plans of the Mount Mulligan workings prepared by Lionel Ball in 1917, those published by the Royal Commission in 1921, and those in the Powell Duffryn report of 1949 shows that no extraction occurred close to the main dip at any time during the mine's life. However, a large quantity of timber was purchased, apparently for this task, from

30 The much wider implications of the Mungana Scandal are treated in detail in K.H. Kennedy, William McCormack, Vol.2; and a book by the same author, *The Mungana Affair*, St Lucia 1978. This account is concerned only with those aspects of the affair which concerned the state's administration of Mount Mulligan.

31 *Q.G.G.* Vol.134, 1 March 1930, pp.753-754.

32 Harris' step-sister believes he resigned after refusing some undisclosed corrupt offer from "Theodore, Goddard and Reid" (Interview with Mary Wardle, Ravenshoe, 13 August 1976). This offer may conceivably have been connected with the Tarzali timber purchase.

33 Goddard's report on Mount Mulligan, as General Manager, State Smelters and Mines, *A.R.* 1925, p.84. Note that this report refers to the calendar year 1925. The mine plans published in *R.C.* in 1921 do not support this explanation, but no plans of the mine in 1925 survive.

a sawmill at Tarzali on the Millaa Millaa railway. Gossip in the Chillagoe district soon had it that the Mount Mulligan timber purchase was not entirely in order. By 1926, more general comment on the state's management of the smelters and mines was rife, and the Country-Nationalist opposition had begun to raise questions in parliament. In the course of this speculative inquiry, a disgruntled employee at the Chillagoe smelters wrote to the leader of the opposition, A.E. Moore, informing him:

> ...rumour says Mr Goddard, F. Reid and Mr Dunlop warden own a saw mill at Tarzali, that is how F. Reid came to get the order for Mt Mulligan mining timber.[34]

The Auditor-General's report for 1925-26 criticised the unprofitable management of the state smelters, and in passing commented on the 'irregular' nature of the Tarzali timber purchase:

> In May last, an arrangement was entered into between the General Manager, Chillagoe State Smelters, and Tarzali Saw Mill, whereby timber to the value of £2,500 was to be supplied by the Saw Mill to the State Coal Mine at Mount Mulligan for timbering the main tunnel of the mine. The total value of the timber to be supplied was credited by the State Smelters to an account standing in the books of the Smelters against one of the owners of the Saw Mill. Mount Mulligan Mine was to receive the timber, and to credit the value of same against the charges for coal supplied to the Smelters. Up to 30th June last, timber to the value of £911 12s. 11d. only was supplied by the Saw Mill, leaving deliveries of £1,588 7. 1d. still to be made.
>
> In effect, the State Smelters paid an account of £2,500 owing to itself, and allowed the debtor to adjust the account by supplying timber required for the use of another State undertaking.
>
> I consider the transaction was quite irregular.[35]

This report, and further information supplied by Stones, led Moore to ask a series of questions about the state enterprises in the Legislative Assembly on 19 October 1926, eliciting from Mines Minister Jones the information that over 71,000 superficial feet of timber had been purchased for "imperative and urgent" repairs at Mount Mulligan, and that the owners of the Tarzali sawmill were Frederick Reid and Robert Dunlop, who had been Chillagoe mining warden until early 1926.[36] In

34 James Stone to Moore, copy, no date, in Q.S.A. CRS Y10.

35 *Auditor-General's Report 1925-26*, pp.113-114.

36 *Q.P.D.* Vol.148, 1926, p.1182; and Mungana Royal Commission Evidence (Xerox copy, History Department, James Cook University; and Q.S.A. ROY 15-16), Vol.2, p.458. Only 56,000 super feet of timber was purchased.

May 1927 the Auditor-General further investigated the timber purchase and found over 35,000 superficial feet of it, consisting of twelve and six feet lengths of twelve inch square sawn hardwood, still lying unused at Mount Mulligan, despite the supposedly "imperative and urgent" nature of its purchase a year earlier.[37]

Clearly several aspects of the timber purchase were not in order, but fuller information was not available until the Mungana Royal Commission in 1930. However, even on the evidence publicly available in 1927, there are serious discrepancies which seem not to have attracted attention at the time. Jones justified the purchase in parliament in November 1926, quoting information from Goddard and Government geologist Saint-Smith which appeared to provide expert justification for the use of the Tarzali timber in the mine. But the retimbering of the main dip was reported in the past tense by Goddard in his report on the year 1925, whereas the Tarzali timber order was not made until May 1926. Although Jones pretended in parliament that Saint-Smith had recommended re-timbering, it is clear from a careful reading of Saint-Smith's letter to Jones that he was simply reporting the action that had been taken by Goddard before Saint-Smith inspected the mine,[38] and the report from Goddard is evasive, and in places meaningless.[39]

The Mungana Scandal remained simply rumour and inconclusive parliamentary questioning until May 1929, when the Labor party was defeated for the first time since 1915 and Moore formed a government. On 1 March 1930 a Royal Commission was set up to investigate the affair, and further details of the management of Mount Mulligan came to light in the course of its inquiry.

The '"irregularity" of the method of payment, which was the feature of the timber sale which had first attracted notice, proved to be an overstatement arising from a misunderstanding by Auditor-General G.L. Beal of a report by Senior Inspector of Accounts P. McCaffrey.[40] This proved to be merely a "slippery method" of avoiding multiple ledger

37 *Auditor-General's Report, 1926-27*, p.52.

38 *Q.P.D.* Vol.148, 1926, p.1585.

39 *Ibid.*, p.1586. Goddard obviously did not understand what had happened in the mine, and described the creep in terms which are little more than gibberish. He was vague about the time when the creep occurred, and stated that Saint-Smith participated in the decision to retimber the mine, whereas Saint-Smith refers to an inspection of the work already completed; before the timber order was made.

40 Mungana Evidence, Vol.3, pp.896-898.

entries, rather than a fraudulent practice.[41] However, the smelters should not have been involved in payment for the coal mine's materials since the smelter's and mine's accounts were provided under separate parliamentary appropriations.

The quantity of timber purchased - 56,000 superficial feet[42] - was vastly in excess of the amount required, as is borne out by much of it being left unused a year after the purchase.[43] Saint-Smith was found to have played no part in the purchase. He described the original creep as "of no great extent"[44] and stated that he had never been consulted on retimbering it, as Jones had claimed in parliament, but had simply commented on the need to retimber the mine entrance, which had been in poor shape since the explosion of 1921.[45]

Retimbering of the dip did continue after the arrival of the Tarzali timber, but with little urgency. Strang had stopped the work in July 1926 when the Mines Department decided to charge the cost against working instead of development, thus reducing on paper the cost/productivity of the mine.[46] Sawn timber is not normally used in coal mines, both because of its greater cost, and because a round log is more efficient for the task of resisting compression; mine manager Strang claimed "that he would never have taken sawn timber if he was left on his own".[47] In the past, the mine's timber requirements had been met by local contractors working in the vicinity of Mount Mulligan on a casual basis.[48]

Yet Dunlop claimed in evidence that "there was no suitable round timber" available at Mount Mulligan, and also misled the Royal Commission by claiming that "the explosion in Mount Mulligan has affected the structure of the roof to such an extent that it was not safe".[49] This is nonsense if it refers to the creep of 1925, but probably sounded plausible enough when confused with Saint-Smith's earlier evidence on

41 *Ibid.*, Vol.2, p. 684.

42 *Ibid.*, Vol.3, p.690.

43 Used in sets of two six feet posts and one twelve feet beam at six feet intervals, 56,000 super feet would timber 400 yards of the dip.

44 Mungana Evidence, Vol.3, p.690.

45 *Ibid.*, Vol.1, p.323. Note that even a violent creep might dislodge timber, but would be unlikely to damage much of it beyond future usefulness.

46 *Ibid.*, Vol.2, p.669.

47 *Ibid.*, Vol.3, p.688. Strang was also quoted as saying 'there was not a colliery in Queensland which would use sawn timber at such a price.' [that is, the price Goddard paid Reid] (*Ibid.*, Vol.1, p.287)

48 Frank Graham, Bob James and William Barry supplied the mine's timber. (Interviews with Ivy O'Gorman and Bruce Mackey, Cairns, 3 & 4 January 1976.)

49 Mungana Evidence, Vol.2, p.484.

the timbers at the mine entrance. Dunlop also claimed when questioned about the type of timber previously in use at Mount Mulligan:

> It had not been timbered. It has held up by the pack walls. It was mined on the long wall system, and the roof stood down on the pack walls.[50]

This too might have sounded convincing, but was an outright lie. Permanent roadways in Mount Mulligan were extensively timbered, as Dunlop was well aware, having been in the mine on many occasions. While Chairman of the Mount Mulligan disaster Royal Commission he had taken evidence on the damaged condition of the mine timber, and had submitted as exhibits to his report detailed plans clearly showing round timber in Number Eleven Bord.[51] The report on the State acquisition in 1923 had commented: "The amount of timber taken up by this mine is considerable".[52]

Other minor elements of the Mungana Scandal touched on Mount Mulligan. It was suggested, and denied by Goddard, that cement for the construction of Goddard and Reid's *Pacific* Hotel in Cairns was diverted from the state mine's stocks.[53] A generator costing £5,189 had been purchased for Mount Mulligan, although there was no apparent use for it - in May 1930 the generator was still sitting unpacked.[54] Goddard claimed that Theodore (then Premier) had suggested purchase of the generator in case of a breakdown, but later attributed the same suggestion to Jim Harris.[55] Goddard was general manager of Mount Mulligan at the time of all these questionable transactions.[56]

It is apparent from the Mungana Royal Commission evidence that Goddard used his position for the benefit of Reid, Dunlop, himself and others. In his intrusion into the management of the Mount Mulligan mine, he put the mine to unnecessary expense in order to advantage Reid: the Tarzali timber was not required (or was at least grossly in excess of the quantity necessary), did not need to be sawn, nor brought from Tarzali, and was purchased against the wishes of the mine manager. Goddard, Dunlop and Jones all lied or misrepresented the

50 *Ibid.*, Vol.2, p.475.

51 *R.C.*, Exhibits 6 and 18.

52 Charles Baddeley, Report on Mount Mulligan State Coal Mine, 23 July - 11 August 1923, Premiers' Department office copy, p.5. Q.S.A. PRE A782, 23/10633.

53 Mungana Evidence, Vol.1, pp.304-305.

54 *Ibid.*, Vol.1, p.288.

55 *Ibid.*, Vol.1, *cf.* p.289 and 290.

56 Goddard was made General Manager on 25 October 1923, and was replaced in this capacity at Mount Mulligan on the appointment of a Supervisor of State Coal Mines on 1 July 1926. (*Ibid.*, Vol.1, p.16.) He resigned as smelters manager on 31 March 1927, after the Auditor-General's second investigation. (Goddard to Minister for Mines, 31 March 1927, in Q.S.A. A/8558.)

situation in seeking to justify the purchase: by blaming the explosion of 1921, by distorting Saint-Smith's statements, and by misrepresenting the existing system of mine timbering. The surprising thing is that so few of these blatant untruths were detected at the time.

There is reason to suppose that the Royal Commission, preoccupied with larger aspects of the affair at Mungana and Chillagoe, and inexpert in coalmining matters, exposed only a part of the questionable activities practised at Mount Mulligan. While the people of the district were aware of these activities - and possibly others - well before they became publicly known, an intense loyalty to the Labor government and to Theodore personally kept the affair secret. Even fifty years later the subject was treated with caution in interviews:

> [In response to a question asking whether people in Mount Mulligan knew beforehand of the matters raised in the 1930 Royal Commission.]
>
> Ohhh...(laugh)...they must have. But then you see, there's all sorts of arguments, you know, for and against the whole thing.
>
> They were in it all the way, though, weren't they? That's how it was such a success. They sort of bought them from the lowest to the highest. Everyone had his price and they paid it. I think that's why it was hush-hush for so long.[57]

The negligent and corrupt administration of Mount Mulligan from 1923 to 1927, the general condition of Queensland industry in the late 1920s, and competition from the Bowen State Mine combined with the slowdown and closure of the Chillagoe smelters to bring a sharp decline in Mount Mulligan's coal production. By 1927 output had dropped to a little over 20,000 tons, less than half the peak of three years earlier, and there was no significant improvement in the following two years.[58]

The coal industry throughout Australia was reducing production by 1929 in the face of declining demand. The Davidson enquiry into the New South Wales coal industry stated:

> When it is found that the capacity for production...of the mines...exceeds the normal demand to the extent of at least 43 per cent., it is idle to elaborate the consequences...it is evident that there is a radical cause of

57 Interview with Jim McColm and Jock Clarke, Booval, 17 December 1976.
58 See Appendix E.

> mischief which must be balanced partly by an increased demand and partly by a reduction of the over-weighted capacity.[59]

The Moore government, faced with a loss of £400 per week at Mount Mulligan and no possibility of increased demand for coal, decided to close the mine.[60] This suggestion was resisted in Mount Mulligan where continued operation in the mine meant not only financial security, but also the maintenance of a close-knit community; the union branch pressed for continued production on a tribute basis. Colliery Employees' Union President Kilpatrick negotiated an agreement with Mines Minister Ernest Atherton whereby the state-owned mine would be operated by the miners as tributers. The state was to pay the manager's salary, insurance and workers' compensation premiums, and the shilling per ton royalty to the Irvinebank Company's executors. The tributers, represented by a union committee, would sell the coal and pay wages among themselves, and pay the state five shillings per ton royalty on all coal sold or consumed at the mine:

> ...Mount Mulligan today is an object lesson of what workers can achieve by co-operation. The miners employed are jubilant at the success they have attained.[61]

No-one in Mount Mulligan was jubilant; all they had done was snatch survival from the jaws of destruction. The mine was taken over by the union committee on 7 October 1929,[62] and remained on tribute to the state for eighteen years. The survival of the mine and township through that period attests strong community loyalty, although the mine was assisted to some extent by the Moore government's perverse decision to reopen the Chillagoe smelters, which were blown in eight days after the coal mine was taken on tribute.[63] This was a crucial moment in the life of Mount Mulligan. The coal mine really should have died in 1929 when Moore's Nationalist government came to power and the years of Labor's assistance to the northern mining industry ended. But by the greatest good fortune, in that crucial period the Minister for Mines was Ernie Atherton, the local member and the ex-Shire Chairman. To boost the economy of his electorate, the Mount Mulligan mine was permitted to struggle on under tribute, and the Chillagoe smelters - which the

---

59 *Report of the Royal Commission...into...the Coal Industry*, 1930, p.313. For another contemporary view of the economic crisis of the coal industry, see Mauldon, *op.cit.*, 'What is Happening to the Demand', pp.101-108, and 'The Nemesis of Over-Capacity', pp.148-156.

60 *Q.G.M.J.* 14 June 1930, p.232.

61 *Ibid.*, and see *Auditor-General's Report 1929-30*, pp.54-55.

62 *A.R.* 1929, p.39.

63 *Ibid.*, p.38.

Nationalists in opposition had fought so hard to close - were opened again, fanning some life back into the mining industry of the Cairns hinterland.

The tribute provided an austere and insecure existence for the people of Mount Mulligan. The cavil was abandoned and the union committee allotted men places in the mine according to their skills. The committee was not concerned with profitability, but sought to provide employment for as many as possible, with the mine's meagre profit pooled and shared equally. This arrangement provided subsistence, but at a lower level than state wages: the tributers called themselves "kanakas".[64]

Within months of taking over the mine, the union committee was faced by a series of calamities. In February 1930 an abnormal wet season exceeded the capacity of the pumps and flooded the lower levels of the mine, which were the newly developed productive areas of the westward dipping coal-seam.[65] Simultaneously, a drop in metal prices closed the smelters from late January until September,[66] leaving only the depressed railways as a major consumer of coal. With costs raised and demand reduced, the union reluctantly reverted to one shift per day, and laid off about 80 men.[67] In September 1930 the mine generator, brought second-hand from Forsayth fifteen years before, broke down irreparably. Work could not resume until the very end of the year, when the state had purchased and installed a replacement generator,[68] and coal production for 1930 fell to below 12,000 tons, the lowest figure since 1917.[69] The Under-Secretary's Report laconically noted: "the mine has had a run of bad luck".[70]

The following years were a period of austerity and quiet decline at Mount Mulligan. The tribute system administered by the union committee eliminated the incentive of piece-work payment, and served to keep coal production at around 20,000 tons in most years, until the Second World War brought further decline. As the tributers could not

64 Interview with Jim McColm, Ipswich, 17 December 1976. The name refers to indentured Pacific Island labour in the sugar cane fields. *A.R.* 1929, p.39 improbably claimed that the tribute "pool" returned better money than wages. This seems highly improbable, and McColm states the tributers could not maintain earlier wage levels.

65 *A.R.* 1930, p.40.

66 *Ibid.*, p.80.

67 Interview with Jim McColm, Ipswich, 17 December 1976.

68 *A.R.* 1930, p.40. One puzzling aspect of the generator breakdown is that the generator purchased by Goddard in 1924 was still at Mount Mulligan in May 1930. (Mungana Evidence, Vol.1, p.288). It was apparently either unusable or removed before September.

69 See Appendix E.

70 *A.R.* 1930, p.133.

afford to maintain the mine adequately, and the state was reluctant to do so, Mount Mulligan's workings and plant became steadily less efficient. The coal-cutting machines and conveyors installed by Watson nearly 20 years earlier were now obsolete and decrepit, but they were not replaced. Transporting the coal to market was always a problem, as it had to be sent along the winding, cheaply-built narrow gauge railway to Dimbulah. Nothing bigger than four-ton wagons could be used on the line, and the locomotives could haul only ten at a time, so a trainload of Mount Mulligan coal weighed a pathetic forty tons: about the load of a modern semi-trailer. Even had the line been upgraded in the 1930s there would have been few buyers, as the railway demand was constant, the transition to oil-burning ships had diminished the small bunker trade in the port of Cairns,[71] and the Chillagoe smelters obtained almost all their fuel from the Bowen cokeworks.[72]

As ever, extremes of climate worked against the tributers. The mine flooded each wet season, increasing pumping costs and diverting labour to the repair of crumbling pack walls.[73] Alternately, in the dry seasons, the shortage of water could affect mining operations; late in 1935, production was halved because there was insufficient water for the boilers powering the generator.[74] Throughout the tribute period, the state still provided finance for the conduct of mining; the mine's accounts were controlled by the Mines Department, which debited advances and credited coal sales, less its own royalty.[75] Like the Chillagoe company before them, the tributers steadily moved deeper into debt.

Mount Mulligan no longer attracted the adventurous transient miner. The township's population reduced, retaining the more stable, older miners, a higher proportion of them married, who were tied to the town by a mixture of loyalty and inertia. Single men with less vested interest in the town tended to seek employment elsewhere. The school shrank in size from a peak enrolment in 1928 of 139 pupils to 36 in 1943.[76] There was a new community facility in 1936, when the state Health Department built a community hospital in Harris Street, a neat timber

71 Mauldon, *op.cit.*, pp.131-132.

72 In 1936, Bowen produced 18,815 tons of coke. (*A.R.* 1936, p.3.) Chillagoe consumed 6,608 tons of this (*ibid.*, p.109) - most of the remainder was sold to Mount Isa Mines.

73 See for example *ibid.*, p.179.

74 *A.R.* 1935, p.177.

75 *Auditor-General's Report 1947-48*, p.102.

76 Mount Mulligan State School Annual Returns in Q.S.A. EDU AB1477. This dramatic reduction does not necessarily reflect a proportional reduction in the town's population in the same period. A fairly stable population of increasing age and low fertility could account for this decrease in enrolment.

building with a nursing sister in charge. The community seems to have become very close in the 1930s, having little contact with the outside world.[77] A tradition survived in Mount Mulligan through this difficult period: 19 September was observed each year as a holiday in memory of the men who died in 1921.[78]

In 1937, the tributers undertook the first major redevelopment of the underground workings since the mine opened. A new adit, Number Five, was opened a few hundred metres north of the mine entrance, and driven south-west to connect with the old workings.[79] It was planned to rebuild the surface workings outside the new entrance, but no action was ever taken, presumably because of the expense of such a move. A light tramway was built to the new adit, but it had been located in an awkward position, perched over a steep gully which would make it terribly expensive to provide haulage machinery or railway access. The opening of Number Five Adit, however, improved ventilation through the extended workings.

Two new developments stirred Mount Mulligan in 1941. The union withdrew from the tribute agreement, and management of the mine passed to an independent committee of eight miners on 29 September. The new management committee restored payment to a piece-work basis and reduced the number of men employed, but the payment of royalty and other aspects of their relationship with the state remained essentially similar to the agreement negotiated in 1929.[80]

More significantly, a new mine, the King Cole, opened on the mountain face south of the gorge. Tableland Tin Dredging (NL) operated a dredge near Mount Garnet, electrically powered by a steam driven generator. To fuel its generator furnace, the company re-opened the old Number One Adit and spent much of 1941 retimbering and developing the old mine workings. The miners marvelled at the handiwork of their

77 There is strikingly little reference to Mount Mulligan in written sources between 1930 and 1947. Government publications largely lost interest in the mine during the tribute, and little happened in the town to draw the attention of the press. Even correspondence from Mount Mulligan became sporadic - the union branch became notorious for failing to present its books for audit. (Correspondence between District Auditor and the Q.C.E.U. Executive, 1933 and 1934, Q.C.E.U. office, Ipswich.)

78 The state school received permission to close on the anniversary of the disaster until at least 1932, but the holiday is not noted after that year in the annual returns. (Q.S.A. EDU AB1477.) The miners observed the day every year until the mine closed.

79 *A.R.* 1937, p.53. Some confusion occurs in the nomenclature of the adits from this date. *A.R.* and *Q.G.M.J.* henceforth refer to the new adit (properly No.5) as No.2, and the mine entrance (old No.2) as No.1.

80 *A.R.* 1941, p.101, and interview with Jim McColm, Ipswich, 17 December 1976.

030 Miners in the underground workings about 1930, most of them still using carbide lamps. Note the timber props and stone packwall at left (Jim McColm)

predecessors in 1907; marks on the rock showed that the adit had been driven entirely by men with picks, without the use of explosives. A ventilating adit was driven from the southern wall of the gorge to connect with the mine workings. The mine's winding machinery was perched precariously at the very foot of the escarpment, from where a precipitous ropeway led down to a coal bin constructed by a siding on the railway.[81]

The opening of the King Cole brought little benefit to Mount Mulligan, as the number of men employed at the new mine was never large, and its development coincided with, and thus absorbed, the laying-off of excess labour by the management committee at the state mine. The two mines supplied separate closed markets - the Mount Garnet dredge and the Queensland Government Railways - and were not in any real sense in competition.

Tableland Tin's coal requirements were not great and the King Cole operated on a modest scale, only once producing more than 10,000 tons in a year.[82] The mine was located in a geologically unstable region of the coal-seam, where faults and rapid crush increased the cost of mining operations. The King Cole worked on a hand-cut bord-and-pillar system,

81 *Ibid.*, p.22.
82 See Appendix E.

and its single track ropeway down the mountain slope enabled only one skip to be handled at any time. But throughout its working life of sixteen years, the new mine was far more efficient than the state mine; the King Cole never employed more than twenty men, compared with 60 to 80 in the state mine in the same period, but normally produced between half and two-thirds the quantity of coal produced by the older mine.[83]

This greater productivity at the King Cole is explained in part by its small size and shorter wheeling distances, and by the greater thickness and better quality of the coal-seam south of the gorge.[84] The coal-seam in the state mine was reducing in thickness and becoming increasingly stone-banded as operations extended to the west and north. In 1942, mining was concentrated on the thicker top seam,[85] but although the coal there was more easily won, it was shotty and poor in quality. The top seam was abandoned in 1944,[86] and mining in the middle seam began increasingly to be channelled to the south-west by the deterioration of the seam in other directions. After 1948, production at the state mine was concentrated on a single face at Number Thirteen Bord to the south of the main dip, beyond what had been the South Section in 1921. The workings in this region were developed as a single semi-circular face, machine cut on the long wall advancing system, and served by three radiating wheeling roads.[87]

In July 1943, the Chillagoe smelters shut down for the last time:

> After their reopening by the State in 1929, and apart from short periods of idleness brought about by shortages of ore supplies and other causes, the Smelters had been in almost continuous operation from that time until their closure. The decision to close was influenced in a great measure by the diminution of ore supplies and the shortage of manpower due to wartime conditions.[88]

83 In the years when full information is available, relative efficiency of the mines was:

Year	**Men Employed**		**Production (tons)**	
	Mt Mulligan	King Cole	Mt Mulligan	King Cole
1947	57	19	16,211	7,696
1955	79	15	20,153	9,299
1956	63	19	15,731	9,068

(*A.R.*'s 1947, p.31; 1955, p.129; 1956, p.136)

84 Interview with Inspector R.N. Hardie, Ipswich, 21 December 1976.

85 *A.R.* 1942, pp.38 and 210.

86 *A.R.* 1944, p.44.

87 *A.R.* 1948, p.98; 1951, p.59.

88 *A.R.* 1943, p.39.

In fact, the smelters had for years operated only intermittently and at considerable loss to the state. Lead production had ceased in 1933, and the smelters' principal function in the later years was to encourage the depressed mining industry by smelting copper ore railed an amazing distance by the gougers of the Cloncurry district. When Mount Isa Mines built a copper smelter to assist wartime production in 1943, that last function was lost. The closing of the Chillagoe smelters had none of the calamitous consequences at Mount Mulligan that it had in 1914 or 1927, as Mount Mulligan had supplied no significant amount of coal to the smelters since about 1930. The total eclipse of the Chillagoe district's mines was reflected administratively by the closing of the Chillagoe mining warden's office, and the incorporation of Mount Mulligan into the Mareeba Mineral Field on 1 January 1949.[89]

The years immediately following the Second World War were a time of fundamental change in the Queensland coal industry. Some traditional markets had declined in importance, but rising population and post-war prosperity led to anticipation of increased railway, electricity generation and gasworks consumption. Mining technology had advanced to the point where fully mechanised extraction was being implemented in new mines, vastly increasing their productivity per man-shift relative to the mines which relied on human effort for hewing, loading and wheeling coal.[90] The new mines in the Bowen Basin - Bluff and Baralaba - were demonstrating the extent and quality of that field.

In November 1947, the Queensland government commissioned a British company, Powell Duffryn Technical Services Limited, to undertake a broad review of the state's coal resources, markets and mining methods.[91] The Powell Duffryn Report, published in July 1949, was optimistic about the prospects for Queensland's coal industry, but recommended increased mechanisation and more rational development of the existing mines. It proposed the redevelopment of the Mount Mulligan state mine on an orderly pattern of rectangular long wall

89 *A.R.* 1949, p.53.

90 See 'Boxflat's Progressive Mechanisation Programme', *Q.G.M.J.* 20 January 1953, pp.17-22.

91 Powell Duffryn Technical Services, *First Report on the Coal Industry of Queensland*, Brisbane 1949, Vol.1, pp.12-13.

districts,[92] and the expansion of its output to a planned 60,000 tons in 1955 to meet the growing coal requirements of the Cairns hinterland.[93]

The report also pointed out, however, that the thinning of the coal seams to the west and north of the Mount Mulligan workings suggested that Ball's 1911 estimate of the coal reserves at 84 million tons was a gross over-statement. Tentatively re-estimating the reserves at a little over one million tons,[94] the report recommended that a drilling program be implemented to test the coal reserves in the vicinity of the state mine:[95]

> The coal from the Mount Mulligan coalfield is being appropriately used, but...the present demand is approximately double the present output and will increase considerably by 1960. Such an increase in output will require considerable expenditure...on colliery plant and...a full consideration of [this expenditure] must await the proving of satisfactory reserves by a drilling program.[96]

The state resumed direct control of the Mount Mulligan mine on 13 October 1947. By that time the tributers owed the state nearly £20,000,[97] but this cannot explain the government's resumption of operations. The debt had to be written off at the end of the tribute, and the mine was less costly to the state under tribute than under direct operation because of the added cost to the state of wages. The state's annual loss at Mount Mulligan increased dramatically after the tribute ended - from £731 in 1945-46 to £18,658 in 1948-49.[98] The state resumption may have been made at the suggestion of the Colliery Employees' Union because of conflict between the miners and the management committee,[99] but, as it coincided with preliminary negotiations between the Mines Department and Powell Duffryn Technical Services, the resumption was probably part of a policy of better co-ordination of coalmining activities throughout the state.

Despite the optimism of the Powell Duffryn Report, the only justification for the state's retention of the Mount Mulligan mine was the need to supply coal to Cairns railways, and even in this market, Mount

92 *Ibid.*, Vol.2, pp.490-491; and see plan of proposed workings, Vol.3, plate 64.
93 *Ibid.*, p.489. The Powell Duffryn Report was seriously in error in predicting major growth in the Cairns coal market.
94 *Ibid.*, Vol.1, p.268.
95 *Ibid.*, Vol.2, pp.496-497.
96 *Ibid.*, Vol.2, p.385.
97 *Auditor-General's Report 1947-48*, p.102.
98 Public Service Commissioner's Office minute, 4 October 1950, in Q.S.A. A/8508.
99 Interview with Jim McColm, Ipswich, 17 December 1976.

Mulligan coal was only marginally competitive. In 1947, railway coal in Cairns cost £2/12/- a ton from Mount Mulligan and £2/16/5 from Collinsville.[100] There was resistance to Mount Mulligan coal from engine crews; fireman despised it because it was dirty, high in ash and clinkered the grate bars. Whenever possible they used cleaner alternatives, even at a slightly higher price.

The only other buyers of Mount Mulligan coal were Tableland Tin, which bought small quantities when King Cole production was inadequate, the Cairns Brick and Pipe Company, two Cairns cafes and a Ravenshoe hotel.[101] Mount Mulligan was reduced to selling coal by single truckloads. There were still grand schemes for expansion: a conference of the Gulf and Peninsula League in Mount Mulligan on the Australia Day weekend, 1950, heard a Mareeba delegate press for the re-establishment of coke ovens at the state mine, but in the face of the size and efficiency of the Bowen works, the proposition was fantastic.[102] The unprofitability of the Mount Mulligan mine was almost universally acknowledged, and production was continued simply to supply fuel to the railway system in the immediate district:

> Private ownership would have ceased operations...years ago, but because of...the geographical position of Mount Mulligan, the Government has found it necessary to continue production.[103]

Much of the surface plant at Mount Mulligan was necessarily updated in the early 1950s, but the Powell Duffryn plan for development of the middle seam was never implemented, and coal extraction was limited to Number Thirteen South for the remaining years of production. There was modest growth: the township expanded with the construction of a Post Office, the Roman Catholic church of Saint Therese, a new hospital and a few substantial private homes. Two events in 1951 greatly increased the comfort and convenience of life in Mount Mulligan: installation of two diesel generators gave the town domestic electricity

---

100 Unsigned Mines Department memorandum, "Price of Coal" 3 September 1947, in Q.S.A. A/8682. The relative costs involved were:

	Mount Mulligan coal	**Collinsville coal**
Price at railhead	41/3	27/8
Rail freight to Cairns	10/9	28/9
Total	52/-	56/5

101 Listed on a memorandum attached to a circular letter from the Under-Secretary, Department of Mines to buyers of Mount Mulligan coal, 7 August 1947, in Q.S.A. A/8682.

102 *Courier Mail*, 26 December 1949.

103 Under-Secretary to Minister for Mines, minute, 3 August 1950, in Q.S.A. A/8508. Private ownership **did** cease operations 27 years before.

031 The surface workings of the King Cole Mine about 1945, looking west (Mary Wardle)

for the first time; and a road was constructed from Dimbulah; the streets of Mount Mulligan were properly formed, and the first motor vehicles appeared in the town.[104]

New facilities for the miners were constructed near the mine entrance: a shower and changing house, lamp room and first-aid room, costing over £15,000.[105] The Under-Secretary for Mines reported: "the building is a most modern type and is a favourable indication of the Government's faith in the mine."[106] This need to state publicly the government's faith in the state mine reflects the uncertainty of the

104 *A.R.* 1951, p.59.
105 *Q.G.M.J.* 20 November 1952, p.926.
106 *A.R.* 1953, p.61.

Mount Mulligan people during the period of equivocal development in the early 1950s. In the hard-headed reconstruction of the Queensland coal industry that followed the Powell Duffryn inquiry, it was apparent that the Mount Mulligan mine operated only on sufferance, to forestall the price rise of a few shillings a ton for Cairns railway coal that would follow the mine's closure. A proposal emerged in 1951 to quarry building stone from the mountain face, but because of the inaccessibility of the exposed stone on the escarpment, the probable unsuitability of the sandstone, and the distance from any likely market, the idea came to nothing.[107] There was probably a small net increase in the population of the town during this period, but many long-established families left Mount Mulligan as opportunities arose elsewhere.[108]

There were sound reasons for pessimism. The prospecting program recommended by the Powell Duffryn Report in 1949 had further reduced the estimate of coal reserves under the mountain. An aerial survey in August 1949 was followed in April to November 1951 by drilling tests along the mountain slope to the north of the state mine, which found no significant quantity of usable coal:

> Sampling has indicated that coal sections of possible economic significance do not exceed 3ft. except in one instance, and that most of these are of inferior quality.[109]

Other events signalled the declining fortunes of the old coal industry. At Tinaroo and Koombaloomba, dams were under construction to supply hydro-generated electricity to the Cairns region. In Mount Mulligan itself, the coal-fired boilers which had powered the mine's generators since 1915 were superseded in 1953 by four diesel generating plants. The reason given was conservation of water:

> The use of these in comparison with steam generation will result in a saving of 14,000 gallons of water per day. The supply of water for the boilers has always been a source of difficulty and expense during the dry season.[110]

But there was an unmistakable irony in the use of diesel engines to supply power to the ageing coal-cutting machines which provided fuel

107 Correspondence between Secretary, Department of Co-ordinator General and Chief Government Geologist, February 1951, referring to a proposal by H.H. Collins, M.L.A.; in G.S.Q. Correspondence file 4-2-22, Department of Mines, Brisbane.

108 *A.R.* 1955, p.56; and interview with Mary Wardle, Ravenshoe, 13 August 1976.

109 *Q.G.M.J.* 20 February 1953, p.106. An unsigned, undated memorandum with administrative correspondence on the drilling program estimates the Mount Mulligan reserves at 750,000 tons, and King Cole's at 'a couple of years at 10,000 p.a.' (G.S.Q. Correspondence file 4-2-22.)

110 *A.R.* 1953, p.61.

for North Queensland trains. And in view of Mount Mulligan's total dependence on the railway market, a further ominous portent appeared in October 1952 when the first ten diesel-electric locomotives entered service with Queensland railways.[111] It was obvious that coal's future in the railway fuel market would be short.

By 1955, coal production at Mount Mulligan was dropping in every year - 25,000 tons in 1953, 20,000 in 1955 - and the population of the town had begun its final decline.[112] In that year a new Inspector of Coal Mines was appointed to the Northern Division; R.N. Hardie, whose reports to the Mines Department were an incisive compilation of data on the relative efficiency of the Northern and Central coal mines, in contrast with the vague narrative of incidents provided by his predecessors. In 1955 he reported the Mount Mulligan mines were producing 1.8 tons of coal per man-shift, compared with 4.9 tons at Collinsville and 38.3 at Blair Athol open-cut mine.[113] Hardie allowed the figures to speak for themselves, but it was apparent that the future of coalmining in Queensland lay with the capital-intensive mines of the Bowen Basin.

The decision to close the Mount Mulligan mines was precipitated by immediate and independent crises in the mines themselves. For some years a horizontal movement had been developing in the escarpment above the King Cole mine. Mount Mulligan's escarpments are subject to steady erosion, with huge blocks of sandstone breaking off and falling spectacularly onto the mountain slope on several occasions since the establishment of the town. Subsidence brought about by crush into the King Cole workings had opened a crack on top of the mountain, running diagonally across the southern corner of the gorge entrance; which threatened to bring a huge piece of mountain down onto the surface workings. Small falls of rock occurred in the gorge in 1956. For several years the crack was inspected for signs of movement each morning before the shift entered the King Cole mine.[114]

In the morning of 13 April 1957, the daily inspection showed that the crack had visibly widened. Hardie ordered the mine closed ten days later, and the nineteen men employed at the King Cole moved to the state mine on the north side of the gorge.[115] Three months later, on 30 July 1957, Tableland Tin's dredge at Mount Garnet was connected to the

111 *Report of the Commissioner for Railways 1951-52*, p.15.
112 School enrolment fell from 91 in 1953 to 53 in 1955. (Q.S.A. EDU AB1477.)
113 *A.R.* 1955, p.129.
114 Interview with R.N. Hardie, Ipswich, 22 December 1976.
115 *A.R.* 1957, pp.57 and 141.

electricity supply provided by the hydro-electric generators at Kareeya, below the Koombaloomba Dam.[116] That market for coal was closed.

On 3 August 1957, with the Mount Mulligan State Coal Mine in a precarious economic condition, the political circumstances changed abruptly. The Labor party which had held office continuously in Queensland since 1932 was defeated at a general election, and replaced by the Country Liberal government of Frank Nicklin. The last vestige of the State Mines policy which had existed since 1915 to create employment in mining districts abruptly vanished; the Country party had no interest in the traditional Labor voters of Mount Mulligan.

Thus when Inspector Hardie was recalled to Mount Mulligan on 28 October 1957 to investigate overheating at the working-face in the state coal mine, he was working for a government that had no reason to keep open an unprofitable coal mine. He found that subsidence in the new workings had opened cracks to abandoned goaf areas at a lower level, and the limited oxygen supply thus introduced had initiated spontaneous combustion. Hardie ordered closure of the mine, and all reclaimable plant was removed in the following days. The Mount Mulligan mine entrances were sealed on 15 November 1957.[117]

It would be oversimplistic to say that the Mount Mulligan mine closed because of heating. Had the spontaneous combustion occurred in a viable mine, especially a gas-free mine, it would have presented an expensive but not insuperable problem. At Mount Mulligan in 1957 it was the final weight cast into the balance of unprofitability. Mount Mulligan had survived much worse technical problems in the past, but there was no longer any political reason for the mine to exist.

Mount Mulligan became a ghost town with a speed and efficiency unmatched in any other North Queensland mining settlement. Since the mining plant and much of the township were the property of the Queensland government, they were dismantled and railed to the state mine at Collinsville. Most of the miners, their families and their houses were transferred to the Bowen field, the first arriving on 7 November 1957, and were resettled on balloted homesites.[118] The tiny business community of Mount Mulligan was removed to Cairns at state

116 *Q.G.M.J.* 20 September 1957, p.649.

117 *A.R.* 1957, p.141; and interview with R.N. Hardie, Ipswich, 22 December 1976.

118 Brisbane *Telegraph*, 7 November 1957.

expense:[119] the top hotel closed its doors on 16 November;[120] the bottom hotel had vanished years before.

In May 1958, the lesser items of state property were publicly auctioned, the town and mine were abandoned and the railway line dismantled. A month earlier the mountain had signalled the end with proper ceremony when 250,000 tons of sandstone, tilted beyond stability by the King Cole workings, fell thunderously from the escarpment into the gorge.[121]

The only building still standing in the Mount Mulligan township is the handsome timber hospital of 1936, which after the abandonment of the town, functioned for many years as the homestead of the Mount Mulligan cattle property. The hospital is now operated as a host farm, where tourists can enjoy an outback experience at a historic place in impressive natural surroundings. At the foot of the mountain, the concrete walls of the power-house, the brick kiln, the frame of the tippler, rusting skips and a large dump of waste coal identify the site as a former coal mine. The most impressive monuments surviving are the brick stack of the cokeworks, still standing in tiny contrast to the vastness of the mountain, and the cemetery with its crisp marble headstones and its anonymous mounds.

Since 1991, the mountain has been owned by the Kuku Djungan Aboriginal Corporation, and is leased to the Queensland Department of Environment and Heritage as the Kuku Djungan Ngarrabullgan National Park.

119 Under-Secretary, Department of Mines to Q.C.E.U. president, 6 November 1957, in Correspondence files, Q.C.E.U. office, Ipswich.
120 *Courier Mail*, 15 November 1957.
121 *Q.G.M.J.* 20 April 1958, p.249.

032 Entrance to the Mount Mulligan mine, 1977 (Peter Bell)

033 Chillagoe smelter ruins from the air, 2004 (Peter Bell)

034 The Drier father and son's grave, Mount Mulligan cemetery, 2004 (Peter Bell)

035 Ruins of the ventilating fan adit, Mount Mulligan, 2004 (Peter Bell)

6.
POSTSCRIPT

"Disasters occur, enquiries are made, and legislation is brought in to prevent accidents."

James Donald, 1947
(*QPD* vol. 191, p. 1,403)

James Donald, MLA for the seat of Bremer in Ipswich, which was then still Queensland's largest coalfield, made this succinct assessment of the means by which mine safety measures evolve during debate on an amendment to the *Coal Mining Act* on 14 November 1947. In a later era, his speech would have said that the process of reform is reactive, not proactive. The amendment was prompted by the deaths of four of Donald's constituents in a coal dust explosion at the New Ebbw Vale No. 3 colliery in 1945. His description of the process is generally accurate, in that reforms are almost invariably prompted by the outcry that follows an especially ugly accident, but he was far too optimistic about its effectiveness. Disasters occur and enquiries are made, certainly, but there have been many enquiries which have then been ignored, and much legislation which has come ten or twenty years too late. And even after this process is complete, there remains the problem of ensuring that what is written in the legislation is what actually happens in the coal mines.

A comparison of the reports published after the investigation of Queensland coal-mine disasters leads to pessimism about the usefulness of their recommendations. Each of the enquiries into the Mount Mulligan, Box Flat and Kianga explosions recommended the establishment of a research facility to investigate safety in coal-mines; each criticised the level of competence of those responsible for decision-making in the mine; each recommended legislative reform, and most conspicuously, each essentially repeated its predecessor's advice on means of coping with coal dust:

Mount Mulligan, 1921:

STONE DUSTING

6. We append copy of the British Stone-Dusting Regulations for inclusion in the Queensland Act, in lieu of stone-dusting regulations contained therein:-

PART 1 - PRECAUTIONS AGAINST COAL DUST

...the floor, roof, and sides of every road or part of a road which is accessible shall...be treated with incombustible dust in such a manner, and at such intervals, as will ensure that the dust on the floor, roof, and sides throughout shall always consist of a mixture containing nor more than 50 percent of combustible matter....[1]

Box Flat, 1972:

<u>3. COAL DUST</u>

...there should be a complete review of the Act with regard to the treatment of coal dust, in accordance with up-to-date world wide knowledge on the subject, with special emphasis being placed on the application of stone dust in working and back-bye places.[2]

Kianga, 1975:

(3) LEGISLATION

It is recommended that:-

...(b) The Queensland Coal Mining Act be amended to provide for:

---

1 *R.C.* p. XLV.

2 Mining Inquiry - Box Flat Colliery: Report, Findings and Recommendations, unpublished typescript, Queensland Department of Mines Library; and see *A.R.*, 1972, p.83.

> (i) stone dust or water barriers on road-ways where it is difficult to maintain compliance with stone dust regulations....
>
> (5) STONE DUSTING
>
> It is recommended that:-
>
> ...(c) Stone dusting must be kept up to specification throughout all underground coal mines and...means of placing combustible dust continuously in the immediate return, must be kept working at all times while continuous miners or other coal producing machines are operating.[3]

When three enquiries over 54 years all offer the same recommendations, then something is wrong with the process of reform. That is not to say that the legislators were inactive; we have seen that the Mount Mulligan disaster led four years later to the enactment of separate colliery legislation. But what was the relationship between the Mount Mulligan disaster and the new safety provisions? The 1925 Act and Regulations provided much more stringent standards for electrical installations, greater control over the use of explosives, made safety lamps compulsory when the air contained even a trace of flammable gas, and banned tobacco and matches from mines where safety lamps were in use.

This was in response to the finding that a plaster shot had initiated a coal dust explosion. The 1925 reforms were silent on both of these issues; the vague coal dust rules of 1920 remained in force, despite the Royal Commission's recommendations. No-one had suggested that electrical installations, gas or matches contributed to the Mount Mulligan explosion. It was strangely as though the new regulations after Mount Mulligan were designed to prevent another Torbanlea explosion.

Nothing was done about coal dust until 1945 when the four miners were killed by the explosion at New Ebbw Vale. Premier Frank Cooper was still the member for Bremer at the time, and the Queensland Colliery Employees Union were in a strong position to press for reform. An amendment to the Act in 1947 brought in comprehensive regulations covering ventilation and coal dust, including standards for the ratio of incombustible dust which must be present in the mine: in other words, mandatory stone-dusting. The new provisions were laudable, but they were neither timely nor new; they were essentially the actions the Mount Mulligan Royal Commission had recommended 26 years earlier. Again Queensland coal mine legislation seemed to be setting out to prevent the disaster before last.

3 *Report on an Accident at Kianga, op.cit.*, pp.13-14.

A new mining era dawned in the 1960s, as the opencut mines of the Bowen Basin began to dominate the Queensland coal industry, bringing a different set of safety problems. Then in the 1970s explosions in the Box Flat and Kianga underground mines killed 30 miners, and it became apparent the 1947 regulations were not enough. The Kianga findings were promptly implemented, and new Rules were drawn up for the detection of methane and control of coal dust.

The 1977 Rules established precise standards to be observed in the distribution of stone-dust in coal-mines, and made mandatory the installation of explosion barriers in proximity to areas of the mine where coal dust is likely to be distributed in quantity. Further Rules in 1978 specified standards to be observed in ventilation and the measurement of flammable gases in underground coal mines. There was also a completely new provision for miners' personal safety:

> A person shall not be belowground in an underground coal mine at any time unless...He is carrying a self-rescuer [i.e. a respirator] or has one available within one metre of his person, ready for immediate use;...[4]

Such a rule might have saved the lives of many hundreds of miners in coal-mine explosions during the past two centuries, since the greatest loss of life has normally been caused by inhalation of toxic or suffocating gas in the explosion's wake. If George Turriff and a few others at Mount Mulligan had carried self-rescuers, they might have walked out of the mine.

With all these measures in place, it caused stunned disbelief in Queensland coal mining circles when two more underground explosions at Moura, not far from Kianga, killed 12 miners in 1986 and 11 in 1994. After the first of these, investigators were able to enter the mine afterward; it was the first time since Mount Mulligan that anyone had inspected the scene of a major Queensland coal dust explosion. The evidence in the mine proved inconclusive as to the initiation of the explosion, but the Warden's inquiry found the most likely cause was that flammable gas had been ignited by the flame of a safety lamp lying on its side.[5] This seems to be the first time that a safety lamp, undamaged and responsibly used, had been blamed for a mine explosion in the 170 years they had been in use.

The second Moura inquiry had even less evidence before it, as there were no survivors and the mine was sealed. It found that there was

4 *Q.G.G.*, 21 January 1978, p.156.

5 *Report on an Accident at Moura No. 4 Underground Mine*, Brisbane 1987.

known to be spontaneous combustion in a goaf area which may have ignited flammable gas.[6] It seems as though coal mine safety regulation may have reached an impasse, for there is little point in doing more sophisticated research and imposing more and more finely-tuned regulations, when experience is showing that coal dust explosions continue to occur, in increasingly baffling circumstances.

Kianga and Moura are only fifteen kilometres apart, and all the mines in the field are gassy. In two of the accidents, miners were sent to work in mines where there was known to be active spontaneous combustion occurring, and methane in the mine atmosphere. The Moura No. 4 explosion in 1986 happened, like Mount Mulligan, in the course of normal production without any warning. Moura No. 2 in 1994 however, followed a day in which the mine management monitored evidence of heating and rising gas levels without warning the workforce. At Kianga in 1975 the methane was known to be nearing an explosive concentration in close proximity to a coal fire; a reading of 4% was recorded nine hours before the explosion. On that day there was a drop in barometric pressure, which was known to increase the rate of gas emission.[7] Stone dusting in the mine had not been kept up to specification. Given that everyone present must have known that the circumstances were tending in the direction of an ignition of firedamp, it is extraordinary that work continued in the mine.

The historical ineffectiveness of reactive legislation as a force contributing to improved safety in coal mines over time can be demonstrated very simply. The means to prevent the loss of life in the Box Flat, Kianga and second Moura explosions did not require the 1947 stone dust regulations, the 1920 "systematic steps" or the 1910 safety lamps rule. They were clearly stated in the very first Queensland safety legislation, the *Mines Regulation Act* of 1881, in a passage drawn word-for-word from the British *Coal Mining Act* of 1872:

> If at any time it is found by the person in charge of a colliery, or any part thereof ... that by reason of noxious gases, or of any cause whatever, the colliery or the said part is dangerous, every workman shall be withdrawn therefrom ... and no workman shall ... be readmitted into the colliery or such part thereof as was found so dangerous until the same is reported ... to be safe.

6 *Report on an Accident at Moura No. 2 Underground Mine*, Brisbane 1996.
7 *Report on an Accident at Kianga No. 1 Underground Mine*, Brisbane 1976.

It may be a sad reflection on the progress of coal mine legislation that this passage was still in force in Queensland with only slight amendments over a hundred years after it was drafted. But it is an even sadder reflection on the conduct of the coal mining industry that it was still being ignored.

It is difficult to see what more mine regulations can do to prevent coal dust explosions happening in underground mines, given that in recent decades there has been a consistent pattern of mines continuing to operate in conditions that are known to be dangerous. Perhaps the solution to coal dust explosions is simply to close the mines that are at risk. In 1993-94, 72% of Australian coal production came from opencut mines.[8] In Queensland the figure was 88%.[9] Why are miners still sent down gassy mines to produce less than 12% of Queensland's coal?

As a final postscript to this description of an explosion of coal dust and its consequences, it has been suggested that a similar event at the other end of the earth six years earlier might have had a previously unsuspected influence on world affairs. On 7 May 1915 the Cunard passenger liner *Lusitania* was torpedoed off the south coast of Ireland by a German U-boat, with great loss of life. The dead included 128 citizens of the USA, then a neutral country. This outrage fuelled a growing hostility to Germany, which culminated in America's intervention in the war two years later.

One puzzle about the loss of the *Lusitania* was that a single torpedo should have caused such a large ship to sink so quickly. Many survivors reported a second, much larger explosion moments after the torpedo's impact, and for decades there was speculation that the *Lusitania* was carrying contraband munitions for the war effort, and that these had exploded.

In the 1990s, Robert Ballard of the Woods Hole Oceanographic Institution investigated the wreck of the *Lusitania*, using a submersible vessel capable of withstanding high pressures at great depth. There is indeed a very large hole in the ship's side, with the ruptured iron plates pushed outward as though by a powerful explosion within the hull.

8 Figures by Australian Bureau of Statistics from Joint Coal Board sources.

9 Figures from Coal and Mineral Industries Division, Department of Primary Industries and Energy.

However, its location is not a cargo hold or magazine, but a coal bunker, which would have been nearly empty at the time of the U-boat attack. Ballard's theory, still controversial, is that the torpedo initiated a coal dust explosion in the bunker which caused catastrophic damage to the *Lusitania*'s hull, causing the ship to sink very quickly.[10]

10 R. Ballard, *Exploring the Lusitania*, Toronto 1995, pp. 194-95.

APPENDIX A

Letter from Walter Filer to his sister Kate, 25 September 1921, describing rescue work at Mount Mulligan.

25th Sept. 1921
c/- Post Office
Mungana

Dear Kate,

Glad to get your letter. Sorry your holiday is over. I am glad you enjoyed it so. Well Kate I have had a holiday for 4 days but an enforced one worse luck. Fourty miners were called from here to volenteer to the relief of Mt Mulligan after the explosion. I was among them. We arrived on the Tuesday night after the explosion and went down the mine immediately. They had recovered a dozen or so. By Thursday all were found. Some trouble was experienced owing to so few men being available who knew the run of the mine. Some delay was caused before the last 3 bodies were found. Every man below was killed bar Evans the underground mine manager & it's doubtful if he will live. It's was an awful job Kate going along with boards picking up dead corpses. The last were simply awful. I was with 2 others when James & 2 other dead were found. We had searched all no. 12 and some old workings too &

[page two]

coming back we found off the main drive more old workings & seeing rails pulled about we concluded that they must be somewhere about as only 3 bodies were missing and James was one and he was engaged on rails. Well we went along and we nearly fell over him about 400 yards from where he was working. putrid what well I leave it to you can imagine our horrible task I shall never forget it. Some say the explosion killed them instantaneous but from my observation I should say in the parts farthest away from the force the men had a few seconds to think anyway. Why some were found 300 yards from their work. Their billies & cribs & even lamps in some cases were found a good way from where they were picked up showing after their lights went out which would be immediately of course they had run for life only to be overtaken by fumes and fall dead. Of course most were undoubtedly blown to death instanly. It was pittiful to see the poor fellows. One or two had a smile on their faces but most were

[page three]

unrecognizable. I have to use the pencil as my mate is writing home to his wife at M Morgan who was anxious about him. There was a risk to the rescue party of course as there might have been a fall again & gas loosed and as we were all using naked carbide lamps and keresene lamps nothing could prevent us being blowed up too. I found one chap kneeling down with his head on his arms. He must have been praying. Others were lying face down with their nose on the ground showing they had time to thrown them selves down & bury their noses to try & escape being smothered. It was nothing but a procession of coffins from the pit to the morgue & to the cemetary. They could not dig the graves fast enought. The poor widows were clustered at the mouth of the tunnel to identify their husbands & sons. Alas it seems cruel that the God above cannot prevent such awful disasters. Think of it Kate 76 miners & only 1 brought out alive well half dead too. The mine itself was not damaged to any great extent. It could be retimbered etc & worked again in a short time. Ah well it's all over now & I never wish to see Mt Mulligan again. I hope I have not shocked you Kate but I tell you the truth as I was there & picked up & carried them right out on the stretchers. Talk of the war it was 4 & _ days the last

[page four]

few had been lying undiscovered. One man Grant had been walked by in the search a dozen times & then he was only found by someone noticing his hip about 4 inches square buried below a bit of a fall. Of course the smell was bad near him, but 7 or 8 were got near him and one could not go by the smell. We used to use plenty of phenol and had masks but I tell you after a few hours below one was glad to return to the mouth. You see Kate in a coal mine you do down the mine by a long tunnel not like a metal mine in a cage down a shaft. Of course I was strange to the coal mine. I would not work in one thats all I know. The drives are only about 2'6" to 3' in places. How they filled trucks I can't imagine. Cross cuts they call boards and twists are gates & gigways I was puzzled. We just kept in sight of one another so as not to get lost. I tell you its a maze to a stranger. Trusting you are well as I am. I hear some talk of us all being paid off now & the smelters being closed as the coal is not available. They are working only the copper furnace I hear & have paid off 60 men. I thought they could use wood. Anyway its only a charity job I reckon & shall be prepared for a close down anytime. so only write one letter & I will let you know if possible next mail.

Your loving Brother Walter

APPENDIX B

Schoolchildren throughout Queensland were encouraged to write letters of sympathy to children of Mount Mulligan after the disaster. A reply to one of these letters is reproduced here.

Mt Mulligan
State School
nov the 23 1921

Dear Isabel Maur
Sandford
Mackay

Dear Schoolmates

We thank you for your kindness & for yours letters of sympathy. Some day I hope to have the pleasure of meeting you. The accident happened at 25 past nine on Monday the 19th of September and they got all the men out some on Monday Tuesday Wednesday Thursday and Friday. The explosion started up at the fan and then in the tunnel. the blacksmith shop got blown to bits. The man who was in the shop got blown 200 yds aways from the tunnel and after the explosion they went down the [mine] and worked all night and day looking for the men Everyday the people used to have breakfast dinner and tea up at the mine.

Mt Mulligan
North Queensland State School
Herbert Smithson

Herbert Smithson, the writer, is shown in the photograph of Mount Mulligan schoolchildren on page 36; seated front row, second from left. His father, William Robert Smithson, was killed in the Mount Mulligan disaster.

Herbert Smithson later became a coal miner. He was killed in an accident at the Collinsville State Coal Mine on 29 June 1942. (*A.R.* 1942, pp.206 and 211)

APPENDIX C

AUSTRALASIAN MINE ACCIDENTS CAUSING MORE THAN FIVE DEATHS

Mine		Date	Type	Dead
Kaitangata	NZ	21 Feb 1879	Explosion	34
Australasian	Vic	12 Dec 1882	Flooding	22
Bulli	NSW	23 Mar 1887	Explosion	81
Hamilton	NSW	22 Jun 1889	Roof fall	11
Eclipse	Qld	4 Feb 1893	Flooding	7
McEvoy	Vic	20 Jul 1895	Flooding	6
South Broken Hill	NSW	18 July 1895	Roof fall	9
Brunner	NZ	26 Mar1896	Explosion	67
Stockton	NSW	6 Dec 1896	Fire	11
Dudley	NSW	21 Mar 1898	Explosion	15
Mt Kembla	NSW	31 Jul 1902	Explosion	96
Brilliant	Qld	14 Oct 1904	Fire	7
Stanford Merthyr	NSW	29 Oct 1905	Explosion	6
Mt Morgan	Qld	5 Sep 1908	Roof fall	7
North Lyell	Tas	12 Oct 1912	Fire	42
Kulumadau	PNG	6 Apr 1914	Runaway skip	6
Ralph's	NZ	12 Sep 1914	Explosion	43
Mt Mulligan	Qld	19 Sep 1921	Explosion	76
Golden Horseshoe	WA	6 Dec 1921	Cage fall	6

Mine		Date	Type	Dead
Bellbird	NSW	1 Sep 1923	Fire	21
Dobson	NZ	3 Dec 1926	Explosion	9
Wonthaggi	Vic	15 Feb 1937	Explosion	13
Glen Afton	NZ	11 Sep 1939	Gas	11
Collinsville	Qld	13 Oct 1954	Gas	7
Strongman	NZ	19 Jan 1967	Explosion	19
Box Flat	Qld	31 Jul 1972	Explosion	17
Kianga	Qld	20 Sep 1975	Explosion	13
Appin	NSW	24 Jul 1979	Explosion	14
Moura No 4	Qld	16 Jul 1986	Explosion	12
Emu	WA	13 Jun 1989	Flooding	6
Moura No 2	Qld	7 Aug 1994	Explosion	11
Pike River	NZ	19 Nov 2010	Explosion	29

APPENDIX D

Population of Mount Mulligan in 1921

175 people, including 55 women, are named as residents of Mount Mulligan in the state electoral roll (Division of Cook, Subdivision of Chillagoe) in 1921. While the limitations of the electoral roll as an indication of population are obvious, the Mount Mulligan figures can be given greater credence than might otherwise be the case because of their updating before the October 1920 election. A problem arises in defining Mount Mulligan residents, however, since a number of coal miners are listed as residents of Woodville, Wolfram or Thornborough, in the same subdivision. There was obviously a high rate of short-term movement among the Hodgkinson mining communities. Where these men are known to have been in Mount Mulligan at the time of the disaster, they are included in the total above.

In addition, 41 of the miners killed, and 13 of their wives or mothers resident in Mount Mulligan do not appear in the electoral roll,[1] raising the known population to 229, including 68 women, if it is assumed no-one had left or arrived in Mount Mulligan in the year since the roll was revised. References to newly-arrived miners, the trend in school enrolment, and the continuing development of the mine and surface workings all suggest a net increase in population during that period. 74 children were enrolled at the Mount Mulligan school in the last quarter

1 *R.C.* pp.165-166 lists the victims and their dependants.

of 1921,[2] and four of the miners who were absent on the morning of the disaster were not registered as voters. The addition of these gives a known population of 307.

Perhaps 20 other names can be found in newspaper references and business directories, and an arbitrary allowance must be made for unaccounted categories of people such as those between school-leaving and electoral registration ages. This latter group was small, because school leavers who could not find work at the mine or in the town's few businesses usually left Mount Mulligan. Ivy O'Gorman stated there were 5 single girls in Mount Mulligan in 1921.[3]

350 thus seems a reasonable estimate of Mount Mulligan's population at the time of the disaster, keeping in mind the normal day-to-day fluctuation common in North Queensland mining towns. Bruce Mackey[4] confirmed this in very broad terms by putting the population at "between three and four hundred".

2 Mount Mulligan State School Annual Return, Q.S.A. EDU AB1477.
3 Interview at Cairns, 3 January 1976.
4 Interview at Cairns, 4 January 1976.

APPENDIX E

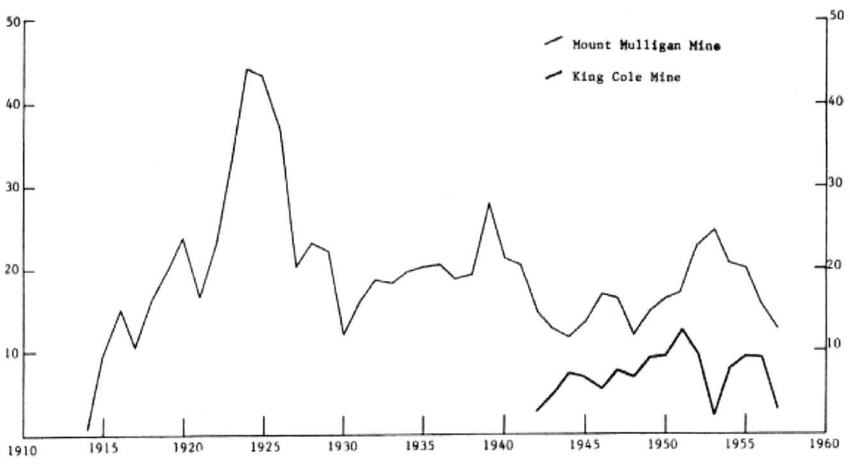

036 Coal production at Mount Mulligan 1914-1957 (x 1,000 tons)

APPENDIX F

The Death

There is no way of knowing precisely who died at Mount Mulligan, because of poor record-keeping before the disaster, the anonymity of some of the dead miners, the difficulty of identifying many of their bodies, confusion in counting both how many dead were recovered and how many were buried, and the removal of some bodies for burial elsewhere. No coronial enquiry was held into the disaster, and no cemetery burial register exists. There were probably 75 miners killed, but there may have been one more. This list is compiled principally from two official sources, both of which give 75 names: (a) the list from Chillagoe Limited reproduced as Exhibit 22 in the Royal Commission report, and (b) the list of miners and dependants in the report on the Relief Funds Act, which was based on more research and is more accurate. One miner's name is given in full only on his headstone in the Mount Mulligan cemetery.

Name	Dependents	From	Notes
Adam, Thomas	Unknown	England	T. Adams in (a)
Adcock, Thomas	Wife, 2 children	Herberton	
Beattie, James	Wife, 3 children	Ballarat	
Bell, Irving	Mother	England	
Bollen, Herbert	Wife, 2 children	Broken Hill	
Butcher, Frank	None	Charters Towers	
Butler, Donald	Mother	Tasmania	
Camm, Thomas	Wife	Toowoomba	T. Cann in (a)
Cairney, John	Wife, 3 children	Broken Hill	J. Carney in (a)
Carson, James	Wife, 4 children	Wolfram	
Casloff, Alick	Wife, 3 children	Mount Mulligan	
Cole, William	Unknown	Wales	
Conoplia, Peter	Wife, 4 children	Mount Mulligan	
Cunningham, James	Wife, 2 children	Sydney	
Doyle, Philip	Unknown	Dublin	aka John Long
Drier, John	Wife, 2 children	Mount Mulligan	
Drier, Jonathon	Posthumous child	Mount Mulligan	Aged 17
Evans, Thomas	Wife, 1 child	Victoria	Mine Manager
Fisher, William	Wife	Howard	
Fitzpatrick, John	Wife, 2 children	England	
Fogarty, John	Mother	Victoria	
Gielis, Francis	None	Mount Mulligan	
Grant, Francis	Wife	Mount Mulligan	Deputy
Hall, Albert	Wife, 2 children	Mount Mulligan	
Harrison, Harry	Wife	England	
Hawes, Cecil	3 children	Sydney	
Hawes, Thomas	None	Mount Mulligan	
Henry, John	Wife, 1 child	Mount Mulligan	
Hutton, Edward	Wife, 2 children	Mount Mulligan	
Hutton, Thomas	Wife, 3 children	Herberton	
Hynes, Thomas	Wife, mother	Mount Mulligan	
Jackson, Hugh	Wife, 1 child	Brisbane	
James, George	Wife, 5 children	Mount Mulligan	
James, Robert	None	Mount Mulligan	Aged 15
Joachimzik, Louis	Wife	Abermain, NSW	Name on grave
Johnstone, William	Unknown	England	

Name	Dependents	From	Notes
Keirs, William	Wife, 2 children	Cessnock	W. Kerr in (a)
Latimer, Frank	None	Brisbane	
Leary, Robert	Mother	Mount Mulligan	
Lewis, Oliver	1 child	Wollongong	aka Jack Lawson
Liversidge, Sydney	Unknown	Sydney	
Lomax, Jack	Wife	Mount Mulligan	
Loughrie, James	Sister	West Wallsend, NSW	
Mansfield, William	Wife, 1 child	Sydney	H. Mansfield in (a)
Marks, Percy	Mother	Townsville	
Martin, Harold	Wife, 3 children	Sydney	
Mounsey, George	Unknown	Melbourne	
Minogue, Paul	Sister	Victoria	
Morgan, Edward	Wife, 4 children	Chillagoe	
McColm, Samuel	Wife, 7 children	Mount Mulligan	
McCormack, Roland	Mother	Mount Mulligan	Aged 16
McIntyre, Duncan	Wife	Mount Morgan	
Nixon, John	None	New South Wales	
O'Boyle, James	Wife, 1 child	Mount Mulligan	
O'Grady, Martin	Unknown	Unknown	
O'Halloran, John	Wife, 1 child	Wonthaggi	
Ostle, William	Unknown	England	Wilson Ostle in (a)
Parkinson, Thomas	Wife, 2 children	Mount Mulligan	Deputy
Pattinson, Frederick	Wife	Mount Mulligan	
Pattinson, Robert	None	Sydney	
Reay, James	None	New South Wales	
Regan, John	Wife	Broken Hill	
Riseley, Ernest	Unknown	Tasmania	
Ruming, Harold	Parents	Koorboora	N. Ruming in (a)
Seymour, Sydney	Parents	Wonthaggi	
Smithson, William	Wife, 4 children	Mount Mulligan	
Spiers, Robert	Wife, 1 child	Mount Mulligan	
Stevens, William	Wife, 5 children	Wonthaggi	
Swift, William	Unknown	Wonthaggi	T. Swift in (a)
Taylor, Thomas	Wife, 2 children	Mount Mulligan	
Templeton, Robert	Unknown	Wollongong	
Thompson, Robert	Unknown	England	

Name	Dependents	From	Notes
Thompson, Wilfred	Unknown	England	
Turriff, George	Wife, 2 children	Wonthaggi	Body found 1922
Wheeler, Thomas	Wife, 2 children	Wonthaggi	R. Wheelan in (a)

SOURCES

Queensland State Archives

A/8481 Mines Department: Use of Permitted Explosives in Collieries, 1922-1938

A/8508 Mines Department: State Coal Administration

A/8558 Mines Department: Chillagoe State Smelters

A/8682 Mines Department: Marketing State Coal and Coke, 1942-1948

A/8695 Mines Department: Exhibits in action the King vs. Goddard, Reid, McCormack and Theodore over the sale of Mungana Mines to the Qld. Govt. 1931.

A/8715 Mines Department: Reports, Chillagoe, H.I. Jensen.

A/9222 Railway Department: Hard Batch Series - Chillagoe Railway, 1897-1921

A/9230-9232 Railways Department: Hard Batch Series - Dimbulah to Mt Mulligan

COL 139 Correspondence records relating to the supply of rations to Aborigines, 1888-1902

COL/A 366 Colonial Secretary's Office: General Correspondence Records, 1883

CRS/Y1-14 Mungana Supreme Court Case - Evidence, exhibits and miscellaneous papers

EDU AA 728 School Admission Register, Mount Mulligan, 1933-1957

EDU AB 1477 School Statistical Returns, Mount Mulligan, 1914-1957

EDU/Z 1930 School files (correspondence) Mount Mulligan

JUS 54-57 Reports, forms of agreement, memoranda and correspondence relating to the Chillagoe Railways and Mines Limited, 1898-1920

JUS G199 Justice Department: Letter book 19 September-15 October 1921

JUS R15 Register of coroner's inquests depositions, Book 16, 2 February 1921-18 August 1922

PRE/A 524 Premier's Department: In-letters, 12-31 May 1916

PRE/A 782 Premier's Department: In-letters, 1-12 November 1923

PRE/A 848 Premier's Department: In-letters, 1921-1925, relating to Mt Mulligan disaster

ROY 15-16A Royal Commission of Inquiry into Mungana, Chillagoe, etc.

Chillagoe Company Annual Reports: irregular copies 1900-1919 with correspondence in A/9222 and JUS 54

Company Registers

23/1913 Chillagoe Limited

277 book 11 The Chillagoe Company Limited

29 book 9 Chillagoe Proprietary Limited

Other Archival Material

Geological Survey of Queensland Correspondence File 4-2-22: Coal - Mt Mulligan. Department of Mines, Brisbane

Register of Deaths, General Registry Office, Brisbane

Miscellaneous correspondence and accounts relating to Mount Mulligan. Queensland Colliery Employees' Union office, Booval

Register of Deaths, Cook District, 1899, Cooktown Courthouse

Papers in Private Possession

Ledger; Chillagoe Limited: Mount Mulligan Coal Mine (September 1915-June 1923), in possession of Mr and Mrs A. Hardaker, Chillagoe Historical Centre

Letter from Thomas McCarthy to Edwin Desailly, 14 March 1883, in possession of Norman Desailly, Noble Park, Vic. (Concerns the murder of Charles Desailly.)

Letter from Walter Filer to Kate Filer, 25 September 1921, in possession of Kate Antcliff, Bardon. (See Appendix A.)

Letter from Herbert Smithson to Isabel Maur, 23 November 1921, in possession of Isabel Harris, Mackay. (See Appendix B.)

Miscellaneous certificates, other documents and Clarke Medal of J.T. Watson, in possession of Jack Watson, Slade Point.

Queensland Government Publications

Queensland Government Mining Journal

Queensland Government Gazette

Queensland Industrial Gazette

Queensland Parliamentary Debates

Queensland Statutes

Queensland Parliamentary Papers:

Annual Report of the Under-Secretary for Mines, 1897-1977

Report of the Public Curator, 1922-1933

Report of the Commissioner for Railways, 1913-1958

Report of the Auditor-General, 1920-1949

Report of the Royal Commission into the Torbanlea Colliery Accident, 1900

Report of the Select Committee on the Proposed Branch Railway from the Chillagoe Company's Railway, at 24 Miles, 63 chains, to Mount Mulligan, 1912

Report of the Select Committee on the Chillagoe and Etheridge Railways Purchase Bill, 1917

Report of the Select Committee on the Chillagoe and Etheridge Railways Bill, 1918

Further Report of the Select Committee on the Chillagoe and Etheridge Railways Bill, 1918

Report of the Royal Commission into the advisableness of Establishing State Iron and Steel Works, 1918

Mount Mulligan Colliery Disaster: Report of the Royal Commission, 1922

Report on the Mount Mulligan Relief Funds, 1922

Geological Survey of Queensland Publications

222: L.C. Ball; *Notes on Coal at Mount Mulligan, near Thornborough*; 1910

237: L.C. Ball; *Mount Mulligan Coalfield*; 1912

239: B. Dunstan; *Coal Resources in Queensland*; 1913

Report on the Establishment of State Smelting Works in Queensland, 1909

General Rules: Collieries (n.d., about 1924)

Powell Duffryn Technical Services Limited: *First Report on the Coal Industry of Queensland*, 3 volumes, 1949

Queensland Mining Guide, 1959. (Revised at irregular intervals.)

Report on an Accident at Kianga No.1 Underground Mine on Saturday 20th September 1975: Warden's Enquiry, 1976

Report on an Accident at Moura No. 4 Underground Mine on Wednesday, 16th July, 1986, Brisbane 1987

Report on an Accident at Moura No. 2 Underground Mine on Sunday, 7 August, 1994, Brisbane 1996

Queensland Mines Rescue Station, Ipswich: Guide Book, (n.d.)

State Electoral Roll, Division of Cook, Subdivision of Chillagoe, 1920-1922

Map: *Town of Mount Mulligan*. Department of Public Lands, 1944

Publications of Other Governments

Bulli Colliery Accident: Report of the Royal Commission, New South Wales, *V.&P.*, 2nd session 1887, Vol.4, pp.271-459

Mount Kembla Colliery Disaster: Report of the Royal Commission, and *Conduct of Mr Rogers, as Manager, Mount Kembla Colliery*, New South Wales, *V.&P.*, 1903, Vol.5, pp.1-1226

Report of the Royal Commission into the Coal Industry, Sydney 1930

Report of the Royal Commission into the Safety and Health of Workers in Coal Mines, Sydney 1939

de Keyser, F. and Lucas, K.G. *Geology of the Hodgkinson and Laura Basins, North Queensland*. Commonwealth Bureau of Mineral Resources Bulletin 84, Canberra 1968

Resources and Industry of Far North Queensland, Canberra 1971

Preliminary Report of Her Majesty's Commissioners appointed to inquire into Accidents in Mines, and the Possible Means of Preventing their Occurrence or Limiting their Disastrous Consequences, 1881. Irish University Press facsimiles of British Parliamentary Papers: Mining Accidents, Vol.10

Final Report of Her Majesty's Commissioners...into Accidents in Mines..., 1886. Irish University Press facsimiles of British Parliamentary Papers: Mining Accidents, Vol.11

Imperial Mineral Resources Bureau, *The Mineral Industry of the British Empire and Foreign Countries: Coal Mining Accident Statistics 1912-1922*, London 1967

National Coal Board, *Final Report of the Working Party on Coal Dust Explosions*, London 1967

Ministry of Fuel and Power, *Coal Mining: Report of the Technical Advisory Committee*, London 1945

Rice, G.S., Jones, L.M., Egy, W.L., and Greenwald, H.P., *Coal Dust Explosion Tests in the Experimental Mine 1913 to 1918 Inclusive*. United States Bureau of Mines Bulletin 167, Washington 1922

Wells, A.T., "The Late Permian Mount Mulligan Coal Measures, Queensland", in H. J. Harrington (ed), *Permian Coals of Eastern Australia*, Bureau of Mineral Resources Bulletin 231, Canberra 1989, pp. 175-177

Newspapers and Directories

Australian

Australian Worker

Brisbane Courier

Cairns Post

Common Cause

Courier Mail

Daily Mail

North Queensland Register

Post Office Directory (Queensland)

Pugh's Almanac

Queenslander

Sunday Mail

Sydney Mail

Sydney Morning Herald

Telegraph (Brisbane)

Townsville Daily Bulletin

Truth (Brisbane)

Walsh and Tinaroo Miner

Worker

World's News

Newspaper Cutting Books and Files held by:

Australian Bureau of Meteorology, Brisbane

John Oxley Memorial Library

Queensland Coal Owners Association

Queensland Colliery Employees Union

Queensland Newspapers Library

Unpublished Typescripts

Bell, P., Coal Mine Safety Legislation in Queensland 1854-1978, paper at First International Mining History Conference, University of Melbourne July 1985

Bell, P., "History", in Allom Lovell Marquis-Kyle Architects & Austral Archaeology, Chillagoe Smelter Conservation Plan, report to the Queensland Department of Environment and Heritage, 1993, pp. 6-24, 105-122

Chatterjee, P. K., A Critical Review of Coal Mine Disasters in Queensland and New South Wales since 1920, University of Queensland Department of Mining and Metallurgy report to MIM Holdings Ltd, Brisbane 1980

Dixon, L.H., Stratigraphic Studies adjacent to the Great Dividing Ranges, Northeastern Queensland; 1957: Company Report No.336, Mines Department Library, Brisbane

Explosion at Appin Colliery on 24th July 1979, report of His Honour Judge A. G. Goran, Sydney 1979

Mining Inquiry - Box Flat Colliery: Report, Findings and Recommendations; 1972: Mines Department Library, Brisbane

O"Mara, J.H., Paleozoic Stratigraphy and Relevant Geologic Structure of the Chillagoe and Mount Mulligan Areas, Northern Queensland: 1957: Company Report No.150, Mines Department Library, Brisbane

Rees, R., History of the Bowen Cokeworks, manuscript, Bowen c. 1985 (Copy from writer: former Manager of cokeworks)

Roach, W., History of Coal Mining in Queensland; 1969. (Copy from writer: formerly Chief Inspector of Coal Mines.)

Waddell, A.F., Odd notes on Mt Mulligan, N.Q.; 1951. (Microfilm in University of Queensland Library.)

Whitmore, Ray, Coal in North Queensland, paper at Australian Historical Association "Peripheral Visions" Conference, Townsville 1989

Woodward, O.H., John Moffat of Irvinebank; 1962. (James Cook University Library, North Queensland Collection.)

Interviews

Jock Clarke, Booval, 17 December 1976

Mary (Nellie) Franklin, *née* Hourston, Malanda, 14 August 1976

R.N. Hardie, Bundamba, 22 December 1976

Elsie Kirkwood, Ashgrove, 13 May 1976

Alf Leary, Bulimba, 21 January 1976

Bruce Mackey, Cairns, 4 January 1976

Jim McColm, Booval, 17 December 1976

Mark Morgan, Chillagoe, 27 June 1978

Ivy O'Gorman, Cairns, 3 & 5 January 1976

Bill Roach, Brisbane, 7 May 1976

Doris Smith, *née* Watson, Salisbury, 14 May 1976

Mary Wardle, formerly Grant, *née* Richards, Ravenshoe, 13 August 1976

Jack Watson, Slade Point, 6 March 1977

Les Weatherston, New Farm, 22 November 1975

Books and Monographs: Queensland History

Beale, E., *Kennedy of Cape York*, Adelaide 1970

Bedford, R., *Naught to Thirty-three*, Sydney n.d., [1944]

Bernays, C.A., *Queensland Politics during Sixty Years, 1859-1919*, Brisbane n.d., [1919]

Bernays, C.A., *Queensland: Our Seventh Political Decade 1920-1930*, Sydney 1931

Bolton, G.C., *A Thousand Miles Away*, Brisbane 1963

Borland, H.A., *From Wilderness to Wealth*, Cairns 1940

Borland, H.A., *One Hundred Years, North Queensland Dates and Events*, Brisbane 1945

Borland, H.A., *Mareeba: Meeting Place of Waters 1893-1946*, Brisbane 1946

Borland, H.A., *Roadway of Many Memories 1876-1951*, Brisbane 1951

Carron, W., *Narrative of an Expedition Undertaken under the Direction of the late Mr Assistant Surveyor E.B. Kennedy for the Exploration of the Country lying between Rockingham Bay and Cape York*, Sydney 1849: facsimile Adelaide 1965

Central, Western and Northern Queensland Today, Toowoomba n.d., [1914]

Fitzgerald, R, *"Red Ted": the Life of E. G. Theodore*, St Lucia 1994

Jack, R.L., *Northmost Australia*, 2 vols, Vol.1, London 1921; Vol.2, Melbourne 1922

Jones, D., *Trinity Phoenix: a History of Cairns*, Cairns 1976

Kennedy, K.H., *The Mungana Affair: State Mining and Political Corruption in the 1920s*, St Lucia 1978

The Life of A.J. Draper, Cairns 1931

Mulligan, J.V., *Guide to the Palmer River and Normanby Gold Fields, North Queensland, Showing the Different Roads to and From the Etheridge River, Cleveland Bay, and Cooktown, with Map of the Palmer River and Adjacent Gold Fields, and Journal of Explorations*, Brisbane 1875

Murphy, D.J., *T.J. Ryan: a Political Biography*, St Lucia 1975

Pike, G., *The Men who Blazed the Track*, Cairns 1956

Pike, G., *Pioneers' Country*, Mareeba 1976

Thompson, M. and L. Townsend, *A Pictorial History of Mareeba*, Mareeba 1981

Tindale, N.B., *Aboriginal Tribes of Australia*, Canberra 1974

Trezise, P.J., *Quinkan Country*, Sydney 1969

Young, I., *Theodore: His Life and Times*, Sydney 1971

Books and Monographs: Coal Mining

Agricola, G., *De Re Metallica*, 1558: trans. H.C. and L.H. Hoover, New York 1950

Atkinson, W.N. and J.B., *Explosions in Coal Mines*, London 1886

Australasian Coal and Shale Employees" Federation, *Report of First Miners" Convention*, Sydney 1925

Beard, J.T., *Mine Gases and Explosions*, New York 1908

Blainey, G., *The Rush that Never Ended: a History of Australian Mining*, Melbourne 1963

Bulman, H.F., *Colliery Working and Management*, London 1906

Elford, H.S. and McKeown, M.R., *Coal Mining in Australia*, Melbourne 1947

Ellis, M.H., *A Saga of Coal*, Sydney 1969

Galloway, R.L., *A History of Coal Mining in Great Britain*, 1882: facsimile, Newton Abbot, 1969

Galloway, R.L., *Annals of Coal Mining and the Coal Trade*, 2 vols, Vol.1, 1898; Vol.2, 1904: facsimile, London 1971

Galloway, W., "Colliery Explosions and Rescue Appliances", in W. S. Boulton (ed), *Practical Coal-Mining*, (vol. 5), London n.d. [c.1910], pp. 57-120

Harris, H.C., *The Colliery Manager's New Guide*, London 1937

Hill, D. and Maxwell, W.G.H., *Elements of the Stratigraphy of Queensland*, 2nd ed., Brisbane 1967

Hughes, H.W., *A Textbook of Coal Mining*, London 1904

Hunter, D. *The Diseases of Occupations*, London 1975

Jack, R.L. and Etheridge, R., *The Geology and Palaeontology of Queensland and New Guinea*, Brisbane 1892

Jevons, H.S., *The British Coal Trade*, 1915: facsimile, Newton Abbot 1969

Kerr, G.L., *Practical Coal Mining*, London 1922

Long, P., *Where the Sun Never Shines: a History of America's Bloody Coal Industry*, New York 1989

Mason, E. (ed.), *Practical Coal Mining for Miners*, 2nd ed., 2 vols, London 1951

Mauldon, F.R.E., *The Economics of Australian Coal*, Melbourne 1929

McKeown, M.R. (ed.), *Coal in Australia*, Melbourne 1953

[Ross, E.], *Miners' Federation of Australia: 50th Anniversary*, n.d. [Sydney 1965]

Poole, G.G., *Leigh Creek Coalfield: History and Development*, Adelaide 1946

Power, F. Danvers, *Coalfields and Collieries of Australia*, Melbourne 1912

Reynolds, J., *Men and Mines: a History of Australian Mining 1788-1971*, Melbourne 1974

Rosen, G., *The History of Miners' Diseases: A Medical and Social Interpretation*, New York 1943

Ross, E., *A History of the Miners' Federation of Australia*, Sydney 1970

Standards Association of Australia, *A Report on the Coal Resources of the Commonwealth of Australia*, Sydney 1955

Thomas, P., *Miners in the 1970s: a Narrative History of the Miners Federation*, Sydney 1983

Thomas, P., *The Coalminers of Queensland: a Narrative History of the Queensland Colliery Employees Union*, Ipswich 1986

Whitaker, J.W. and Willett, H.L., *Colliery Explosions and Rescue Work*, London 1946

Whitmore, R. L., *Coal in Queensland: the First Fifty Years*, St Lucia 1981

Whitmore, R. L., *Coal in Queensland: the Late Nineteenth Century 1875-1900*, St Lucia 1985

Whitmore, R. L., *Coal in Queensland: from Federation to the Twenties 1900 to 1925*, St Lucia 1991

Woodruff, S.D., *Methods of Working Coal and Metal Mines*, 3 vols, Oxford 1966

Books and Monographs: Disasters

Austen, T., *The Entombed Miner*, Perth 1986

Ballard, R., *Exploring the Lusitania: Probing the Mysteries of the Sinking that Changed History*, Toronto 1995

Barton, A.H., *Communities in Disaster: a Sociological Analysis of Collective Stress Situations*, Garden City, U.S.A. 1969

Dingsdag, Donald, *The Bulli Mining Disaster 1887: Lessons from the Past*, Sydney 1993

Disaster!, Melbourne 1977

Hinze, H. [pseud: Pope, David], *The Fish John West Reject: Cartoons by Heinrich Hinze*, Canberra 1995

Lemon, A. and M. Morgan, *Poor Souls, They Perished: the Cataraqui, Australia's Worst Shipwreck*, Melbourne 1986

Lucas, R.A., *Men in Crisis: a Study of a Mine Disaster*, New York 1969

Piggin, S. and H. Lee, *The Mt Kembla Disaster*, Sydney 1992

Woodward, O. H., *A Review of the Broken Hill Lead-Silver-Zinc Industry*, (2nd edn), Sydney 1965

Journal Articles

Bell, P., "'If you take something from Mother Earth, she will retaliate': Legends from the Mt. Mulligan Coal Mine Disaster", Royal Historical Society of Queensland *Historical Papers XI*, No. 1, 1979-80, pp. 89-102

Bell, P., "The Origins of the North Queensland Coal Industry" in K. H. Kennedy (ed), *Readings in North Queensland Mining History Volume I*, James Cook University 1980, pp. 251-271

Bell, P., "Watson, James Thomas 1872-1938", *Australian Dictionary of Biography Supplementary Volume*, Melbourne 2005, pp. 398-399

Cochran, S.F., "The Coal Industry", *Australian Quarterly*, Vol.35, 1963, pp.66-72

Cottrell, W.F., "Death by Dieselization: A Cast Study in the Reaction to Technological Change", *American Sociological Review*, Vol.16, 1951, pp.358-365

Crivelli, R.L., "History of the Coal Industry in Australia", *Journal and Proceedings, Royal Australian Historical Society*, Vol.16, 1930, pp.151-160

David, B., "Nurrabullgin Cave: Preliminary Results from a pre-37,000 year old Rockshelter, North Queensland, *Archaeology in Oceania 28*, 1993, pp. 50-54

Davidson, C.G.W., "The Coal Industry in Australia", *Australian Quarterly*, Vol.20, 1948, pp.53-65.

De Jersey, N.J., "The Chemical and Physical Properties and Classification of Some Queensland Coals", *University of Queensland Papers*, Vol.3, 1949

Dunne, E.F., "Brief History of the Coal Mining Industry in Queensland", *Historical Society of Queensland Journal*, Vol.4, 1950, pp.313-339

Foskett, A., "Mount Mulligan", *Walkabout*, Vol.20, 1954, pp.36-37

Grainer, John, David, Bruno, Cribb, Roger, White, Bruce and Kuhn, Hilary, "Nurrabullgin - 'A mountain, once seen, never to be forgotten'", *Rock Art Research 9*, No. 1, 1992, pp. 74-77

Hagan, J. and Fisher, C., "Piece work and some of its Consequences in the Printing and Coal-Mining Industries in Australia, 1850-1930", *Labour History*, No.25, pp.19-39

Jensen, H.I., "The Geology, Mineral Prospects and Future of North Queensland", *Queensland Geographical Journal*, Vols 34-35, 1920, pp.23-36

Johnson, L.W., "A History of the Collie Coal Mining Industry", *University Studies in Western Australian History*, Vol.3, 1957, pp.7-50

Kennedy, K.H., "'Sons of the Manse': a Memoir of the Reid Brothers in North Queensland", *Lectures on North Queensland History No. 4*, James Cook University 1984, pp. 1-35

Kirkman, N., "Mining on the Hodgkinson" in K. H. Kennedy (ed), *Readings in North Queensland Mining History Volume II*, James Cook University 1982, pp. 170-193

Lou-U (pseud.), "Mt Mulligan-Finis", *North Australian Monthly*, Vol.4, 1958, p.24

May, S., "Queensland Place Names", *Local Government*, 1964. Bound Xerox copies of a series of articles, held by John Oxley Library.

Menghetti, D., "Bowen Coke Works: State Enterprise or State Subsidy?", *Journal of Australasian Mining History 3*, 2005, pp. 97-114

Mitchell, G. and Piggin, S., "The Mount Kembla Mine Explosion of 1902: Towards the Study of the Impact of a Disaster on a Community", *Journal of Australian Studies*, No.1, 1977, pp.52-69

Morrison, A.A., "Militant Labour in Queensland 1912-1927", *Journal and Proceedings, Royal Australian Historical Society*, Vol.38, 1952, pp.209-234

Morton, C., "Who Killed Mt Mulligan?", *North Australian Monthly*, Vol.4, 1958, pp.15-16

Murphy, D.J., "The Establishment of State Enterprises in Queensland 1915-1918", *Labour History*, No.14, 1968, pp.13-22

Old Hand (pseud.), "Mt Mulligan", *North Australian Monthly*, Vol.4, 1958, p.27

Pike, G., "James Venture Mulligan", *Historical Society of Queensland Journal*, Vol.4, 1951, pp.494-508

Quarantelli, E.L. and Dynes, R.R. (eds), "Organisational and Group Behaviour in Disasters", Special issue of *American Behavioural Scientist*, Vol.13, No.3, 1970

"The Report of the Committee on Explosions in Mines", *Engineering*, Vol.95, 1913, pp.164-165

Richards, F., "Customs and Language of the Western Hodgkinson Aboriginals", *Memoirs of the Queensland Museum*, Vol.8, 1926, pp.249-265

"Stone Dust and Coal Dust Explosions", *Engineering*, Vol.94, 1912, pp.164-165

Stoodley, J., "Queensland Miners' Attitudes towards the Need for Safety Regulations in the late Nineteenth Century", *Labour History*, No.14, 1968, pp.23-33

Tramp (pseud.), "Tragic Colliery Explosion", *Cummins and Campbell's Monthly Magazine*, Vol.5, 1935, pp.9-12

Watson, J.T., "Explosions and Fires in Mines", Institution of Engineers of Australia *Transactions*, Vol.5, 1924, pp.25-37

Watson, J.T., "Waste of Coal", Institution of Engineers of Australia *Transactions*, Vol.5, 1924, pp.191-209

Theses

Bell, P., The Mount Mulligan Coal Mine Disaster 1921, BA (Hons), James Cook University 1977

Birrell, M., T.J. Ryan and the Queensland Labour Party 1901-1919; B.A. (Hons), University of Queensland 1951

Bray, P., E.G. Theodore and the Queensland Labour Movement 1909-1925; B.A. (Hons), University of Queensland 1958

Kennedy, K.H., The Public Life of William McCormack 1907-1932; PhD, James Cook University 1973

Kirkman, N.S., The Palmer Gold Field 1873-1883, BA (Hons), James Cook University 1984

Murphy, D.J., The Establishment of State Enterprises in Queensland 1915-1918: B.A. (Hons), University of Queensland 1965

Murphy, D.J., T.J. Ryan: A Political Biography; PhD, University of Queensland 1972

Other

Too Young to Die: A television documentary by the Australian Broadcasting Commission, shown in Queensland 12 November 1971 to commemorate the fiftieth anniversary of the Mount Mulligan disaster